D0894838

*Soviet*

*Educators*

*on*

*Soviet*

*Education*

# *Soviet Educators on Soviet Education*

EDITED AND TRANSLATED BY Helen B. Redl

FOREWORD BY FRITZ REDL

*The Free Press, New York*
*Collier-Macmillan Limited, London*

WITHDRAWN
UTSA LIBRARIES

Copyright © 1964 by The Free Press of Glencoe

A DIVISION OF THE MACMILLAN COMPANY

*Printed in the United States of America*

All rights reserved. No part of this book may be reproduced or transmitted in any form or by any means, electronic or mechanical, including photocopying, recording, or by any information storage and retrieval system, without permission in writing from the Publisher.

Collier-Macmillan Canada, Ltd., Toronto, Ontario

Library of Congress Catalog Card Number: 64-20309

*Second printing, November 1967*

*For Julia*

# Contents

## *Part Four—Children's Literature*



## *Part Five—Pioneers*

# *Foreword*

*Fritz Redl*

FOR PROFESSIONALS in any field it is a great experience when a curtain, which has blocked communications between them and their opposite numbers in another nation or culture, lifts. Whatever may continue to separate nation from nation, culture from culture, and whatever unbridgeable differences may remain between the over-all value outlooks in each setting—not everything that pertains to the specific task of a given professional undertaking is different. Some of the problems the engineer faces in constructing a daring new type of bridge, the medical researcher is up against in his search for as yet unknown bacteria, the public health worker encounters who is saddled with the task of spreading health information into remote areas, are likely to be similar enough. The desire of people engaged in comparable jobs and tasks to communicate with each other is natural and strong.

For the educator this is just as true—perhaps even more so. Thus, when official channels of communication and travel between the Soviet Union and ourselves opened up several years ago, the eagerness with which Americans grasped the chance to "go and see for themselves" was enormous. We literally inundated our Russian counterparts with visits to their classrooms, their camps, their children's institutions, their research institutes, in the hope of catching a glimpse of Soviet Education, of the Soviet School, and the Soviet Child.

Only—the painful discovery was soon forced upon us that the removal of passport troubles does not remove all blocks to communication. Some of those blocks seem to sit deep, indeed. Let's not even mention those which are due to philosophical or personal bias, political controversy, or downright prejudice—"for" as well as "against." These are obvious enough and not too difficult to spot, and I would guess that anyone who is too tightly in the grip of those blocks would not have opened the covers of this book. More difficult to trace and overcome are those blocks to communication which stem from the enormous complexity of the task of linguistic and conceptual translation, and those which are related to the problem of familiarity with the over-all cultural scene within which one observes a classroom or a child. And let us not forget to list the need for knowledge of the history of a country or even of a specific region, and a number of similar factors without which so many phenomena, even though clearly "seen," can hardly be understood.

As soon as we get to talking about understanding an educational system, we have, of course, to add to all this the demand for considerable familiarity with the educational field, and a high level of sophistication in those disciplines upon which it is grounded, such as education, philosophy, group psychology, and child development.

Here, by the way, we run into special troubles, and I cannot help but feel somewhat envious of my colleagues from other disciplines. Anyone visiting a surgical operating room or a plant for the production of agricultural machinery would hardly feel impelled to bring home exciting "findings," unless he happened to be equipped with the appropriate training in the fields related to these activities. Nor would he have to be afraid of being considered either conceited or stupid if he simply admitted his inability to form any judgments when pressured into generalizations after his return home. Since opinions on children and schools still seem to be exempt from such demands of scientific modesty and honesty, it is not surprising that the well-meaning travelogues delivered by those who went to the Soviet Union to see for themselves often turn out to be more confusing than enlightening and leave some of the most pressing questions unanswered, or produce "answers" which by their very naiveté seem to indicate the existence of a communicational block.

Making this statement, I add that I am using the term "communication" in the context of these introductory remarks in the widest possible meaning of the term. I am not referring only to what goes on when two people talk with each other (and even this, by the way, should include all the "nonverbal" communication exchanged through voice tones, facial expression, posture, gestures, and so forth). I use the term here in the still wider connotation which it has assumed in some of the more recent communication theories and literatures; namely, anything a given situation "tells me" about what is going on. This, of course, is stretching it a bit, for obviously there need not be any intention in the situation to tell me anything, except that I may be observant enough to receive the "message" it happens to contain. To use just one oversimplified example: An experienced teacher, visiting a classroom of a colleague in his own country, will not have to wait for all the things his host may be able to tell him about it. The very arrangement of furniture, the type of material pinned to the bulletin board, the pictures or hortative proverbs painted like a frieze around the room, and many other details, may tell him much of what is going on—sometimes more than his host wishes to reveal. However, this kind of nonverbal communication in the widest meaning of the term is no less subject to the dangers of misinterpretation and misunderstanding than the verbal one. As soon as host and visitor belong to different systems or cultures, both will have to guard against the temptation to read "into" what they observe something entirely different from what it really means, while missing the "message" it conveys. In short —there is no escape from the need to search for the proper *frame of reference,* without which even nonverbal signs cannot really be "understood."

When my wife and I started out to "go and see for ourselves" —fortified, on our first trip, by a generous grant from the Ford Foundation—we had some of the prerequisites for coping with problems of communication about educational systems: both of us are professional educators, both of us have worked for years with children in a variety of different settings, in Europe as well as in the United States, and one of us is thoroughly familiar with the Russian language, history, and literature, and with many other aspects of "Russian life." In spite of this—or was it even because of it?—the question: "How do we really know what we see?" plagued us continuously, and the constant search for a frame of reference was probably about as painfully urgent for us as for anybody else; even those processes of communication which didn't happen to be a problem to us, kept impressing us with their importance at every step.

This is certainly not the place for another travelogue, nor for a dissertation on intercultural communication as such. But perhaps a confessional about the pangs of our communicational consciences might be a proper introduction to a book which is obviously based on the impression that "having been there is not enough. . . ."

## § How Do We Know What We See?

The biggest danger to all human insight lies, of course, in our greed for premature generalizations. In our own areas of specialization we are, of course, quite aware of this. When we switch from our special domain into areas of exploration somewhat remote from it, or when we leave the well-cemented paths of scientific rigor as practiced in our daily tasks and venture into terrain as exciting but also as unpredictable as "travel abroad," our pride in scientific restraint is suddenly put to a hard test. For —if we really stick to our resolve not to generalize too fast—what will we have to tell or show when we come back home, what would we have to contribute but a few cute stories without a point? Especially in a country as huge and full of contrasts as the U.S.S.R.—how can one be sure that a few weeks, a few months, a few years of travel, or even planned and repeated trips, give one "enough" data to be sure of the inferences one thinks one might draw? No wonder that many a book, article, back-home report by even otherwise quite sophisticated writers is likely to ignore some of the following facts: That the country so glibly referred to by the American traveler as "Russia" is in itself a "collective" composed of fifteen republics, with enormous differences in culture, national characteristics, historical, socioeconomic-political details, to say nothing of the wide range of styles of living and folk customs even within the territory of any one of them; that for some of the boys and girls so summarily stereotyped under the label of the "Russian Child," Russian is a second language taught in bilingual schools, with their own native tongues entirely different from it in root, syntactical design, and even in script; that the difference between life in a Western type metropolis such as Moscow or Leningrad and in remote rural areas surpasses anything which our own imagination of differences between "town and country living" may have dreamed about; that some of the schools whose classrooms you may happen to observe had to be hastily built after the city had been 80 per cent destroyed—the list of relevant issues is endless. Suffice it to remember how careful we should be in whatever conclusions we draw.

There were some points at which this problem of premature generalizations gave us, too, a hard time, in spite of our firm resolve to the opposite. We were, of course, quite aware of the pitfalls listed above, but we thought that if we kept the range in terms of locale, language, nationality, age of children, etc., somewhat constant, we should be able to generalize within a given area. This idea seemed substantiated by the obvious fact that textbooks, over-all teacher training, equipment, and prescribed curriculum or play activity would be expected to be quite uniform unless we wandered too far from a given district. We could not have been more wrong, as we soon discovered, for, just when we nearly decided we need not look into another school with the same toys, routines, and games, we were forced to concede that great differences might exist between two schools even just a mile or so apart, in terms of over-all atmosphere, deviation tolerance toward child behavior, flexibility of child handling, and general "warmth" of the communication tone between adult and child. The gamut ranged all the way from highly formalized, rigidly structure-conscious, and heavily efficiency-oriented—with the children becoming props invented to show how efficiently things can be done—to unusually casual, proudly flexible and relationship-focused styles of child care, with the emphasis noticeably on the production of a "warm place for kids to spend the day in." We never were able to find out just what accounts for the existence of this amazing discrepancy, even when the over-all variables are held constant. Our hunch—based on our previous experience in countries with similar over-all school and child care orientations rather than on actual study of the U.S.S.R. situation—would be that two factors are crucial: The first just the impact of the director's personality on the rest of the staff and the atmosphere of the place; the other the "security" in the director's position in the specific bureaucratic power domain. As in any bureaucracy, the person who doesn't have to prove anything because he is well trusted and accepted in the official power hierarchy can afford to ignore the letter of the law and encourage his staff to live its spirit; the one who isn't so sure how those above might misinterpret what he does would therefore spread much more letter-consciousness into the handling of day-to-day events.

There is another way for distortions, gaps, or downright misleading elements to enter the communications from those who have been there to those who have not. That one is even worse than the problem of premature generalizations, if for no other reason than that we are less aware of it, and it is thus harder to recognize its impact. To restrain from drawing too far-reaching conclusions from incidents we witness should not be too hard. But there is another possibility: even if we have many incidents to draw from, and sort them carefully so as to avoid the pitfalls of the variables mentioned above, what happens if our original interpretation of each of them was incorrect to begin with? To reach incorrect conclusions from an insufficiently large or insufficiently critically sorted sample of observation is one thing, but how do we know the observations we add up were correct?

The trouble with distortions and wrong communications does not begin at the moment when we start adding up what we saw. *It actually begins the very moment we open our eyes in order to look.* For: How do we know what we see?

Let me illustrate this with an experience from our trip. Someone we had met en route, whose high level of sophistication in his own discipline is beyond doubt and who had just come back from a trip to the U.S.S.R., complained bitterly about the amount of "regimentation" the "Russian Children" are exposed to, even on their playgrounds. "No wonder they are all so well behaved." We were told the exact city and place where this could be observed any morning, so that we could go ourselves and see, in case we had any doubt. We did, and here is what we think we saw. The scene: the equivalent of a city playground with a summer vacation program carried on for about 400 children, the population changing from day to day. On that specific morning, several hundred of those children were engaged in a wide variety of activities, from box hockey and chess to ball games, most of them operating in smaller clusters in different areas, spread all over the terrain, supervised by adults—youth leaders, parents, or student-volunteers. At 10:45 one of the theater groups was to put on a fairy tale performance in a large auditorium nearby, as a contribution to youth service. Now, this theater building was somewhat removed from the main areas of activities; it would take about four to five minutes to get the youngsters over there. The signal for the program change was given, the adults rounded the children up into loose marching lines, and marched them singing over to their fairy tale show. Once at the door, the lines broke up, the children rushed in with the usual restless scramble for preferred seats so universal in the human species of that age in large crowds before exciting events. They broke ranks; there was obviously no expectation that they would be seated in any special way, the auditorium was just being "filled" with as many as wanted to come. The children formed a large mass audience, with adults sprinkled around here or there keeping an eye on events at large. Now, it is unquestionably true that if you walked in on this scene at 10:45 A.M., you would have seen a large number of children, lined up about three abreast, "marching" somewhere. Yet something else is equally obvious for anyone who has ever found himself in the role of a playground supervisor in a similar situation: If widely assorted groups of children have to be moved some distance in large numbers at a given time, you had better create some pattern for this type of "transition," if you want to avoid bedlam and mayhem. In short, the scene witnessed simply used marching as a natural transitional device designed to reduce confusion rather than to regiment souls. It could be observed in any large camp or playground in any country. Whether it spells "regimentation" *must be read not from the formation in which the transit occurs* but from the over-all purpose of the event, and from *the atmosphere in which this transition takes place, and the deviation tolerance with which adults guide the event.* As it happens, for us this situation was easy enough to "read." We had seen—and participated in—similar scenes so many times in our own professional lives, and had spent considerable effort ourselves training staff in handling such "transitional moves" with the skill it takes to avoid "regimentation." However—it did give us pause to wonder! This time we were lucky, since the special event to be looked at and communicated about happened to be right up our own alley of professional sophistication. But how will we know whether we have the appropriate frame of reference within which to judge an event in other observational situations which do not happen to come so close to the chance factor of our professional competence and experience? How, then, will we really know what we "see"?

In the same scene, by the way, we witnessed a short interlude, as a matter of chance. While the youngsters were "marching" to their auditorium with their adult group leaders, we sat down on a bench near their path with one of our Russian hosts who was not directly involved in the transition process. Excluded from some of the conversational content between him and my wife because of my language barrier, I had ample leisure to look around and watch the children.

All of a sudden I noticed that one of the youngsters—a boy of about nine years—was getting restless and angry and started "wrestling" with another boy, as kids anywhere will do when they get somewhat out of line or bored with official routine. However, things got worse between the two of them. It seemed to me that their mutual excitement began to snowball. Both children were getting "high" in the process. The adult group leader made some rather casual attempts to get them back into line, but they were both much too excited by now to pay any attention to her. They punched and poked each other away from the marching column, and soon rolled over on the ground in the direction of our bench, now fighting with so much fervor that both of us, as well as our Russian host, had to move our legs aside so as to avoid their unintentional kicks. Our host, by the way, seemed unaffected by all this. Finally, our first boy's opponent won the fight with a heavy slug, recovered his composure quickly, and ran back into his place in the marching line. His victim, however, was left in a state of fury. Struggling between rage and tears, he ended up combining both in a neatly circumscribed temper tantrum. He eluded the adult who tried to grab him back into line, hid behind a tree trunk, first pummeling it madly, then crying. The adult left him alone and the group walked on. Nobody seemed to pay any attention. After more display of his battle between anger and concern, he visibly pulled himself together and ran over in the direction of the theater hall.

My question: Was this a "Soviet Child"—and why not? Was the adult's handling of the incident due to trained policy or simply to a personal feeling that it was better to give up and wait for someone else to handle it, or perhaps even an attempt to avoid a scene because of the presence of people who were obviously visitors? What did it all mean? If we had observed this same boy listening quietly and absorbedly to a lecture beyond his comprehension, would we have been inclined to assume that he must be a "typical Russian schoolboy"? But why should this incident be less "typical"? What we saw was clear enough. We can observe it hundreds of times on our own playgrounds. How do we know what to make of it? Under which category should the incident be recorded in our minds? Should we say: "It seems that their children are more 'human' after all, more like ours. . . ." Or: "It seems they too have a smattering of 'actor-outers' in their midst." Or should we perhaps first find out what else was involved and say nothing unless we can do just that? And—a thought that would make us shiver: let's assume we have several hundreds of beautifully observed and described—but wrongly interpreted—incidents like this one in our satchel, will we be strong enough to withstand the temptation of numbers magic and pretend we have a right to "generalize" because of the large number of "data" we have piled up?

## § Characteristic—of What?

When one travels in somebody else's country, one seems to develop an uncanny urge to consider anything one finds interesting as also "characteristic." Now, in the wider meaning of the term, this is not entirely without foundation, for if we keep the frame of reference vague enough, almost anything will turn out to be "characteristic" of something. But the question remains: characteristic *of what?*

Our first thoughts usually go in either of two directions: What a child is seen doing may be considered characteristic in the more literal sense, namely, expressive of what he is, of his character and personality. It may also strike us as characteristic, less of the child as a person then of the child as a product of the educational system and therefore indirectly of the system that has produced him. Thus, the sight of an obedient child will be presumed as evidence of how wonderful the child is, or how effective the system seems to be that produces such a child—or both. Up to a point, there is no quarrel with this. Also, there is no doubt that the U.S.S.R. has some wonderful children sitting in their classrooms and that, on the whole, Soviet child behavior is generally easier on adult nerves than some of the developmental noise ours produce. However, the point under discussion right now is this: child behavior need not necessarily be primarily "characteristic" of either of those factors. Among the many other items which may account for it, I would like to single out for discussion one which is too often ignored.

Some things children do seem to be part of a deeply ingrained "tribal custom" rather than an expression either of their character or of the educational system in vogue. It may even date back to time immemorial, or at least long before the history of whatever system happens to be in power at the time. In fact, some of such behavioral clusters are like "rituals" in which children engage. I hope I can use this concept without too much entanglement in terminological complications. One illustration may suffice.

Among the items most frequently listed as memorable in back-home reports by American visitors to Russian schools is the enormous respect which children seem to have for adults, the high level of discipline in their classrooms, the amazing amount of courteousness, politeness, and the lack of rebellion with which youngsters seem to take the authority role of the adult for granted. Yet the behavior described does not have to be "characteristic" of either the Soviet Child or the Soviet School as such. Rather, it may be the manifestation of a deep-seated ritual prescribed wherever Child meets Adult in an Official Authority role which has been in vogue for centuries not only in pre-revolutionary Russia but also in other European countries. Of course, those youngsters stand up when an adult enters their classroom. Of course they are expected to remain standing until given a sign to relax. Of course they keep within an established ritual of the way "pupil" is to act when "teacher" confronts him with a question. Of course they keep a stiff upper lip, as long as the official situation lasts, even if they get somewhat tired, bored, anxious, or even critical and disgusted with the lack of consideration by a given adult in a given moment. To me, who had taught in "Gymnasiums" in Vienna for many years before coming to the United States, this scene felt like a *déjà vu*. It was a repetition of what I had been used to as a child in Imperial Austria, or as a teacher in post-monarchical Vienna. In fact, I had another sense of *déjà vu* when I stopped, after our first trip to the U.S.S.R., for a few days in Vienna and revisited the very gymnasium which I had gone to as a child. I happened to walk through a nearby park with the present director of that school. From a distance, I saw two youngsters coming toward us, rather wildly pushing and poking and giggling and "fooling around" as youngsters will do when let out after the stress and strain of a highly disciplined day at school. The moment they spied us from afar, behavior and posture changed abruptly. They stalked past us with respectful erectness of body, taking their caps off their heads in a great sweeping gesture with the appropriate "*Kuess die Hand, Herr Direktor*" clearly exclaimed. Hardly were they behind us when they resumed their previous horseplay with increased giggling hilarity, occasionally throwing a glance back to make sure they were "out of sight."

This "European Ritual of Child Meets Adult in Authority Role," by the way, works both ways—for those less familiar with it I ought to add: European adults put heavy stress on it—in general, it seems to me, heavier stress than we might be inclined to in the United States, a few exceptions to this statement granted. European adults get downright punitive if denied their "court ceremonial." On the other hand, they don't expect this obedience to last longer than the duration of the ritualistic situation. While an American educator might be more concerned if children behaved respectfully only to his face but broke out into giggles or misbehavior when not watched, the European adult seems to me, in general, more inclined to expect that "kids will be kids" and take it for granted that, in the absence of controls from without, a lot of behavior might occur which we are better off not seeing.

In short, it is hard for the foreign observer to know just which behavior is really characteristic of either a child's character or a system's present effect, and which happens primarily as part of "custom" so ingrained one doesn't even notice it any more. Even here at home the distinction between behavior that is characteristic of the person who does the acting versus behavior in the context of a commonly accepted ritual may not always be an easy one. For instance, with the elevator rituals as firmly established as they are in American hotels, I would hesitate to draw too binding conclusions from the way men take off their hats when a lady enters as to their chivalry and real respect for the other sex.

## § Complications from Within

That cross-country and cross-cultural communication may be complicated by the hurdles of linguistic problems is so obvious it hardly needs repeating here, except that I would like to make sure that we add to the strictly "linguistic" ones those complications which only start with word meanings, but are actually due to much more complex differences in conceptual formulation, all the way up to issues of philosophy and basic outlook on values and beliefs. The pages of this book will contain ample evidence of the complexity of linguistic and conceptual translation and communication; let me go on to another phenomenon which the introspective observer on a foreign scene is bound to be caught up in and which seems to me in need of more official recognition than it has received in the past.

This phenomenon I like to describe under the term of "emigration neurosis"; it seems to hit many of us who moved, in our adult years, from the cultural and sociopolitical framework in which we grew up to a different one. I do not want the term "neurosis" taken too literally, and what I am referring to is really a disturbance of the thinking process, as separate from other "neurosis-like" adjustment pains an emigrant may go through. Without detouring too far in introductory lines, let me try to draw the analogy I think this move holds to the internal blocks to observation and communication which I experienced so strongly during my recent attempt to grasp the meaning of life for children and educators on the "Russian Scene." For I am convinced that this is more than a chance similarity. I really think that all intercultural communicants may go through similar internal complications and "phases" as students of somebody else's country and institutions. While one is observing a culture pattern which is new and puzzling, and while one tries to keep one's eyes wide open and one's judgment as decontaminated as possible from obstructions of all sorts, the following struggle seems to me to accompany such laudable goals of intellectual purism, and one finds oneself passing through "stages" like these:

1. Temporary overemphasis on the impression that "it is all so different," to the exclusion of noticing obvious similarities or even identities with back-home phenomena.

2. Temporary overemphasis—after the first phase is about to abate—on the impression that "it is, really and way down deep, all the same anyway," ignoring the obvious differences one has by now become accustomed to, stored away, and taken for granted.

3. Overestimation and overglorification in back-home reports of some of the "good" things one has discovered, which came as a surprise, for they were not anticipated in one's image before one set out on the trip.

4. Underestimation—or even negation—of the fact that we

"have some of the same things and conditions back home"—and this referring to "good" as well as "bad" items.

5. Overweighting of positive as well as negative impressions of the "here and now"; insisting that "this could never happen at home"; something like a naive post-situational distortion under the impact of present excitement and surprise.

6. Sudden fits of limitless and reckless "judgmental expertise" even in people who are otherwise modest, aware of the limits of their competence and experience as well as of the potential complexity of the new situation.

7. Temptation toward a "triumphant or disgusted sneer" when one meets up with evidence that is contradictory to what one knows the people at home are still naive enough to assume.

8. Temptation to isolate and overrate as evidence minor occurrences which happen to be related to a "hot" issue in back-home debates, but may not be very meaningful within the context in which they are observed. (Oh, yes, there was—or wasn't—one baby that was being swaddled . . . or: I did come across a child who sucked his thumb, . . .)

9. Sudden switch from observational conscientiousness to fits of "historical apologia" for back-home conditions as well as controversial phenomena in the new country.

10. Escape from the painful and laborious task of observing and understanding into orgies of "adaptational acrobatics" or "counter-adaptational pride." (Exaggerated happiness in being so popular with and well accepted by some figure on the local scene, or exaggerated pride in having stuck to one's guns so well in an argument with a local representative in spite of risks involved.)

11. Wasting time on anger at and constant internal argument with false back-home impressions or mistaken reports at home by unperceptive, biased, or naive compatriots.

12. Sudden urge to play "devil's advocate" either on the present travel scene or in imagined controversies after return home.

13. Occasional overidentification with hardships one observes, to the detriment of remaining firm and realistically critical of actual shortcomings of services, equipment, implementation, or over-all design of situations and institutions observed.

14. Occasional fits of despair of ever understanding anything, especially when one, in the grip of "complexity shock," becomes respectful of the limit of one's equipment, time, and the basic knowledge that would really be required to grasp it all in its full meaning.

15. Sudden shock at the mere idea of one's own "back-home destiny" the facing of which one happily postponed for a while; namely: (a) I will be misunderstood and misquoted, no matter what I say; (b) I won't have anything to tell them, or doing so will only make me obnoxious; they won't believe anything that doesn't fit their preconceived notions anyway; or I might even, inadvertently, be used to feed their already existent distorted stereotypes; (c) Anticipatory anger at all the silly questions and wrong expectations one will have to cope with after return, and the certainty that sticking to our complexity demanding statements will only bring us the accusation of being conceited, non-communicative, or devaluating the listener's ability to "understand."

Fortunately, not all of this hits all of us all of the time—but of all the angles to be considered when we want to predict the possible complications which may throw themselves between us and the people with whom we want to communicate and the situation we need to communicate about, I would want to advocate strongly that this list of issues be looked at more closely than has been done in the past.

## § Communication Troubles— Even at the "Source"

No matter how good the back-home reports from site visits by Americans to the U.S.S.R. may be, how skillfully we may learn to avoid all the communication traps described above, how long our lists of "schools visited, children observed, Soviet Educators talked with" have become—there is no substitute for reading what the Soviet Educators write. To understand fully what basic goals and principles underlie all the things they do and say when we meet them, we need to go back right to the source.

This book has attempted to help the American reader to do

just that. It also has taken the firm stance that the American reader needs as direct an access to Soviet education theories and beliefs as can be provided, so that he can draw his own conclusions.

Yet—the complexities of the process of communication we have sketched in relation to a trip abroad do not leave us alone, no matter how close we come to the original source in the form of the printed word.

Some of the pitfalls in "translating" from one language medium into another, are obvious and well enough known. Unfortunately, though, linguistic know-how and conscientiousness are not enough. Even the question of just how "literal" a translation should remain, or how far it can venture into being "free" without becoming distortive, is not a simple one. Also, how much conceptual precision can be safely sacrificed on the altar of readability constitutes a type of decision the translator may have to make at every step. In order for him to make it wisely, more than knowledge of the language and a good dictionary are required. Since every translation will be criticized by those whose linguistic conscience is tighter than their conceptual one, and also by those whose demand for the "original flavor" outweighs their interest in linguistic or conceptual precision, just a few of the communication pitfalls which confront the reader —or the translator—shall be briefly listed here.

The Russians have a word the translation of which is quite obvious and suggested in any dictionary you may want to consult: *pedagogical*. Now, it so happens that many times when they talk about children and schools, this term is used by them for situations in which we—with the same meaning in mind—would much more naturally use the word "*psychological*." In short—in a considerable number of instances the terms pedagogical and psychological are, for all practical purposes, used as synonyms. Since the American reader is so much more comfortable with the one than with the other, wouldn't it be wise to take the linguistic liberty of substituting "psychological" wherever we can do so without any damage to the meaning involved? This seems a reasonable way out, and certainly tempting in terms of increased readability. Yet—another risk becomes imminent at once. If we did so, the frequency and ease with which the word "psychological" would be seen turning up in Soviet writings would easily mislead us into assuming that their familiarity with, belief in, or even obsession with "psychology" is about the same as we would expect to find in American literature on education and child behavior. Nothing could be further from the truth! Thus —while not distorting the meaning of each passage where the word "psychological" would be correctly substituted for the word "pedagogical," the nonliteral translation, if too liberally applied, would distort our over-all picture of Soviet philosophy and would tempt the reader into false assumptions about its premises.

In this book, therefore, a dual approach has been chosen. Where it was at all correct and advisable, the phrase containing the word "psychological" was preferred. Yet, in a majority of the situations, the term "pedagogical" was stuck to stubbornly, in spite of its linguistic clumsiness and probably at the cost of some irritation to the American reader, simply in order to avoid the danger of over-all confusion about theory warned against above.

Unfortunately, there are cases where no translation—"literal" or "free"—can span the great distance in culture, philosophy, or linguistic custom. In those instances nothing but a special clarification can rescue the reader from distortional temptations. For, just as in direct communication described above, the need for the search for a correct frame of reference is always with us. The fact remains that the use of professional terms is related not only to issues of terminology or professional lingo: it may actually imply the acceptance or rejection of a whole theory of behavior and thought, or even of a whole credo of politico-philosophical convictions.

How important this may become is best illustrated by a term for which an extensive clarification was deemed necessary in this book. In Soviet educational literature you will find the adjective "conscious" appearing and re-appearing in all sorts of, to the American reader, unexpected combinations. Now, whenever we read the adjective "conscious," the first antonym that most readily comes to mind is "unconscious." Even Americans who know little about Freud—and would care less if they did—have by now been made to expect some sort of reference to the fact that feelings, emotions, thoughts may be motivating child behavior even though the child himself may not be aware of this at the time. That a person may harbor an "unconscious grudge" against a teacher or parént occasionally, has, by now, become commonplace in our literature. *For the Russian writer, no such theoretical belief is implied!* Most of the time, this is not at all what he is talking about when he uses this term. As the editor points out in her Introduction, the Soviet educator's use of the adjective "conscious" is designed to evoke a whole cluster of sociopolitical or characterological issues rather than remind him of an item of psychological theory, as it might his American counterpart.

H. B. Redl has painstakingly struggled with this problem of conceptual, professional, philosophical, and cultural frames of reference. In places where the reader might be irritated by knowing a much more "readable" word than the one she has stuck to in her translation—or, on the other hand, where he might wonder about the right one has to travel so far afield from the dictionary, as she had to do at times, let me assure him that there was a deliberate reason. Her book quite willingly sacrifices ease of readability in some places in favor of retaining the original flavor or conceptual precision of a thought. Yet it tries equally conscientiously to help the reader see similarities and recognize analogies in basic issues, whenever the choice of a more familiar term would facilitate such communication for the American reader. Basically, neither being "free" nor remaining "literal" should be considered a translational virtue in its own right. He who is eager to communicate complex issues with as little distortional residue as can be achieved, must be ready to alternate between both.

# *Introduction*

THIS BOOK brings together a representative selection of old and recent materials dealing with the education and rearing of children in the U.S.S.R. Soviet educators make a clear distinction between the two processes, as will become apparent in this book.

My firsthand experiences with parents, teachers, and other educators in the U.S.S.R. suggested the idea of assembling a sourcebook of this kind. These personal contacts made it clear that much of the material available in the United States on the subject of Soviet education and child-rearing practices reflects the unavoidable biases and cultural misunderstandings of the observers. It seemed useful to make available to an American audience the original writings in Soviet educational philosophy.

The book includes two kinds of selections. One group focuses on the basic philosophy underlying both child-rearing and education; the other is chosen from the literature on its implementation. Hopefully, these selections will illuminate those influences in the daily lives of Soviet children which contribute most to their development from infancy to adulthood. Philosophy and technique are so closely interrelated that it is not possible to understand the second without a knowledge of the first.

Anton S. Makarenko, Nadyezhda K. Krupskaya, Anatoly V. Lunacharsky, and S. T. Shatzky established the foundations of the Soviet educational system, each contributing significantly in a certain area. The selections from their writings trace the beginnings of this system. Makarenko is, of course, widely read in many countries. He is known as one of the "fathers" of Soviet education. His work after the Revolution with homeless children originated widely accepted practices which remain in use to the present day. Krupskaya, the wife of Lenin, was one of the main architects of the organized youth movement, which has had tremendous influence not only upon the lives of the Soviet children but also upon the development of the whole society.

The Soviet point of view stresses the responsibility of *all* adults for the education of the young. Thus, the concept of "educator" requires a broader definition than that used in the United States. For this reason Kornei Chukovsky (whose stories have become very familiar to several generations of Russian children), though not an educator in the strictest sense of the word, is included in this selection. Furthermore, his brave defense of the right of children to be exposed to fairy tales, against the vehement opposition of many Soviet educators—among them the powerful Krupskaya—proved to be of great educational importance. This issue, by the way, may sound familiar to those American readers who are cognizant of a similar educational controversy over children's literature in the United States.

A good portion of this book is drawn from the writings of those educators concerned with practical implementation of educational theory. These selections emphasize the various problems with which educators are concerned, and the extent to which the writers are constantly attempting to find new and better methods for achieving their stated aim—to bring up the new Soviet generation prepared for the tasks which will be set before them.

A word of caution: although I have attempted to include a representative selection from the spectrum of Soviet pedagogical literature, this selection is by no means comprehensive. Nevertheless, the writers represented here come from different regions of a vastly heterogeneous country; some come from Moscow or Vladivostok, while others have worked in the villages of Azerbaidzhan or Russian Georgia.

At no point in this volume is there an attempt to draw either specific or general conclusions about Soviet education or to pass value judgments. Instead, it offers a few glimpses into what to the West remains largely *terra incognita.*

The process of translation ordinarily involves many problems; when the subject-matter covers many culturally different institutions, the difficulties are compounded. There are organizations in the Soviet Union that have no counterpart in the United States. Moreover, the literal translation of some Russian terms results in the use of English words whose meanings are so contextually different as to be misleading. Some of these must be singled out for definition.

**Academy of Pedagogical Sciences, RSFSR**

Scientific institutions whose members are the most outstanding scientists of pedagogy. Created in 1943 by government decree in cooperation with the ministry of Education, RSFSR. It is composed of thirty-two full and sixty-nine associate members. Its purpose, in accordance with the decree, is to cooperate in developing education on a nationwide basis, to conduct research, and to implement its findings in practice as well as to publish professional journals and magazines. All members are recommended by scientific institutions, individual scientists, or by scientific groups. They are elected during the plenary session by secret ballot. APS coordinates its functions with institutes of pedagogy and pedagogical psychology. The general assembly of distinguished and full members is the governing body. In the interval between plenary sessions the presidium takes over as the executive authority. It consists of one chairman, two vice chairmen, one secretary, and seven members—all elected by the general assembly for a period of three years. Only full members are eligible for this office.*

**Bezprizornye**

This term, widely used after the Revolution, denotes children without parents or legal guardians. It has no implication of "delinquency" attached to it. However, since during the post-revolutionary years such children had nobody to take care of them, they ganged together in wayward hordes, living off the land as best they could. The American reader may be familiar with Makarenko, who gathered such youth into collectives to re-educate them, or he may have seen one of the first post-

* *Pedagogitchesky Slovar*, Akademiya Pedagogicheskich Nauk, RSFSR. Moscow, 1960. Vol. I, pp. 31-32.

revolutionary Russian movies, "The Road to Life," which dramatized the solution to this problem. As soon as the country recovered from the first phases of post-revolutionary disorganization, the State accepted its official responsibility for all children without parents or guardians. Since then, the phenomenon of children who roam the street for lack of shelter and food disappeared, and the temporary connotation of "delinquency," which had clung to the term *bezprizornye* during those years, became obsolete. The American visitor to the U.S.S.R. should be aware of this; when we still cling to it, the Russian educator becomes grossly incensed, since it implies to him that we either are ignorant of history or do not believe their assurances that all parentless children are now cared for by the State. The term that comes closer to what we have in mind when we talk about "delinquents" is "hooligan."

**Beznadzora**

Refers to children who are without adequate adult supervision. They are, from an economic and legal point of view, "cared for," that is, they have a family and a home in which to live. However, for a variety of reasons their parents or guardians do not seem to give them sufficient supervision, so they spend too much time "in the streets," thus missing the proper educational training. They, too, are not considered "delinquent," though a continued state of such educational neglect may later turn some of them into "hooligans."

**Camps**

Every child (aged six to fourteen) in the U.S.S.R. is entitled to at least one month of experience in a camp situation during his vacation time (in most parts of the country during the summer, but in Siberia it is during the winter). Sometimes the children stay for longer periods. All trade unions, as well as offices, agencies, and so forth, maintain camps which they fully support. All children of the people working in a given place are invited to participate.

**Collective**

A group of people with the same interests working together toward a mutual goal. For example, a children's collective may mean a classroom, play group, or pioneer group.

**Commissariat of Education of the U.S.S.R. (*Narkompros*)**

Created after the October Revolution by the Second Congress of the Communist Party. A. B. Lunacharsky was the first commissar. On March 15, 1946, the above name was changed to *Ministry of Education of the U.S.S.R.* Its tasks are to create, execute, and maintain curriculum instruction, research, organization, administration, coordination, select textbooks, put into practice the law of compulsory attendance. The minister is personally responsible for fulfilment of these tasks.

**Compulsory Education**

Soviet children enter first grade at age seven. The period of obligatory school attendance has now been increased from seven to eight years. The completion of a full secondary education (eleven years) is not obligatory. The eleventh year was added after the school reform of 1958. Schools in the U.S.S.R. from primary to university level opened their doors to about 40 million students at the start of the 1962-1963 school year.*

**Conscious**

Conscious, used as an adjective to nouns such as discipline and behavior, in many instances is almost equivalent to the American term "goal-directed" (conscious discipline).

**Consciousness**

Consciousness is the higher form of reflecting reality, characteristic only of human beings inseparably linked with language ability by which it transmits knowledge and thoughts. With the help of words man marks, deliberates, and acknowledges his impressions. Consciousness enables man to become goal-directed and to regulate his behavior as well as influence that of others. This form of reflecting reality is a result of evolution of the brain and the social development of the species.†

**Consciousness in Learning**

This term implies a didactic principle expressing the need to create a conducive environment which would facilitate the task of learning as well as the process of absorbing and retaining knowledge. This principle is inseparable from initiative, activity, and independence of students and its roots are diametrically opposed to dogmatism. As its main premise it holds the following characteristics: (1) Understanding of the advantages of educa-

* UNESCO, *Courier*, December, 1962, p. 34.

† *Pedagogitchesky Slovar*, Akademiya Pedagogicheskich Nauk, Moscow, 1960, Vol. II, pp. 374-375.

tion by those engaged in it. (2) Total comprehension of the material under study. (3) Utilizing personal experience and observations during the learning process. Its practical significance grows in accordance with the development of the Soviet society and its movement toward Communism. Didactical means directed toward achieving conscious mastery of knowledge are linked directly with the total process of developing the cognoscible elements of memory, thinking, speech, and imagination in the learners, while formulating such personality characteristics as initiative, persistence, and will power. K. D. Ushensky (1824-1870), a Russian pedagogical theoretician, arrived at the conclusion that children are motivated toward learning when they clearly understand its meaning and when they can engage in independent study. Conscious mastery of knowledge is achieved when the practical meaning of learned generalization or rules become understood and when it appears that with its help new phenomena may be explained and new problems solved. To achieve it tasks demanding active thinking and independent work should be used systematically in the learning process. The clarity of presentation, inferences and conclusions arrived at depend on the degree of conscious assimilation of material under study. The higher manifestation of conscious learning reflects itself in the ability to implement successfully the acquired knowledge in practice while analyzing it in the light of learned theoretical principles. This process fosters the development of the most valuable characteristics in the learner.*

**Dialectical Materialism**

The theory of reality advanced by Karl Marx and Frederick Engels and adopted as the official Soviet philosophy combining elements of traditional materialism with the method of Hegel's dialectic and maintaining the independent objective reality of matter and its priority in both time and logical importance over mind.†

**Discipline**

(i) "means that the children know how to work collectively without disturbing anyone and helping each other in difficulties."‡ (ii) A. S. Makarenko, a famous Soviet educator, elaborating in detail the concept of discipline in general and that of students in

* *Ibid.*, Vol. II, p. 375.

† *Webster's Third New International Dictionary* (Unabridged), Merriam Co., Springfield, Massachusetts, 1963, p. 1932, col. 3.

‡ N. K. Krupskaya, *Pedagogical Works*, Moscow, 1959, Vol. 3, p. 576.

particular, says: Discipline is a means to accomplish successfully collective tasks, an inner freedom which helps to maintain more secure attitudes, and conscious awareness of the necessity for developing the habit of behavorial controls.

(iii) "Soviet school develops in the students initiative, independence, an ability to subordinate, promptness, and self-control. It creates in the youngsters a new, critical approach to shortcomings and, simultaneously, respect for the school authority, for the teacher, for adults, for the general point of view of the collective, for experience of previous generations. The teacher's trust is combined with setting high standards and demands."*

**Educators**

The Soviet school system makes a clear distinction between subject matter teachers and those whose main task is to "bring up" children. (For details see *School Internats.*) Though the Russian term in translation, namely, "upbringers," is rather a clumsy one, it was considered important to retain the delineation of functions. Subject-matter teachers are referred to as teachers.

**Hooligan**

Usually an older child or adolescent who commits some antisocial act. This term is closest to our acting-out delinquent.

**Kandidat member A.P.S.**

Provisional member of Academy of Pedagogical Sciences.

**Kolkhoz**

Collective farm, a system under which the people own the land and tools collectively.

**Komsomol**

See listing under *Oktyabryata.*

**Janusz Korchak (Henryk Goldschmit) (1878)**

Famous Polish educator. A physician by profession, he became interested in education. He wrote many popular articles and books for parents and also some for children. He died during World War II in Treblinka, together with the children who were in his care in the Warsaw Ghetto, August 5, 1942.

**Materialistic point of view**

Implies a view based upon the theory of dialectical materialism. (See *Dialectical Materialism.*)

* *Pedagogitchesky Slovar,* Akademiya Pedagogicheskich Nauk, Moscow, 1959, Vol. 1, p. 343.

**Morals**

(In many places in this text used interchangeably with ethics.) A process of formulating moral (ethical) characteristics of personality, and habits of behavior.* V. I. Lenin demanded that "The whole process of upbringing, educating, and teaching the contemporary Soviet generation should be in the spirit of Communist morals."† The basic content of Communist morals (ethics) is to create and foster Soviet patriotism, proletarian internationalism, Communist attitudes toward work and communal property, socialistic humanism, optimism, self-discipline, collectivism, camaraderie, honesty, ability for criticism of oneself and of others. The foregoing characterizes the moral makeup of outstanding Soviet citizens and exerts profound influence upon their behavior. The first conceptions of morals as well as habits related to them are formulated in the home. Later, the school as well as Pioneer and Komsomol begin to play a very important role in fostering their further growth and development.

**Oktyabryata, created in 1924**

The first step on the road to membership in the Communist Party. The name originated to commemorate the Revolution of October 1917. The children in this group were as old as the Revolution, hence, the name *Oktyabryata*. This group consists of students in the primary grades (ages eight to ten). In order to be chosen by the class collective, pupils must obtain good marks and exhibit excellent behavior in school and at home.

**Pioneer, created in 1922**

The second step on the road to membership in the Communist Party. After "graduating" from *Oktyabryata,* the children (ages ten to sixteen) become Pioneers (also elected by the class collective).

**Komsomol, created in 1917**

The third step on the road to membership in the Communist Party. These are the older high school and university students and working youth (ages sixteen to twenty-three). It is more difficult to be promoted from Pioneer to Komsomol. The adolescents and young adults remain there until age twenty-seven or older, unless invited earlier (very rarely) to join the Communist Party.

* *Ibid.,* Vol. 1, pp. 771-772.
† V. I. Lenin, *Collected Works,* 4th Edition, Vol. 31, p. 266.

**Parents' Committee**

After debating whether to use the term PTA or leave Parents Committee, it was felt that since the structure is entirely different (see Chapter 9) we would use the original term.

**RSFSR**

Russian Socialist Federated Soviet Republic.*

**School Internat**

The English term "boarding school" is not an appropriate one to use since the philosophy, goal, purpose, as well as the socio-economic status of children who attend, are entirely different from those established in the Soviet Union. Hence, we took the liberty to leave the original Russian term. Soviet children go to school and live on the premises. They see their parents one day a week during their Sunday visit home. They get one month's vacation (in summer) usually to spend it with their family. The curriculum of a school internat is exactly the same as that of a day school. The emphasis is not only on academic achievement but also on vocational preparation and practice.

**Sovkhoz**

State-owned farm.

**Stakhanov**

Alexei G. Stakhanov (born 1905), Russian miner who devised a system of higher production.

**Stakhanovite**

A worker in the U.S.S.R. whose work is considerably above average and who is therefore awarded recognition and special privileges.†

**Virgin Lands**

Young people volunteer to develop virgin lands until now barren and unpopulated to build cities and towns as well as agricultural settlements. They begin industry and agricultural production. Sometimes they also find and develop natural resources which until that time have not been developed.

**Youth Patrol (druzheniky)**

Since vandalism and hooliganism increased, voluntary brigades

* Robert J. Schwartz, *Complete Dictionary of Abbreviations,* T. Y. Crowell, New York, 1955, p. 156.

† *Webster's Third New International Dictionary,* unabridged. Merriam Company, Springfield, Mass., 1963, p. 2221.

consisting of university students, workers, professional people, retirees, etc., wearing armbands to indicate their function, patrol the streets during the late evening hours and night to prevent antisocial behavior of youth.

This glossary is not meant to be complete, nor should it be considered a substitute for a more thorough study of any one of the meanings involved. I hope, though, that the flavor of the ideas and the nature of the institutions referred to in these terms will become clearer to the reader as he rediscovers them in the context of the selections which follow.

*Part One*

# *Philosophy*

The philosophy of a school system is the basis from which all its methods and implementations stem. Each observation of a visitor or of a reader must rest upon the understanding of philosophical principles involved; otherwise the view becomes distorted and meaningless. I felt that the first part of the selections should help the reader to find his way through a maze of different approaches toward child-rearing problems.

However, these selections by no means represent the total concerns of Soviet educators. The attempt here was to extract from the abundance of materials a few, in diversified areas, which may be of special interest to the reader, and which also would serve as a transition to a different environment.

# 1 *Heredity and Upbringing*

*G. S. Prozorov*

CHILDREN'S APTITUDES vary consderably. Marxist science does not deny the existence of these differences. "From each according to his ability, to each according to his needs" is the ideal we strive for. In our socialistic society, which is the first step toward Communism, this principle is already in practice.

Creation of the material as well as the spiritual prerequisites for a planned transition toward Communism will bring about the allotment of necessary goods.

The aptitudes of people are different and always will be. The term "aptitude" implies all the individual's personality characteristics, which in turn determine his fitness in specific areas, and also his functioning at the highest level of his abilities.

Equality, for which the Communists fought and are still fighting, never was assumed to imply "equal abilities." Communists strove to create conditions under which everyone would have equal opportunity to manifest and develop his potential.

There are no people completely devoid of any ability. Thanks to the variety and richness of human endeavor, everyone has aptitude in some area, which he can successfully utilize. The higher the social motivation of his function, the greater his stimulation to work, and the better the achieved results. The

G. S. Prozorov, *Heredity and Upbringing*, Uchpedgiz, Moscow, 1960, pp. 3-43.

responsibility in raising children is to develop fully their potential, and to bring up the youngsters as active, socially minded members of a society in which they would eventually create new material and spiritual values. This (psychic) human development is independent of any hereditary laws.

Each child is endowed by nature with some individual physiological characteristics which represent potentialities. The task of education is to create favorable conditions under which these potentialities would blossom into full development. What is being transferred by heredity is not ready-made abilities, but only the prerequisites for their development; that is, certain physiological characteristics of the organism which demand further development are transferred from parents to children in accordance with biological laws of heredity. These hereditary prerequisites may develop, but they may wilt, depending on prevailing conditions, the nature of the educational influence, and the whole system of upbringing and teaching to which a given child is exposed. Theoretically, it is possible for equally gifted children to achieve different levels of development, as well as for unequally gifted children to reach the same developmental level. This of course can be proved by many examples in real life. Everything depends on the conditions under which the children grow up, and how their abilities are fostered. Hereditary inclinations determine neither the whole process of the child's growth nor the realization of his individual potential.

Natural inclinations are mainly hidden in peculiarities of the human nervous system. But the nervous system does not remain static in its development. Conditions of life and of upbringing can reinforce or shatter the nervous system. Native abilities by no means totally determine future personality characteristics and behavior. The great Russian physiologist I. P. Pavlov wrote:

> The mode of human and of animal behavior is conditioned not only by inborn native characteristics of the nervous system but also by influences which were and are exerted upon the organism during his individual existence, namely, that of continuous upbringing and education in its broadest concept.
>
> Therefore, besides the above-mentioned characteristic of the

nervous system, its very important peculiarity, that of high flexibility, is continuously apparent.*

Fullest development of native abilities can be achieved only by a well-organized method of upbringing. In this process the leading role is played by specific activities. Concrete, practical work in a given field is the better way to foster growth of ability, and lack of experience may leave native potentiality undeveloped and hidden.

A. M. Gorky persistently stressed that innate ability is only a spark, which may either die out or develop into a flame. There is only one way, he says, to develop native talent: namely, through hard work and great demands upon oneself.

No matter how gifted one is, any task requires first of all effort and strength. Just as the development of a strong body is fostered by a healthy daily routine of work and rest, personal hygiene, and physical fitness, the native abilities need favorable conditions in order to blossom. What physical exercise does for the body, mental training does for the mind.

The ability of the student to study develops during the learning process. This developed capability helps the pupil to master subject matter. Realizing the close relationship, experienced teachers strive not only to furnish the pupils with knowledge but also to provide them with individual tasks which they have to fulfill independently. The method which fosters realization of potentialities is one which, as N. K. Krupskaya says, "does not provide the pupil with ready-made solutions" but forces him to think, to analyze.

Since abilities grow and strengthen during activities, it is necessary not to limit the child to a one-sided action, but to supplement his studies with physical labor. The "law of strengthening school ties with life and the further development of the national system of education in U.S.S.R." strongly supports the above premise.

The system of education wherein intellectual and physical work tasks are united and placed at the same level was discussed by Karl Marx in his *Kapital,* where he claims that "synchroniz-

* I. P. Pavlov, *Collected Works,* Vol. III, Book 2, Academy of Science, U.S.S.R., 1951, p. 269.

ing both of them is better for the child than devoting oneself without interruption to one kind." In this way, he said, each provides a rest from the other and refreshes the pupil's strength.

This system makes the basic task of learning easier, and furnishes the pupil with useful and necessary working habits. With correct supervision, the child can acquire many good working habits appropriate for his age and school curriculum. The speed and ease with which the student will be able to absorb new material and to retain new knowledge depend largely on his aptitude in the given area. But all children, regardless of their native abilities and their development, must acquire the habit of working hard.

It is wrong to give children the impression that unsuccessful attempts indicate lack of ability, they may lose belief in their strength, and be unwilling to make further effort. It is also wrong to suggest that, without any effort on the part of the pupil, ability alone will assure him his goal. It is false to assume that gifted people can master knowledge effortlessly in a chosen field through inspiration alone. "Inspiration does not like to prompt lazy ones," said Tchaikovsky.

The prominent Soviet pedagogue and writer, A. S. Makarenko, believed that "while to be lazy is wicked, to be talented and lazy is horrifying." Children must be taught to work regularly and honestly to the best of their ability, and to perform not only their school assignments but also their household chores. Those who do not develop diligence during their childhood years become adolescents and adults who are fit for neither advanced study nor productive work.

Usually, knowledge that is easily acquired without being firmly imbedded is quickly forgotten. A student with great promise, who in a secondary school excelled because of his talents, may fail in an institution of higher learning because of bad study habits. It is for this reason that the school and home alike must foster a systematic approach to mental tasks, and a realization that one should depend more upon real effort and hard work than upon talent. Special abilities not only do not excuse one from work; they set additional demands. Our students must be reminded in school as well as at home of Marx's saying: "The road which leads to the glowing height of knowledge is not a comfortable one, but a hard one, and only those who are not afraid of labor manage to reach its top."

Sometimes it is said that genius or talent conquer all. This statement cannot be substantiated. Certainly, some geniuses could be named who had to overcome many difficulties before their greatness was acknowledged. However, even such people as Lomonosov and Gorky, who succeeded in developing their capacities despite unfavorable conditions, cannot serve as an example that geniuses always fulfill themselves, because many more fail to develop their creativity in an adverse environment.

The backwardness of nations which until recently were colonies is explained not by biological characteristics of "racial inequality," but by the effects of suppression. Such nations, once liberated, begin immediately to develop their economy and nurture their native culture. Many peoples of Russia, such as Karelians, Uzbekiens, Tadzhikiens, Kazakhiens, Kirghiziens, and Bashkiriens, who were not only suppressed but rendered almost extinct under tsarism, blossomed during socialism. For the first time in human history a social system was created which guaranteed to each child, regardless of his nationality, sex, and parental background, conditions favorable to the development of a well-rounded personality and the full exercise of capabilities. This is the decisive difference between a capitalist and socialist system.

The communistic re-education of the society, says the Decree dealing with the School Reorganization, "is closely tied to the upbringing of the 'new man,' who will harmoniously combine spiritual richness, morality, and physical fitness."

The task of the school and the home is to rear the children in a communistic spirit, develop in our youth a materialistic world outlook, and foster communistic ideology and behavior.

In order to clarify the decisive role upbringing plays in personality development, let us examine the limitations of heredity factors in relation to education. In the formulation of a person's view of the world, the decisive ingredients are the environment, educational goals, and the normal development of the child—not biological heredity. In case the child acquires religious or nationalistic prejudices, the only way to effect a change is to influence his consciousness; only the method of purposeful education can free a human mind from prejudice and superstition.

Heredity cannot hinder the development of such personality characteristics as honesty, truthfulness, and integrity. Each child can be brought up to live in accordance with high social ideals. The same is true with regard to work habits. Only a physical handicap can serve as an excuse for preventing mastery of relevant work.

Sometimes, when people comment "like father, like son," they are referring not to hereditary similarities but to the father's personal influence upon his son, and also to the environmental condition of the son's upbringing. A child's character is malleable. A withdrawn youngster (whose undesirable traits can be attributed to an unhealthy home environment) may, when educated skillfully, become an active member of a collective.

Frequently, children become rude or nervously sick because of an unhealthy relationship between their parents, and the ensuing fights and subtle conflicts that children witness in their family. When a child is surrounded by brave, lively adults who can overcome life's difficulties without undue complaint, he acquires the same characteristics. He grows up physically and mentally fit and healthy.

Pampering a child has a strongly negative effect upon his upbringing. It weakens his will power, renders him incapable of overcoming even the slightest difficulty, encourages unjustified demands toward adults in his immediate environment, and produces an egotistical and callous nature. No less negative is the effect produced by unwarranted strictness and constant threatening. When a child recognizes that the demands made on him are just, rather than designed to create fear, he will respond willingly. If, however, fear is the only operative, inevitably his effort will be paralyzed, his mental development blocked; eventually, he will turn to lies, cunning, and hypocrisy.

It is absolutely wrong to be inconsistent with a youngster, i.e., sometimes lavishing too much praise on him while at other times reprimanding or punishing him too severely. As a result of such inconsistency, the youngster grows up to be nervous, harassed, and unstable.

There are instances when single character trends are conditioned by biological causes. For example, a high degree of tension is often related to a weak physical state, resulting in the tendency to tire easily and become irritable. This condition can be ameliorated, but to achieve a change it is necessary to include pedagogical as well as medical measures. A well-balanced diet, gradual physical exercise when the child is ready, a firmly followed daily routine of work and rest, and more time in the fresh air, would offer the correct pedagogical-medical approach to diminishing or even eliminating the problem.

Clearly, then, we can conclude that heredity does not predetermine future character trends. Personality develops through the process of upbringing. For example, the personality of Ilya Ilich Obolomov, I. A. Gontcharov's famous hero, was the product not of heredity but of the prevailing environmental conditions of Tsarist Russia and of the education he received.

The better the educators and parents know a child, the better are the results achieved by well-organized, purposeful upbringing. Knowing a child means understanding the developmental stage he is in and recognizing his characteristics as an individual; both these elements are subjects of scientific study and research in the field of pedagogy. Parents, too, must be exposed to pedagogical findings, especially those which deal with the developmental peculiarities of different stages in the child's life. Once the general characteristics of a particular age group are understood, there is a need for a thorough study of the child (or young or older adolescent) as an individual.

Children of the same chronological age are unlike one another. There are no two identical youngsters. Just as the knowledge of the laws of nature helps one to master it, and the discovery of laws which govern the development of society enhances the possibilities of revolutionary changes, the understanding of a child creates an opportunity to influence him successfully.

All educational measures should take into consideration specific characteristics of the child; the development of his capabilities is possible only when there is a real understanding of his individuality.

Early interest evidenced by a child in a given area should not be immediately interpreted as a manifestation of his genius or exceptional talent. Not infrequently, hopeful parents, at the slightest indication of a child's interest in music or art, immediately see the boy as a future Mozart or Moussorgsky, or consider any of his paintings as good as Renoir's or Repin's. Of course, there are sometimes signs of talent in early childhood. Mozart's genius became apparent at the extremely early age of three. But this is an exception rather than a rule. Generally, children's early interests do not last long and change frequently, depending on their situation. Nevertheless, parents must pay attention to them.

Though native inclinations may appear early, lack of clearly pronounced interests during this period must not concern parents too much; abilities which later develop into talents more often are demonstrated at an older age. In an attempt to define capabilities, extreme caution and thoughtfulness should be exercised. There are too many examples of serious errors of judgment, wherein people who in their youth were considered untalented in a certain field, later contributed greatly to this given area of human endeavor. Isaac Newton in his childhood did not show any ability for studying, but this did not prevent his becoming a learned physicist.

K. S. Stanislavsky, an outstanding actor-director and creator of the "method" school of acting, wrote: "True talents are often hidden deep and it is difficult to bring them out. Therefore, many times the now well-known actors failed their first tryouts or barely passed them. (Chaliapin, Kniper [wife of Chekhov].)"

The Russian author C. T. Aksakov was fifty-six years old when he printed his first book. The great Russian writer of fables, I. A. Krylov, started to create in his forties.

Talents may appear at any given stage of human life, and it is never too late to begin to develop them.

Some parents complain that their children have a bad memory, which they blame upon hereditary factors: "My daughter's memory is just as bad as mine," or, "She studied and studied, thought she knew it well, but now she forgot it all, because she has such a bad memory"—says a mother, using these rationalizations as excuses for her child's lack of acquired knowledge.

Obviously, the quality of people's memory varies considerably. Therefore, we can come to only one practical conclusion: One must intensify his effort to improve and develop memory through continuous practice which directs his habits toward concise thinking and efficient learning.

There are pupils who read through their home assignments only once, and believe that they have really absorbed the new material. This way of "studying" is harmful not only because it is superficial but also because it does not help to develop the memory. Students who cram a few days before finals quickly forget almost everything they have studied in this way. To retain subject matter, it is necessary to create in the cortex a definite system of associations. The more links that become developed in the process of absorbing the given material, the better remembered is the content. Mechanical memorization does not help; only clear comprehension of the text enables its mastery and the establishment of lasting associations. Automatic absorption is permissible only when the character of the material calls for it. For example, when studying foreign languages, one must often memorize words or even whole phrases; however, in a logically linked and connected text, this method only hampers and tires the memory, rather than stimulating its growth.

It has been mentioned that when a child is told about his "bad heredity," he uses it as an excuse to justify such failings as lack of effort and attention. Only a student who is always fully attentive becomes a good one. Psychology differentiates between two kinds of attention: voluntary, which means purposeful concentration on a given subject or occurrence, and involuntary, which takes place automatically, irrespective of our will.

Like memory, attention also can be strengthened by practice. The ability to direct attention can be cultivated by deliberate training. The formation of this habit should be started at a very early age.

Holding a child's attention can be accomplished by stimulating his interest in a given subject. Parents should support and develop children's interest in learning first of all by exhibiting an interest in school and its curriculum. However, it is not possible to sustain the entire learning process solely on the basis of interest. Not all home assignments, for example, can be made to seem equally stimulating. Honor students make progress in all subject matters, even though not all subjects challenge them equally. Sheer will power, exerted during classroom sessions as well as during home study, can be of enormous help when applied to the kind of subject matter which does not inspire great natural interest.

Instead of being concerned about heredity, one should strive to instill neatness, obedience, concentration, purposefulness, strong will power, and attentiveness, through the application of correct methods of upbringing.

Thinking, which is the leading psychic process, must receive special attention not only in school but also at home. On the ability to think depends the capacity to analyze, to judge, to search for and find interrelationships, and to summarize and to generalize. The single most important aim of teaching is to develop the pupil's mental ability; and the best way to achieve this is to stimulate independent thinking. At all times, such effort should be supported and rewarded.

The thinking process begins when a need for understanding arises. The parents must try to develop the child's ability to think by stipulating systematic exercise and specific training of the brain rather than by relying upon heredity.

Will power is essential to action, especially to any undertaking which is geared to develop one's own personality, self-education, erudition, special abilities, and individual character traits. It manifests itself mostly when difficulties and hindrances have to be overcome. A strong-willed person always subordinates his wishes and desires to the moral principles by which he lives.

An individual whose fleeting desires rule his life is weak. If one is clever and talented, but without a strong will, both characteristics become quite useless. Strong will plays a decisive role in acts of heroism. Great purposefulness and a strong will are characteristic of all fighters dedicated to a cause. Unwavering determination to reach a given goal is of basic significance to any task, whether the goal be a scientific task, an educational one, or the job of child rearing. Endeavors which require will power are always conscious; because of this, the development of will power in children is closely tied to the growth of consciousness, to the working out of his views of the world, his ideals, and his strivings.

A clearly formulated world outlook is one of the most important factors in developing a strong will. Lack of firm opinions and beliefs weakens the will and makes it unstable. On the other hand, it is not sufficient to influence consciousness alone. All good intentions must become accomplished deeds in order to make the will genuinely strong.

The first and basic indication of a strong will in an individual is a determination to complete each given task with persistence (a very valuable characteristic) regardless of hindrances and difficulties.

It is important that adults regularly check to be sure that children have fulfilled the duties requested of them. Often a youngster, although he understands the necessity of a given assignment, gets carried away by games or something else equally exciting and is inclined to avoid the task; but realizing that his activities will be checked by his parents, he will give up the more interesting activity in favor of the necessary one.

In the process of education, even minor incidents are significant, because the child reacts to each of them. Some parents wonder whether they should insist that the youngster put his toys in place each evening, so that he will learn order early. Developing such a habit fosters the acquisition of will power. In case the child does not want to clean up, depriving him of his toys for a time until he agrees to place them where they belong proves to be a good educational measure.

Will power develops best under the favorable conditions of collective work, when the child learns systematically to fulfill clearly defined tasks.

Older children should be instilled with a desire to train and educate themselves. An interest in spiritual growth and the development of positive character traits increases considerably during adolescence. This interest must be supported and stimulated, because in this developmental stage the method of self-improvement plays a pertinent role in the development of the whole personality.

Work education, through the systematic participation of children in socially meaningful tasks as well as in household chores, fosters their physical and mental abilities and develops characteristics which are needed and useful for study and for any future activity.

Observations of children in school and at home prove that a bad memory, weak will and short attention span usually occur in children who are excused from all physical work. They are not able to do anything independently. The laziness their parents complain about is not an inborn characteristic. It develops as a result of parents' faulty philosophy of protecting children from any demands for physical work. Work is an indispensable tool in the formation of character. Knowledge and habits play an important role in accomplishing any physical task; without them no work is possible. To work means to express oneself through action, to enrich one's intellectual horizons, and to develop one's capabilities.

One of the most important duties of parents is to condition their children to physical work. "The Decree to strengthen the ties of school with life and to further the development of the national system of education in U.S.S.R." considers it necessary to "prepare children very early for active participation in socially meaningful work. Youths of fifteen or sixteen and older must be included in all feasible socially useful work, and it is necessary for their subsequent educational experience to be closely linked with those of productive labor in the national economy."

The work education of children must begin in the family before they start school. When they are still very young, they should be taught to fulfill certain duties at home; for example, to make their own beds, clean up toys, sweep the floor, set the table, etc. In this way they will learn to be self-reliant and independent. They must learn to be responsible for the accomplishment of any tasks given to them, of short or of long duration. This participation in house chores is the first very important step in work education.

Pedagogical science differentiates between the concept of

"development" and that of "education." "Development" refers to the process of organic and psychic changes the child undergoes passing through the developmental stages of infancy, childhood, early and late adolescence, young adulthood, and finally mature adulthood.

"Education means a system of organized, purposeful influences to which the child is exposed by parents at home, teachers in school, and other educators in extracurricular groups."

The processes of a child's development and education are so closely linked together that they are almost inseparable. It is impossible to visualize one without the other.

The influence of the older generation upon growing children and youth stimulates their developmental process. The better the child's education, the healthier becomes his development.

Since the child's development helps to broaden his educational possibilities, a process of dialectical interrelationship takes place.

While the child learns to communicate verbally by proceeding from word repetition to talking and finally reaching an ability to differentiate between various word meanings and their complicated usage, his vocabulary becomes enlarged and his memory enriched. He goes through a process which is not only educational but also developmental.

Each generation inherits from the previous ones vast achievements in culture, art, and technique. Thanks to education and upbringing, the growing generation has an opportunity to utilize these resources in their lives and to enrich them further by new discoveries and inventions for the future descendants.

The practical conclusion from all that has been said above is that one must actively help the child's development through a purposeful education rather than by depending on his native, inherited abilities.

A correct upbringing should stimulate his positive, natural capabilities and eliminate any negative characteristics he might have inherited.

The task of Communist upbringing is to raise a well-rounded, harmoniously developed young generation. While we are striving to create a society in which each individual will utilize and realize his potentialities through productive work in his chosen field, we always emphasize the diversity which exists between individual potentialities and individual needs.

In order to prepare the generation now growing up for the demands of a Communist society which will soon become a reality, we do not rear them by methods which would eliminate the differences existing between individuals. On the contrary, we utilize means which foster the fullest development of each individual; we must satisfy more and more the continuously growing variety of interests, requirements, and inclinations, as long as they are not directed against the common interests of the society.

A harmonious development means one which utilizes to their maximum all the native abilities useful to society. A child exceptionally talented in one specific area should not be forced to develop other areas of human endeavor equally well at the expense of his manifested talent. But neither should one go to the extreme of giving a talented youngster only a one-sided education. It should not be forgotten that a contemporary man cannot be considered educated without mastery of the school curriculum, which provides a basis for his future studies. In the process of acquiring knowledge the capabilities of youngsters which need special development become apparent.

The educational process is especially important to children and youth, although adults also may and should be responsive to it. But educating adults is an entirely different process, since their personality is already formed, while youngsters are still engaged in the development of theirs. It is much easier to affect children, whose nervous systems are more flexible than those of grownups. The youngster, whose organism, intellect, and character are still growing, is particularly receptive to correct methods of upbringing.

Nevertheless, there are some adolescents whose behavior contradicts the established morality norms of the Soviet man. These failures are brought about not by hereditary factors, as some parents would like to believe, but by poor upbringing. The task of the Soviet family and school is to develop in youth high moral values and readiness for independence in life. The moral values are expressed not in words but in deeds. "Show your point of view not through words but through deeds," said Lenin.* This means that the individual's morality is determined by his behavior.

When raising youth we must remember Lenin's statement, "The Communist upbringing of youth should not be a sweet preaching of rules of ethics. This does not constitute an education. . . . Only through toiling together with workers in industry and in agriculture is it possible to become a real Communist."† "All education should be arranged in such a way that in each day time should be found for the youth to solve a practical problem of common significance, no matter how small and simple the task might be."‡

In order to achieve the goals of communistic rearing of children and youth, it is necessary to provide them with practical work experience, socially meaningful, which they are ready for. "Without work and struggle," said Lenin, "theoretical knowledge acquired in Communist pamphlets is absolutely meaningless, since it continues to perpetuate the isolation of theory from practice, which composes the most repelling characteristic of the old bourgeois society."§ Children and youth must realize that their work brings real gain to their family or city, town or village. Otherwise the education which takes place is not Communist in spirit.

The child visualizes life in accordance with his environment as well as with the way his family and the people around represent it to him. The actions and relationships he witnesses teach him more than what the parents tell him. In order to educate children correctly the family life must be well organized and conducive to good upbringing. The parents must watch not only their children's behavior but also their own, since children often imitate parental behavior.

* V. I. Lenin, *Collected Works,* Vol. 29, p. 270.
† Lenin, *Collected Works,* Vol. 31, p. 270.
‡ *Ibid.,* p. 274.
§ *Ibid.,* p. 260.

Only when both parents have the same world outlook and when they agree for the most part upon the same educational approach can they bring up their children successfully.

Habits cultivated in early childhood play an important role in behavior, attitudes toward tasks, duties, and responsibilities. Human life would be much more complex if we had to think through each step of our behavior and every minor work detail instead of doing them automatically.

Early childhood should be called the period not only of play but also of the development of habits necessary for the entire life, which the parents must instill early in the child. Since these habits are taught mainly by practice and by training, the primary effort should be placed on their firm establishment in the child. While he will understand later why they are so important, at first it should be sufficient that adults realize their necessity and usefulness. Eventually these habits will influence the youngster's comprehension and feelings and will help to develop his inner orderliness. All successful educational efforts combined together bring about the development of the so-called "second nature" of an individual.

Correct upbringing is not dependent upon heredity. Children grow up as industrious individuals who are able to face and overcome difficulties as well as negative occurrences as an integral part of their life experience.

The decisive role which upbringing plays in the development of personality as well as the importance of practice in widening all recognized capabilities such as thinking, attention and memory, do not negate heredity completely. An examination of the whole history of humankind verifies the positive role heredity has played in human development.

When the very same irritations are elicited in certain parts of the brain during a prolonged period of time (many generations), they will definitely change the structure of the nervous tissue, and according to the laws of adjustment these changes may take hold and become hereditarily transferable. I. P. Pavlov proved that conditioned reflexes, being individually acquired, may change to unconditioned reflexes, which become reinforced by way of hereditary transmission.

According to the biological laws of hereditary, the brain, the hand, and other organs of the human body become more developed with the passing of many generations. Under the influence and stimulation of work and of social relationships, the human brain improves, as does the ability to think; and the sensory organs become perfected.

This biological part of human personality did not play a decisive role in the development of human society. The factor which differentiated the human being from the animal kingdom was work. Though man walks erect and has his hands free for toil, though his speaking ability changed his brain and he built working tools, though he earns a living and meets his social needs, still he is not completely free of animal characteristics. Frederick Engels in his book *Anti-Dühring* implies that there may be only quantitative differentiations between the degrees of bestiality and humanness. While it is obvious that primitive man was ruled by his animal instincts subordinated to his biological nature, in time human social needs played a role which steadily grew in importance. In the process of meeting them, man changed and perfected the biological structure of his personality.

Each generation inherits, of course, the developmental level of biological personality structure which was reached by their predecessors. But human beings are not limited by it; they can progress, perfecting and enlarging their achievements in controlling nature and changing it by their action. In this process each individual also changes his own nature. By this historical course of action human society as well as the individual develops.

These changes in human nature are strengthened by way of hereditary transmission. This provides the individual with an opportunity to eliminate negative characteristics of heredity while fostering the positive ones. Therefore, parents must take care of themselves to make sure they have health, strength, and endurance. Healthy parents produce healthy children, while sick parents produce sickly children. Daily routines of work and rest, normal diet, fresh air, body hygiene and cleanliness of clothing and living quarters are all indispensable conditions for fostering the health of parents and their children. Parents who overindulge in alcoholic beverages bring great harm to their children because of the negative effect upon the whole organism. Alcoholism of parents produces hereditary aftereffects in children who often are weak not only physically but also psychologically.

The childhood of youngsters whose parents are drunkards is a very difficult one. Instead of receiving love and care, they suffer great hardships. Such children become sick and nervous adults. Alcohol often breaks up the family. Parents forget about their responsibilities; children often witness fights, which have a harmful effect upon their nervous systems and their whole development. Sometimes parents even treat their children to wine, thinking it will not do them any harm. This view is absolutely wrong, because the organism of a child is much more susceptible than that of an adult.

Parents who want their children to grow up as healthy individuals must give up excessive use of alcohol.

The education of the child begins the moment he is born. The necessary prerequisites for further development and for formulation of the personality manifest themselves in early childhood. The concern for children should be expressed before that by creating favorable life conditions for the mother.

The physical as well as psychic well-being of the woman during pregnancy is one of the facts which determines the growth of the embryo. Living one life with the mother until his birth, he becomes grossly affected by her fear, worries and disturbances. The future father should keep all of this in mind. When the husband and future father, as well as others mindful of all these important factors, act correctly, there will be no reason to complain that the child's sickness is hereditary.

And so the decisive role in the development of personality is played by purposeful education in school and at home. The task of the parents is to create such conditions of life and engage the child in those activities which will foster in him the development of a Communist world outlook, and behavior which will make him a builder of the Communist society. Every child needs education, no matter what his native abilities; without it he cannot develop his capabilities.

Differences existing among people are not the result of heredity, but of education. People often do not develop to their highest potential only because they lack favorable living conditions and correct upbringing.

In a Socialist society, where the whole environment fosters the development of the Communist world outlook, and where the efforts of the government and of society are directed toward improvement of economic living conditions as well as toward providing greater cultural and educational opportunities, the role of upbringing becomes most decisive.

# 2 *Self-Discipline in Adolescents*

*V. A. Krutetsky*
*and N. S. Lukin*

## § Introduction

ALTHOUGH THIS BOOK is designed primarily for teachers, student teachers, upbringers, pioneer leaders and others involved in educating and raising adolescents, it is hoped that it will be helpful to parents also.

The period of adolescence presents certain specific problems. Many teachers consider this developmental phase particularly difficult for achieving self-discipline. Often teachers, not sufficiently familiar with the psychological characteristics of this age, do not know how to deal with the problems that arise.

In adolescence a great change takes place in the student's school environment. His teacher, whom he knew well for four years, becomes replaced by many new ones; at the same time the teenager is introduced to an enriched curriculum. All of this demands special adjustment and brings about a change in existing relationships. The student does not consider himself a child any longer and wants to be treated as an adult, for which, of course, he is not yet ready.

V. A. Krutetsky and N. S. Lukin, *Self-Discipline in Adolescents,* Uchpedgiz, Moscow, 1960, pp. 3-15, 167-228.

During adolescence he also undergoes many physical changes (this period marks the beginning of his sexual maturation) which have a strong influence upon him and which require much of the teacher's attention. Parents as well as anyone who works with teenagers must understand this adolescence period.

Since the purpose of this book is not to discuss general physical and psychological characteristics of adolescence, we will limit ourselves to considering them only as they relate specifically and directly to the process of acquiring discipline.

Our task is to spread knowledge and experience gained by schools in dealing with these problems, and also to popularize the results of observation and research of Soviet educators. The main goal of this book is not to submit a list of practical "do's" and "don'ts," but to discuss ways and conditions under which certain personality characteristics develop.

Though this book does not encompass the entire rich experience in the area of developing self-discipline in adolescence, we will consider our task accomplished when this book is used by teachers, who work with adolescents, as well as parents.

## § Discipline and Self-discipline

While building communism, new characteristics of man are being developed. When the spiritual growth of the Soviet people takes place and their individual interests become subordinate to those of the collective, self-discipline becomes of the utmost importance. One of the most responsible tasks of the Soviet school is fostering it in students.

*What Is Discipline?* The constitution of the U.S.S.R. interprets the concept of discipline as follows: The basic duties of Soviet citizens are to obey the law, to approach social responsibilities honestly, and to respect the rules of socialist society. These are the qualities the school must bring out in the future generation.

When we speak of students' discipline, we have in mind the discipline which consists in obeying the rules set in the school, at home, and in the street and in conforming to the requests and demands of teachers and parents. Students who do not follow these regulations cannot be considered self-disciplined. But discipline imposed from without is not in itself satisfactory. Even an ardent egotist may successfully follow these rules though he disregards interests of the collective.

True discipline is composed of various relationships in a collective. A man with a well-developed "inner" sense of discipline is able successfully to control his behavior through deep-seated feelings of responsibility. He respects the collective, acts according to its interests, subordinates his aims and goals to those of the collective, and not only is immune to negative influences (the necessity of developing this last characteristic was often pointed out by A. S. Makarenko) but also actively fights to strengthen self-discipline in the collective. He reacts decisively to any infringement of discipline, even in the most trivial instances.

A. S. Makarenko talked constantly about "discipline of struggle and of conquest." A self-disciplined student is characterized less by restrained behavior than by "the what and how" of his action.

The discipline cultivated in our schools and in society at large is a conscious discipline, where the need for its existence, as well as its goals, are clearly understood. This comprehension must express itself in a deep inner conviction regarding the indisputable necessity for discipline, and as a result firm habits of behavior supporting this belief should be established. Only then will a student voluntarily and willingly fulfill his responsibilities in the best possible way. A student becomes self-disciplined without being forced. He feels morally uncomfortable when he violates a trust or does not fulfill his duty. Even when the task is an unpleasant one, he still derives pleasure from demands he sets for himself.

This student behaves in a self-disciplined manner not only in a collective and when others watch him but also when he is alone and even when no one will be able to find out. This behavior in solitude best indicates man's level of self-discipline, says Makarenko.

*To summarize, self-discipline is the ability to as well as the* *habit of controlling one's behavior, of subordinating it to the rules and demands of the collective and of the society,* and *of performing in accordance with social responsibilities.* A man with a well-developed inner discipline firmly and exactly follows the accepted rules of behavior and obeys the authority in charge. In other words, "in the Soviet society, we consider a self-disciplined man one who, under any circumstances, is always able to choose correct behavior most beneficial for society, and who finds in himself strength to follow this through."*

There is a distinction between self-discipline as a temporary condition and behavior and self-discipline as a personality characteristic, says Professor Levitov. It is important to keep this differentiation in mind while working out educational methods.

Interest in subject matter or in activity motivates the student's self-discipline, although there are instances when overstimulation may result in the breaking down of controls. Although sometimes the fear of repercussions or a desire to join a club where good marks are a prerequisite may produce temporary improvement, lasting results are achieved only without ulterior motives.

Well-developed self-discipline is significant in fulfilling "must" tasks without conflict which would hamper accomplishment. Here, Levitov indicates, the behavior proceeds in accordance with set rules and demands. In other instances there are circumstances which preclude breaching of discipline, but this conforming is inherent in the situation itself, not in the student's inner motivation.

The durations of time during which the student remains self-disciplined vary greatly. As soon as the situation changes, the behavior is altered. For example, a lesson becomes boring, stimulation disappears, and so does the discipline. There is no anticipation of reward or punishment, hence the student gradually loses self-control, gets out of hand. When the teacher's demands become vague, the student's determination for self-disciplined behavior vanishes. It is important to point out that there are situations when otherwise self-disciplined pupils exhibit undesirable behavior. This usually occurs when the subject matter

* A. S. Makarenko, *Collected Works,* Vol. IV, 1957, p. 362.

or activity is dull, or when the student considers a given task unnecessary, or when the goal is nebulous and the demands unfair and erroneous or unclear. Obviously truly self-disciplined youngsters do not lose their control and do not change their behavior even under such conditions.

Self-discipline of students must occur not only in a school situation and during studying but also in any life situation. This is not sufficiently recognized by teachers, especially in respect to self-discipline for labor, where the school demands lag behind tasks life sets for school age children as well as those who are finishing their schooling.

The main concern of industrial leaders is how best to develop labor discipline, a task for which our schools do not provide sufficient help. For example, students or workers who just finish secondary school come to work late and leave early. When reprimanded, they become indignant. This lack of discipline produces conditions impossible for normal work. Old foremen and workers complain bitterly about these working habits acquired in school workshops and in school supervised field practice where not enough attention was paid to the development of healthy working routines.

When life and activities are correctly organized, the development of self-discipline as a characteristic is closely related to other personality traits, and it occurs as a final result of the entire process of bringing up children in school and at home, not as the outcome of isolated, singular, "special" methods of rearing and educating youngsters.

The goals and appropriate means of bringing about self-discipline are of a distinct class character. The school in a class system fosters discipline, which reflects particular interrelationships existing between people under a given system.

The change of a social system brings about modification of discipline's goals and character cultivated in society at large and reinforced by learning in school. "Each new social order demands the creation of new relationships between people and discipline,"* said Lenin. The socialist revolution in the U.S.S.R.

* V. I. Lenin, *Collected Works,* Vol. 23, p. 475.

transformed the "discipline of exploitation to that of free choice and conscience"* where collective solidarity, relationships, and duty are the most important factors.

Subsequently, the demand for conscious discipline in a Soviet school derived from needs inherent in the socialist society engaged in building communism. The Soviet method to develop self-discipline, although it utilizes coercion and punishment, is not built on these basically; otherwise, the goals and methods would have produced contrary results. Needless to say, physical punishment, which is still practiced in some families, is out of the question.

Many parents, especially the older generation, do not understand that it is impossible to raise a conscientious, self-disciplined, strong-willed worker by methods of physical force. We must secure our educational goals through interesting and socially useful collective activities.

Students in grades five and six are going through a phase distinguished by instability, swinging from self-discipline to undisciplined behavior. Often reacting impulsively to joy, enthusiasm, or indignation, students forget completely about teachers' requests and their own personal promises. Then the impulse subsides and the younger adolescent often becomes overwhelmed with guilt feelings. He has great difficulty in admitting his mistake, a fact adults often do not take into consideration, believing it an expression of stubbornness and willfulness. In reality, the youngster is afraid to appear ridiculous and childish and to lose face. In other words, he does not want to lose his human dignity.

Students in grades seven and eight are quieter; they are better able to evaluate their actions. Occasionally, often unexpectedly, outbursts occur.

It seems to us that it is premature to consider the adolescent's self-discipline as an imbedded characteristic of his personality. He is in an interesting phase when this formation takes place. We observe a high level of self-discipline only under special conditions, in particular areas; otherwise on the whole it does not yet manifest itself. Rare is an adolescent whose self-discipline

* *Ibid.*, Vol. 27, p. 240.

is always evenly spread. This expectation is not realistic for this stage of development. More often we meet a teenager who is lively, active, at times mischievous, enthusiastic, serious, thoughtful, and responsible for his behavior. Our numerous observations prove that these adolescents grow up to be good comrades, workers, and genuine patriots of our Fatherland.

When, during this period, an adolescent exhibits demoralization, rudeness, irresponsibility, and insolence, the educator must work very hard to effect a change and to teach him respect for order and discipline. The best helper in this difficult task is the student collective.

## § Some Educational Methods and Techniques of Influencing the Adolescent

Self-discipline is the result of the school's entire educational process. Though, as Makarenko said, special methods alone do not produce conscious discipline, they are of significance to teachers and other educators. Skillfulness in selecting the right method to affect the student's behavior is very crucial. In practice, teachers as well as parents use various methods. Some are successful, others are not. Some are accidental, others systematic and consistent. Many techniques stem from accepted systems of upbringing, others are arrived at from psychological findings which at times conflict with generally accepted pedagogical conditions and demands. Some of these methods will be pointed out here.

Obviously, suggestions to use these or other practical methods and techniques cannot fit all cases. The teacher must deal with each individual or his specific characteristics. Situations, although similar, contain many variables.

Many teachers quickly become disillusioned in various methods of influencing the adolescent, since they expect quick, positive results. However, it is extremely unrealistic to expect an adolescent with behavior problems suddenly to transform into a self-disciplined teenager.

When most unexpected discipline problems occur and the teacher or upbringer has to react immediately, the correctness of his response depends greatly on an intimate knowledge of his student. The means chosen are determined by the psychological environment and the character of the student, the collective, and the teacher, as well as individual peculiarities of the pupil. The approach to each case is also dictated by pedagogical tact, by the individuality of the teacher, and by his relationship with the collective of adolescents.

In order to work successfully with the student, the teacher or upbringer must know him, his family environment, the methods he is most accustomed to. A careful evaluation of all possibilities should precede any action. Often a teacher, especially an inexperienced one, fails because he is blindly imitating another teacher or a commonplace pedagogical pattern. The same measure which one teacher uses successfully may prove to be useless to another. The obvious explanation lies in the individual differences among students and teachers. For example, the variation of voice intonation, fluctuation, and pitch may have been the crucial factors. On another occasion, if the teacher who failed with his colleague's technique chooses his "own" method, one he feels comfortable with, he may get excellent results.

Each teacher must be aware of his strengths and weaknesses, anticipate results of his action, and analyze carefully the pros and cons of each technique *before* setting it in motion. He should search for his *own* methods instead of imitating others.

The teacher's age plays a significant role. What adolescents willingly accept from an older teacher may prove disastrous for a younger one. When an experienced teacher teases or jokes with adolescents, they perceive it as an honor, while, if an inexperienced teacher attempts the same the youngsters regard it as an insult.

The verbal influence, most commonly used in schools, is often unjustly criticized. Of course, this approach gets out of hand when used exclusively as a basic technique for bringing about self-discipline. This method can be very useful when skillfully interwoven with practice in the area of self-disciplined behavior. Verbal communication is related to any and all methods of influence upon the adolescent. But words and intonations used vary considerably. They may convey insults, humiliations, and shattering effects, or build up faith and strength, be pacifying, reassuring, and encouraging. Often a great deal depends on the teacher's ability to recognize the correct timing for giving and for withholding communication. Under certain conditions words support and protect the strength of educational measures. The teacher must always follow through on his promises as well as intentions. This creates in adolescents faith and trust in his words and deeds.

The teenager quickly becomes aware of this characteristic. He does not reason, just follows directions given to him by the teacher whose authority is accepted indisputably and whose word he believes. When the teacher is careless in his promises and neglects following through his objectives, he stimulates the breaking down of discipline. "I will not quiz you next time, we will continue with presentation of new material," announces the teacher, but next time he proceeds to question students against their protestation. As a result he loses his authority.

An experienced teacher, self-assured, never shows his doubts to the pupils, who can always sense a teacher's uncertainty. He must be sure of himself and render firm support to the accepted educational line. Since all teacher's demands must be met by his students, he must set his standards in relation to existing possibilities, never above the level of student's performance.

Many teachers resort to threats which they do not follow through and which only create bad feelings and resentment. Experienced teachers utilize verbal communication as an educational means with lesser frequency, but with much greater effect.

The pedagogical literature indicates that reprimands and instructions should be clear, objective, sensible, and emphatically stated. Never should feelings of annoyance, anger, and irritation color their content. All directions as well as orders should be geared to the adolescent's achievement level, and none of these measures should be misused.

The direct verbal method so often employed in a school situation has many variations. A behavior problem occurs in the classroom. A disturbance which first appeared to be minor is threatening to get out of hand. The immediate reaction of the teacher (many times interference on a verbal level suffices) can prevent its spreading.

The adolescent respects firm words and demands which reflect the strength of the educator. At this age, youngsters rebel against oververbalization. Teachers and upbringers who have a thorough understanding of teenagers know that a brief reprimand such as "Shame on you," "Wise guy," or expressive looks or gestures can be more successful than a flood of words.

Curiously, even experienced teachers give in to temptation and shower the youngsters with words, spoiling the effect they tried to produce.

For example, an excited adolescent rudely reacted to his teacher's remark. The indignant teacher ordered him to remain after school. Later, when the boy, feeling guilty and ashamed, tried to apologize, she bawled him out, spoiling the whole effect she wanted to achieve. Disgusted, the boy again began to contradict rudely.

Suppression and prohibition are the two most commonly used forms of direct verbalization, but to make them effective, basic conditions must be met. Forbidding must not be misused, since the adolescent strongly resents any unfair attempts to hamper his initiative and independence. When too many "dont's" are restraining his behavior, he is forced to break rules.

For instance, a teenager runs down the stairs. "Where are you running, can't you walk?" reprimands the teacher. The boy stops, slowly walks by the teacher, but as soon as her back is turned he breaks into a run. This kind of reaction to prohibition becomes habitual, hence the meaning of the teacher's command gets lost. Suppression and prohibition, only when followed through, are effective.

Teachers, upbringers, and parents must remember that adolescents will rebel if they were not taught to follow orders. The younger the child the more receptive he is to adult directives. An adolescent who cherishes his independence and "freedom," who considers himself "almost a grown up," has difficulties in accepting any prohibitions or restrictions, even when they are justified and fair. Sometimes limitations of his activities induce him to break rules. Successful practice at limit-setting requires a great deal of patience on the part of the educator. Often parents, teachers, or upbringers forbid adolescents certain games or friendships with some of their peers, only to discover that their demands were disobeyed and that the teenagers secretly continued their relationships and activities. This defiance, derived from a need to assert one's self and to do something *daring,* can be overcome only by patience and persistence. Since he views any limit-setting as an infringement upon his independence and the willingness of the adult to accept his "grownupness," it is important to convince him that the teacher is not attempting to deprive him of either. Of course, some limits should be set without hesitation and firmly followed through. If it is possible, a tactful approach should be utilized. The educator skillfully guides the teenager and provides him with an opportunity to arrive at an independent decision. "Think carefully and then do the best you can." In such instances the adolescent often decides to ask advice voluntarily and follow it. This, of course, is different from coercing the youngster to conform by means of persuasion and promises.

In case no other avenues are left open, firmness and authority must be used. The adolescent must learn to accept a lot without arguments, as a part of his later adjustment to life as a working adult.

The method of postponing an action proves to be a very helpful one, especially when the adolescent or teacher or both are overexcited, but unfortunately this approach is seldom used in a school situation. This gives the teenager a cooling-off period during which he has a chance to re-evaluate his deeds and to avoid the talk with his teacher.

Undisciplined adolescents react strongly to irony and witty mockery which embarrasses them in front of others, especially their peers. They do not like to be laughed at, and have difficulty in finding a way out without losing face. Since older students are more resourceful in their replies than younger ones, who often do not catch the irony, this measure should be used mainly with adolescents.

It may seem that this suggestion contradicts the findings of other authors as well as our own in the book *Psychology of an Adolescent,** but in reality it does not. First, crude, vicious, humiliating taunting is not permissible with adolescents. Second, teenagers are not able to take even good-natured teasing when it relates to weak and sensitive areas, such as shortcomings of character and physical development. Third, the irony specified here relates exclusively to undesirable behavior as observed in a given situation, indicating that this kind of acting is out of character with this particular teenager who, when he wishes, can correct it. Fourth, the teenager admits his guilt and the fairness of the irony, and last, adolescents, especially older ones, appreciate genuine wit, even if it is directed against them.

There is another way of working effectively with an adolescent, which utilizes some of his other developmental characteristics, namely, his pride and dignity. A skillful manipulation of his self-esteem almost assures excellent results.

Teaching moral values is another method of influence upon young adolescents. Unfortunately, many parents, teachers, and upbringers do not fully appreciate this as an educational method. Others exhibit skepticism and negativism, though such an outstanding teacher as A. S. Makarenko considered them very useful. Obviously, even ideally conducted discussions would not bring about self-discipline. Most helpful in achieving conscious discipline is the direct experience in a collective. As A. S. Makarenko stated, all moral discussions should be supported by practical implementation.

Since our young generation is brought up in a spirit of conscious discipline, Makarenko's theory, which states that a full understanding of discipline is necessary, remains our guiding thought.

Practice is the best way to achieve self-discipline and its comprehension; objections might therefore be raised that special interpretation is superfluous. There is ample proof to the contrary, however. Most adolescents are slow in analyzing and generalizing their experiences independently. Therefore, this drawn-out proc-

* V. A. Krutetsky and N. S. Lukin, *Psychology of an Adolescent,* Scientific Pedagogical Press, Moscow, 1959, p. 106.

ess can and should be speeded up with adult help. Furthermore, the adolescent cannot examine all elements of his experience by himself, and often, when he attempts to, he arrives at the wrong conclusions. For example, many young adolescents believe that class discipline is needed not for students, but for teachers, in order to make their teaching conditions easier. Our observations and studies, as well as those of other pedagogues, proved that in most cases infringement of discipline occurred as a result of erroneous or immature moral concepts. Teenagers often confuse recklessness, mischievousness, and daring with courage, see stubborness as a positive quality, and view rudeness and abruptness as signs of fortitude and manliness. Frequently, adolescents oppose and consider incompatible such qualities as courage and caution, independence and discipline, aggressiveness and self-control, determination and wise deliberation. Some teenagers appraise falsely and develop negative attitudes toward modesty, politeness, courtesy, and affability. As a result, they wrongly evaluate peers' behavior as well as their own.

The pedagogical literature has an abundance of illustrations which throw light on the erroneous concepts of adolescents. The findings of V. I. Asnin, whose work is of great significance, indicate that various levels of comprehending personal and collective discipline prevail among students.

Makarenko felt that in order to achieve self-discipline in adolescents it is necessary to imprint deeply in them the following: (1) The collective needs discipline to achieve its goals faster and better; (2) The individual must discipline himself to fulfill difficult tasks; (3) Each individual member must subordinate his personal interests to the general discipline of the collective; (4) Discipline improves the collective and all its members; (5) Discipline places the individual in a freer, better defended position, assuring his rights and privileges; (6) Discipline manifests itself not only while one is working on a pleasant assignment but also when one is engaged in fulfilling a difficult, unexpected, demanding, and strenuous task, which he knows is essential for the collective.

This discussion must not be boring; it should be built on the analysis of facts, cases, and examples which will illuminate the given situation. This does not mean every rule and demand must be explained to the teenager. He must learn to fulfill demands not only because he understands them but also because the teacher, the upbringer, the collective, or society sets them.

When using the method of explanation, it is important to remember that its effectiveness increases with the growth of the student's intellectual and moral standards. His logical thinking enables him to understand ideas and concepts better, and he becomes more receptive to suggestions.

Reward and punishment are other measures for regulating youngsters' behavior. The first stimulates positive forms of behavior; the second inhibits and stops negative behavior. An incorrect method of punishment, instead of leading to improvement, may deteriorate discipline. As a peculiarity of his stage of development, the adolescent is sensitive to adult appraisal of his personality and of his behavior and at times morbidly overreacts to a real or imaginery injustice.

Taking into consideration the significant role of the collective in the life of an adolescent, it becomes very important that reward and punishment be administered (1) by a collective, or by the teacher supported by the collective; and (2) the collective must be kept informed at all times. Many forms of reward and punishment are successful. Among them, a notice in the school paper, announcement over the school intercom system, a letter to the parents written by the class collective, and public reprimand or praise in front of the class or pioneer group.

While praise is necessary for an adolescent, excessive reward is not healthy because he may become overconfident and conceited. Too frequent rewards become meaningless to him, but a favorable comment by a teacher who is sparing of praise is especially valued by adolescents.

An adolescent, when systematically rewarded and praised for every good deed, considers good behavior merit rather than duty. The method of advance gratification in order to secure desirable behavior works in the same way. As an end result, the teenager may act correctly only because of these rewards. Therefore, the pedagogues rightly recommend using such formulas as, "You fulfill your duty well, just as any member of the Soviet society."

Material rewards, by the way, sometimes have proven to be

risky. Makarenko, aware of this pitfall, used public praise as a higher form of reward.

It is more important to use praise such as a friendly word, nod, or smile to encourage the adolescent when he begins to improve his behavior but still has relapses.

When bestowing reward not upon individual adolescents but on a collective, the praise becomes meaningful only when the achieved goal was truly a common one and the striving for it a united effort. When a collective is considered for a reward, no premium should be given as a summation for achievements of many of its individual members. Only a joint work well done deserves a prize and stimulates further achievements.

There are many ways of rewarding a collective. The reward can be a letter of praise, a pennant, laudatory remarks, tickets to a movie, circus, show. All members, regardless of individual merit, must be praised equally to tie the collective closer together.

In discussing punishment, consideration should be first given to the question: Is punishment necessary to develop self-discipline in youngsters? There are teachers and upbringers who believe that punishment reflects the teacher's inability to cope with a behavior problem in any other way, and that in "ideal" conditions punishment is not a necessary function of the educational process. We disagree with this point of view (even in general). In the process of developing self-discipline in adolescents, punishment is a very significant ingredient, an idea which Makarenko's theory and experience supports. He did not consider this system an "archaic" one, and used it skillfully in his situation as the need arose. Obviously, only careful and wise application is advisable, or else it can backfire. Any mistake in timing defeats the very purpose it is meant to achieve.

Makarenko believes that punishment should not be administered for the purpose of inflicting physical pain, although it should be an unpleasant experience. The punishment should relate the discomfort to the fact that the behavior which elicited it was detrimental to adults or to the collective. The student must regret his mistake and feel displeased with himself, although the nature of his punishment should not imply that his behavior was irrevocable. The punishment inflicted is successful only when genuine remorse results from it.

It may become necessary to exclude a student creating a disturbance during the lesson if he distracts the class collective and if all other methods to get him back in line fail, but the teacher has to realize that this is not always a punishment. Rather, it is a protective measure against the mischievousness of one student interrupting the work of the collective. An artful method of punishment consists in choosing one which the guilty pupil will feel keenly and which would be clearly understood by the collective.

Makarenko points out the necessity of punishment when the adolescent consciously acted against the common interests of the collective in spite of his full understanding of the undesirability of his behavior. And last, punishment should never have revenge or threats as its goal. It should be education, and as such, it should help the guilty one to comprehend fully his misbehavior and to arrive at a conclusion that he punished himself by violating the rules and acting against the interests of the collective. It is always necessary that the punishment be objective and fair. Only actual infringement of discipline, not its suspicion, should be punishable. Also, each case must be judged in accordance with its demerits or the significance of the misbehavior; otherwise, the adolescent feels strongly that he is innocent and unjustly treated instead of experiencing guilt and remorse. When he knows that the punishment is fair, he is able to accept it fully, regardless of its severity.

In deciding upon the best method of punishment, personality characteristics, nature of offense, degree of guilt, age, motivation, frequency of misconduct, the feelings of the collective and of the culprit toward his misbehavior should be considered. It is pertinent to consider seriously the genuineness, if any, of his regrets.

Inflicting a penalty for collective offense upon the entire class collective is not always advisable, since it may bring the misbehaving members closer together. However, this can occur only when the collective is poorly brought up or when they approach their misbehavior incorrectly. On the other hand, individual punishment of certain members is also a bad idea. This diverts the moral conscience of the collective, and in most cases evokes sympathy for those who "suffered for all." Generally we are inclined to believe that collective misbehavior requires collective penalty. But when the collective genuinely regrets its accidental misdoings, it is advisable to forego punishment entirely.

An indirect reprimand is often successful in dealing with adolescents. For example, "You must be a stranger here, young man," says a school director passing a youngster wearing rubbers in the hall. "Oh, no, I'm a student in this school," answers the confused boy. "That could not be possible; all our pupils know that it is bad manners to wear galoshes inside the school."

As was already stated, a penalty set by the collective influences the behavior of adolescents more strongly than that administered by the teacher, upbringer, or school director. Consequently, its importance is doubled. First of all, it provides an educationally meaningful experience for the collective. Second, the adolescent takes the reprimand much more seriously. A joint reprimand by the whole school collective because of an individual's actions which dishonored the collective's reputation isolates the boy from the collective of peers and teachers, and is very difficult to face.

Perhaps an even greater educational effect is produced by the right of the class collective to petition for the lifting of the penalty after a few months of improved behavior. The penalty is revoked publicly, as it was first imposed, in front of the class collective or the entire school. This is valuable because at no time should the misbehaving student be told directly or indirectly that he cannot improve. This implicit expectation of improvement is especially important for an adolescent during the crucial period of the formation and development of character and personality. Even the most undisciplined adolescent must be convinced that he too is able to behave well and, if he really wants to, can improve. As a rule in such cases, the teacher's suggestion is of much greater significance than it pleases us to think. We had many opportunities to observe that distrust which the teacher unwittingly conveys to his student may instigate delinquency. In this way the teacher, instead of safeguarding him from misbehavior and fostering self-discipline, achieves the opposite.

Adolescents are extremely sensitive to distrust exhibited toward them by adults, while too much supervision may stimulate rebellion. The teenager who is told he is bad may then try to live up to these expectations. Often teachers use this approach hoping to sting the adolescent into improving, but they commit an inexcusable error. The feeling that a teacher is unfair may be created not only by his verbal communication but also by his general attitude toward the adolescent.

The teacher's appraisal of the misbehavior should not be expressed in crude and insulting remarks. Humiliating epithets such as "fool," "idiot," "blockhead," "buffoon," "stupid," "dumb," should be eliminated from a teacher's vocabulary, for humiliation will only make an adolescent more rebellious.

Adolescents are often indifferent to a teacher's commanding tone, even when the inflection of his voice is not offensive, if the teacher acts like a commanding officer training his subordinates. This does not mean that no action of the student should anger the teacher and evoke a sharp response. Sometimes it is necessary to show genuine indignation by criticizing misbehavior severely. When the adolescent knows that his action is judged justly and he does not feel he is being insulted, the effect is favorable.

It is as important to feel righteous indignation as it is to maintain calmness and composure, but just as the latter should not be an expression of indifference, the former should not be an expression of loss of control and hysteria. The teacher becomes worked up because he is genuinely irate and because he thinks it is important to his students to realize how he feels, but in this process he must always maintain his self-control. Such displays of anger should not occur too often, because then they lose their impact.

Sometimes one does not need words to express indignation. For example, students, knowing that one of their teachers usually leaned upon the window sill, painted it with chalk, which left a streak on her dress. When the homeroom teacher who had the next period walked in, instead of sitting down on her chair she disgustedly pushed it away. The students, puzzled, asked her what was the matter. When she explained that she was disgusted with the trick played upon the previous teacher, her students explained that they would never do it to *her*. But she replied, "When you are capable of such action, one can expect anything from you." The whole class was embarrassed.

It is important that a teacher who inflicts a penalty admit his error in a situation when he has misjudged the facts. An experienced teacher in such a case unhesitatingly retracts his accusation and admits his fault. Not only does he *not* lose his authority, as many teachers believe, but on the contrary, he strengthens it. Students know how difficult it is for an adult, especially for a teacher or upbringer, to admit a mistake to his pupils. They greatly respect a grownup who, instead of protecting his self-importance, chooses the more difficult road of admitting his fallibility. Of course, the errors must be rare and somehow forgiveable. Such teachers, while ready to admit error, try to avoid them by never drawing fast conclusions.

As a rule, the teacher must react to any misbehavior, but this too has its exceptions. Although the ability to know when to overlook infringements of discipline requires great pedagogical skill and tact, the best teacher can differentiate with sensitivity which instances *cannot be overlooked* and which *must not be noticed.* For example, a teacher saw a student correcting his mark in the teacher's notebook. He decided to ignore it. The boy knew he was caught, and nervously expected the teacher's reaction. Finally, unable to stand the suspense, he approached the teacher: "Please punish me. I cannot take it any longer." But the teacher told him that since he corrected his mark from *F* to *B,* he should prove it the next day. The next day he received an *A* for his excellent assignment. "You underestimated yourself," the teacher told the student. After the lesson the boy voluntarily promised never to do it again. "Thank you. I thought you would complain to my father, but you did not!"

It is important to know how to prevent a conflict from developing and spreading, and, with a joke, to relieve accumulated tension. The educator expresses his artfulness in his ability not only to resolve a conflict but also to prevent its occurrence.

The discussion about physical punishment of the adolescent is basically directed toward parents, since teachers long ago resolved this conflict successfully. This method, even in the most "harmless" forms such as ear or hair pulling, rear or cheek slapping, or just a flick on the nose, is inexcusable. It accomplishes nothing except to assault the adolescent's dignity. Punitive physical measures are harmful at any age, but especially during adolescence.

Some parents believe that these methods are in some cases indispensable, since with their help the adolescent can be forced to do almost anything. Perhaps he may be forced, but never does he become convinced of anything. This alone makes the method unsuitable for use. Most often, such obedience is submissive and false. The punished adolescent tries not to be "caught," which produces the illusion of improvement. Lying, falseness, and hypocrisy are logical results of such upbringing. Let us suppose that by means of physical punishment the adult really succeeded in making an adolescent submit to his demands; suppressing his will by physical means may then make him timid, oppressed, cowardly, or embittered, stubborn, hateful, and vengeful. As Makarenko says, "I have never met any family in which corporal punishment was successful. To hit a twelve- or thirteen-year-old boy means to admit one's own weakness, and it may mean breaking forever any good relationships with him."*

In working with an adolescent, the method of redirecting him proves to be a very successful one. It is known that the teenager many times infringes upon discipline when he does not find positive outlets for his surplus energy, activeness, and mobility; but when, by proper channeling, he becomes engaged in interesting projects, the potential problems of discipline do not materialize.

It is not always easy to stimulate a firm interest in an adolescent, but the areas which seem to intrigue and excite him provide a guiding light for the educator. There is no other age when the capacity for enthusiasm is so overwhelming, and this factor should be utilized to the fullest.

Many infringements of discipline take place between class periods, and they can be avoided by organizing students' activities during recess times. There is no uniform approach to this

* A. S. Makarenko, *Collected Works,* Vol. 4, 1957, pp. 507-508.

problem; different schools develop various methods. Many recommend games as one way of occupying the pupils during breaks between classes. This method is successful with younger school children, but with adolescents it fails, often because space limitations make it difficult to organize active games on a large scale.

Adolescent games during intermission in the playground are useful, but they depend on weather conditions and cannot be planned in advance. Games on a good sports field provide a healthy outlet for accumulated energy, but if the game is relatively disorganized, this will carry over into the following class periods. When a game is well organized, the transition from playground to classroom is less abrupt; it permits the youngsters to calm down and get themselves together for work. Some schools prefer to engage the students in such activities as voluntary listening to music or quiet social dancing. Chess games during intermission are not desirable, since they do not provide a rest for the mind.

Channeling the student's activity toward useful work has significance during class period. A pupil who distracts the attention of the class while new material is being introduced may be asked to assist the teacher or be given some special assignment.

Sometimes the simplest device, even a somewhat artificial one, which creates a diversion of attention can restore order.

It is important to teach youngsters the rules of behavior through organized special practice. Often the lack of appropriate behavior in certain situations comes as a result of the adolescent's ignorance of how to conduct himself, or of his inability to implement what he knows, or of an absence of desirable habits. Some families do not know the desirable rules of social behavior and bring up their children with generally unacceptable conduct, hence, the school role is to fill this void. Adolescents are very susceptible and learn rules fast and willingly as soon as they understand their necessity, provided the learning process is not forced upon them.

It was observed that in some cases adolescents infringed upon discipline when they did not realize they acted against established rules. For example, the students got accustomed to shouting because they were not aware that their voices were raised, or they neglected their appearance. A collective development of self-discipline in adolescents took place in order to correct this kind of behavior. The hard struggle to achieve the objective of establishing positive habits is characteristic for adolescents, especially older ones. This process is closely related to their growing consciousness. The teacher's role is not only to stimulate this self-improvement but also to help the student. In one school an attempt was made to initiate self-improvement among the collective by assigning them three tasks to fulfill:

First task: Control the impulse to run in school during breaks or at other occasions, even if the desire is very great. Be promptly in place immediately after the bell. During class period, concentrate exclusively on subject matter.

Second task: Try to influence a classmate who needs guidance and interest him in some worthwhile cause; ask the teacher or pioneer leader for advice on how to proceed. Prove that you are an organizer who achieves good results.

Third task: Have good manners; show politeness to all, have a clean and pleasing appearance.

Some infringements of discipline are hard to fight. Among older adolescents, smoking is one of them. There are many reasons why an adolescent starts this habit. Adults smoke, and the adolescent considers smoking one of the symbols of his being grown up also; or he may be afraid of being teased by his peers or adults for not smoking. The fight against this habit is a difficult one, but with the cooperation of adolescents, it can be controlled.

To bring about self-discipline it is necessary to provide the adolescent with favorable environmental conditions. Teachers and upbringers must have clearly in mind the personality characteristics they want to develop, as well as those needing special emphasis. Of course, chronological as well as individual differences must be taken into consideration.

Our last point of discussion in this chapter is to analyze the influence of friendship among adolescents upon self-discipline. There are positive friendships which help to develop good habits of behavior, and negative ones which bring harm. The value of friendship is determined less by the individual with whom the student associates closely than by its quality. Let us suppose that a self-disciplined teenager with high moral values becomes friendly with a classmate who is a poor student and a behavior problem. How this friendship should be approached depends upon whose influence is stronger. But even when the excellent student is the follower, the friendship should be rechanneled rather than disrupted. Only when such attempts fail must the relationship be broken. This should be done skillfully and tactfully, since adolescents are sensitive and deeply resent adult interference. Often clumsy, forceful attempts to break up a friendship result in tightening its bonds; if the friendship is then kept a secret from the grownups, they lose all chance at control. The "undesirable" friend must not be laughed at; neither should he be humiliated. Resenting the insults and rebelling against adult interference in their "private" affairs, the youngsters will stubbornly continue the relationship as a matter of "principle." It is better to try to help the adolescent see the weaknesses in his friend and voluntarily give up this friendship. The most effective corrective would be to organize his life and activities in a manner which would promote and stimulate his interests and occupy his time, so that the undesirable relationship is pushed out simply by the demands of his other interests.

Some parents make mistakes in this area. In trying to protect their children from the bad influence of their peers, they isolate them from the collective, while permitting friendship with only a few "chosen" ones. This isolation reflects itself badly in the development of an adolescent, since only within a collective can his personality develop harmoniously. The parents, while guarding him from "undesirable friendships," at the same time prevent his developing a resistance against bad influence which is very much needed in life.

# 3 *Learning from Life to Live*

*E. Krechetova*

## § On the New Road

IN ORDER TO MEET the educational objectives of the new system of public education, each pedagogical collective chooses its own particular way to reorganize the school curriculum. This very complicated and difficult task has clearly defined concrete goals. Its main purpose is to strengthen the ties between school and life which means to develop in youngsters not only academic skills but also ability and proper attitudes toward labor. They must consider work as a primary life necessity and receive genuine vocational preparation.

In the beginning, the school had no curriculum in the area of work education, neither did it receive organized guidance from the Ministry of Education, nor from the Academy of Pedagogical Sciences. Lack of orientation in this direction among students created an additional problem. They perceived secondary schooling only as a step leading them to institutions of

E. Krechetova, *Learning from Life to Live,* XI Series. Pedagogika. Izd-vo "Znanye," Moscow, 1963, pp. 3-29.

higher learning. But competent teachers understood that these two highly important processes cannot continue independent parallel existences without any mutual influence upon each other.

The school administration and teachers, observing the reaction to vocational training among older students, arrived at the conclusion that the school must develop closer relationships with industry, in order to accomplish its task successfully. Teaching additional vocational subjects by specialists constitutes only the beginning of the school reorganization. The final solution to this problem lies in the hands of teachers.

In order to be successful the vocational specialists must also learn about students. The works of Ushinsky, Lunatcharsky, Krupskaya and Makarenko, as well as pedagogical journals, textbooks used in schools, prove to be of great help in exploring this new area. Classical pedagogical theory provides the basic principles upon which the educational process in school and the student-teacher relationship are being evolved. The textbooks are valuable as a guide for establishing a vocational curriculum as a preparation for practical work experience.

We must search for and find genuine, vital, and creative relationships between academic subjects and preparation for labor. It is impossible to visualize the tremendous new task being accomplished without the direct participation and involvement of teachers.

When the change of curriculum was effected, the teachers began to study the industries where the students receive their practical experience. The purpose of this complicated and difficult process was to familiarize the teachers with the concrete conditions of work as well as with its objectives in order to integrate them with other subjects of the school curriculum. This could be achieved only when the created ties were genuine and logical in accordance with real life situations.

Though educators used various ways to solve the new problem, the object was the same: to unite the academic school curriculum with vocational preparation.

## § Together with the Factory

The meeting of teachers of the Russian Soviet Socialistic Republic, which took place in the summer of 1960, was dedicated to the discussion of important problems the school faces during the contemporary period of building Communism. Delegates and guests from Siberia, the Volga Region, Sachalin, Krasnodar region, Voronezh, Ural, Moscow region, etc., came to share with others their first experience with the new Soviet school.

Only now is the Soviet school achieving its great pedagogical goal of fostering a well-rounded academic as well as vocational curriculum which enables youngsters to utilize their newly acquired skills in practice.

The teacher, by penetrating deeply into the factory life and the production process, finds effective ways of relating it to the new curriculum. The enrichment of subject matter is achieved by use of materials acquired in the factory.

Familiarity with the above helps the students to grasp and to retain the theoretical basis of knowledge, since no longer do they learn the laws and rules mechanically; instead, they witness their implementation in practical situations.

Though the teacher has already introduced into his subject matter needed elements discovered in the plant, he continues with his search for ever new factors to inject into the school curriculum.

The students, especially eleventh-grade seniors, are encouraged to use their initiative and to work independently on projects, as well as to be bold in searching for and exploring new findings. The teacher is not afraid that his authority will diminish and that he will lose face before his students when he admits that a question or a method arrived at by a student is not clear to him. He knows his students will respect his scientific honesty, since he too is always searching for new, creative approaches to science.

Each student reports individually to the teacher the subject matter covered in class. In case the task given to students is independent research, the teacher must familiarize himself thoroughly with the topic, which is always closely related to their practical experience. These assignments of individual character foster independence, and enrich the student's scientific and technical viewpoint. This is one of the ways the teacher uses to deepen the acquired knowledge of students and to make it practical by relating it to life by experiences in industry.

Obviously, not all students learn so smoothly. Not everyone develops interests in science. There are loafers whose attitude toward studying is irresponsible and there are also youngsters who do not have the necessary preparation. As you know, students who enter the special ninth-grade classes come from various schools with a different level of readiness. Sometimes it takes half a year to raise the performance of many new ones and to train them in the classroom for practical work experience.

It happens that the teacher, while explaining a topic, senses that not all students comprehend his explanation. Realizing he has lost contact with them, he immediately changes his method to an easier one and uses simpler examples. In achieving his objective—the complete understanding of complex material by all students—factors such as experience, patience, and artful teaching skills are of great help.

When the school's influence upon the older students already working in industry is powerless, the collective of the factory through its Komsomol takes over, using forceful discipline, open and direct criticism which manifest intolerance of all kinds of slovenliness.

## § Maturing Through Work

Lenin wrote: "Knowledge attained by our previous experience is not sufficient. One must strive further to achieve more while changing from easy to difficult tasks. Without this, all progress, even that of building Socialism, is negated."*

In analyzing these new tasks of teachers, Lenin's principle contains the essence of the work and genuine success of creative

* V. I. Lenin, *Collected Works,* Vol. 24, p. 172.

educators. The success or failure of the new curriculum depends greatly upon the cooperation or lack of it between teachers and vocational specialists supervising practical experience of students. To coordinate the new curriculum the pedagogical collective created a committee composed of all vocational teachers and those whose subject matter relates to the industrial part of the curriculum.

One of the most important areas in which the committee renders help to specialists who come to the school from industry is to acquaint them with various teaching methods. There are many instances when the experts become helpless in front of the students, though they master their subject matter excellently. Sometimes they forget the age of their pupils and teach above their level of readiness, or produce dry facts which fail to stimulate the interest of students.

The director of the school, the educational director, and the most experienced teachers attend meetings of the specialists and analyze them in detail. Also, with the director, the experts observe teachers in classrooms and then discuss their impressions.

The school is working to deepen and improve the pedagogically sound industrial education of older pupils. Many factory workers of various qualifications take part in this process. The committee initiates meetings in the factory in which all those who take part in the vocational training of youth in a school situation are included.

The teacher, who always attends these meetings, develops professional relationships with the shop foremen where the students are being trained. Factory workers, to whom this job is new, consult with him frequently.

When some of the factories do not genuinely cooperate, thus depriving the students of real working experience, steps are taken to alleviate the undesirable situation.

All problems and difficulties of the students during their first experience in industry are referred to the committee. In the beginning of the new school system, the primary concern was the change of curriculum in the upper grades. Now attention is focused on grades five to eight, when the connection between school and industry is initiated. Visits to factories and talks with schoolmates already working there mark the casual character of the relationship as it now exists; this of course is not enough. A more organized, systematic approach is needed, in order to create a relationship in depth; to achieve it, the school curriculum must be adjusted accordingly.

The coordinating committee is also concerned with the preparation for work experience of students in lower grades. A good early preparation avoids later problems, because successful teaching is defined by degree of influence the educator exerts, rather than by the number of students taught.

N. S. Khrushchev, in his speech during the XXIInd Congress of the Communist Party, summarized the goals and tasks of Soviet education as follows: "One of the most important tasks of Communist education is to reinforce in everyone's mind the fact that since all accomplishments of the Soviet man benefit him and society, no man can live without working productively. When, out of concern for his comrades, he approaches his assignments with honesty and works diligently at them while keeping up with the set time schedule, he manifests collaboration as well as reciprocal aid, both of which are relevant among people in our new society."

Schools point out many examples where the educational influence of the factory upon youth proved to be very strong. The factory collective many times manages to alleviate problems with which the school seems unable to cope. The students change in the process of being exposed to the life of the plant and to the interests of its collective. As they mature, discipline problems diminish considerably.

Obviously, the working collective can influence young people more than can the school, since it represents not only high goals but also real life, where everything new becomes adopted immediately. The youth who works in the various factories shares with the factory collective all of their hopes, anxieties, successes, and difficulties. The students understand that here people live and work in the spirit of Communism. It is no surprise that each of the young students dreams of becoming an outstanding worker. Many of them continue with the chosen specialization after they finish secondary school. Some remain in the factories and attend night school, while others go on in the same profession to technical institutes of higher learning.

On the other hand, it is incorrect to assume that all graduates select their specialty in the same area. There are many who, though well acquainted with industries, decide upon medicine, pedagogy, humanities, etc. This is natural, since a school population is very diversified in terms of its abilities, individuality, and aspirations. But this active participation in industry proves to be a valuable experience to all students, regardless of their future plans, since it fosters in them a genuine respect for labor as the first life necessity of the new man, while it prepares them to overcome future difficulties.

The program of the Communist Party of the Soviet Union states: "The party considers the development of a Communistic attitude toward work in all members of society as the center of its educational task. Work for the sake of society is the holiest duty of every individual, and any labor, mental or physical, for its benefit, is equally respectable and honorable. It is necessary to use the best models of labor and the best examples of national economy in order to educate all workers."

. . . . .

Time is passing. Schools and industry accumulate experience in the area of educating youth jointly in accordance with the new curriculum, and the graduates begin their independent life with a school diploma and with a certificate verifying the practical work experience.

The coordinating school committee has made great strides since its inception. Their standards are continuously growing; so are the demands they set for themselves and the vocational part of the curriculum. Not satisfied with existing practices, they still search for new, better ways to tie the school with life. The school, while still in the process of reorganization, has to cope with new problems. Though the beginning is already here, new tasks confront the collective.

The training shop brings clarity and organization into the vocational education of students, though stronger control pedagogically could improve the quality of its training. Now is also the time to diversify the existing specializations and make them more complex, which would demand a wider technical horizon and be more challenging. How to accomplish this is a problem yet unsolved by the schools.

Upon being absorbed into the school curriculum, productive work became the primary aid of teachers in educating the new man, and in implementing his knowledge and belief through action.

# 4 *Sex Education*

*T. S. Atarov*

AFTER THE OCTOBER REVOLUTION, the family and marriage in our society underwent a fundamental change. Church weddings were replaced by civil ceremonies which reflected a new content and meaning of the socialistic family. Communist morals became the basis for relationships in the family and in marriage for the majority of Soviet citizens.

Common spiritual interest, love, respect, friendship, and trust, as well as parents' duties and responsibilities toward their children and toward society and government, which mutually assure meeting material needs, are the ethical principles on which the socialist family is built. The interests of the family are synchronized with those of the society and of government.

However, it would be wrong and harmful to assume that the change to a socialist family structure has already been fully accomplished, and that today's structure will remain static. Obviously, there are still various elements in human relationships which reflect many ideological survivals of the bourgeois society. Marxism and Leninism explain that individual growth of consciousness lags considerably behind the industrial and economic development of a society.

Though these undesirable traits are exceptions rather than

T. S. Atarov, *Sex Education*, Medgiz, Moscow, 1959, pp. 3-106.

the rule, they manifest themselves in different phases of social life, such as negative attitudes toward social property or petty bourgeois individualism, or religious superstitions. They appear mostly in the area of heterosexual relationships, as well as in family life. Many individuals, men especially, believe they have a right to have extramarital affairs. Some of the youth, in pursuit of sex only, become involved in relationships devoid of spiritual and ethical common grounds and responsibility. What is even worse, certain women also subscribe to this approach. Naturally, all of this leads to negative social behavior.

Undesirable habits of sexual life are especially difficult to uproot, since they are very deeply imbedded. Individuals' intimate feelings, thoughts, and actions are not easily detected, and because of this they are hard to control. The secret nature of these heterosexual relationships complicates the educational task, even though the results of these relationships are often very serious for the individual and for society at large.

Those who violate established socialist morality try to create a theoretical basis for their conduct. They justify their unworthy behavior by rationalizing that sexual indulgence is a substitute for prostitution, which has completely disappeared from Soviet life. They maintain that no society can exist without some "sexual freedom," that it satisfies unavoidable biological needs, which monogamy cannot meet. These arguments serve only to justify the amoral behavior of these "sexual theoreticians." There is no need to waste time repudiating them, since they are obviously remnants of the old life philosophy surviving in some individuals' minds. It is not true that every society must have prostitution, and that in the event of its liquidation sexual indulgence takes its place. Both phenomena appear simultaneously in capitalistic countries and on a much larger scale than sexual indulgence manifests itself in our country; obviously, then, there is no correlation between such occurrences in a bourgeois and in a socialist society.

Since family and marriage constitute the foundation of socialist existence, which came into being after the October Revolution, the serious task of Communist education is to find a solution to various practical and theoretical problems of everyday life related to the sex life of an individual.

Consequently, since all relationships between male and female (marital and extramarital) such as love, attitudes toward marriage, sexual hygiene, and sexual ethics constitute the essence of socialist existence, it becomes very important to teach our youth respect for human beings, for marriage, and for family, and to teach the true meaning of love.

## § The Role of the School in Sex Education

The Soviet people begin their education in the spirit of Communist morals at a very early age, since the formative years (which exert great influence upon future life) are those of early childhood, when the youngster is still a preschooler.

In a socialist system, the education of the growing generation becomes everybody's task. The methods employed were worked out in, and are constantly improved by, life experience. The best historical traditions in the field of the education and upbringing, and the contributions of outstanding representatives of science and art, have created a curriculum enriched by vast experience.

Youngsters' early exposure to political and social life and the Pioneer and Komsomol movement broadens their education and provides a sound basis for interpretations of tasks inherent in the building of Communism. Coeducational classes, which are established in all schools, are very significant for developing the feeling of camaraderie at work and at play. It is also important to remember that this places upon the teacher and pedagogue the additional responsibility for educating both sexes correctly with a view to their respective roles in Soviet society.

However, as Makarenko wrote: "Many educational methods still remain undecided. No collective of students can exist without a harmonious blend of freedom and discipline, and no collective of teachers can exist without a unified approach."* These words hold true today.

In practice, the "harmonious blend of freedom and discipline" means behavior within accepted moral and rightful norms for

* A. S. Makarenko, *Communistic Education,* 1953, p. 55.

the individual and the collective. The task of the educator is to regulate this behavior within approved limits.

To navigate between freedom and discipline is a really difficult assignment. Obviously the interest of the collective and of the society at large must supersede individual interests and desire for freedom.

Our schools are better at teaching youngsters the curriculum than at preparing them for their future roles as fathers and mothers. One area which is not sufficiently emphasized is the nature of children's developmental stages and related specific characteristics, particularly of their sexual development.

It is true that sex education as such should not be singled out by the school; on the other hand, it should not be ignored entirely. Though the school must not include sex education directly in the curriculum, some place must be found for it in the general process of education and upbringing. Otherwise, only harm will result. This teaching must include discussion not only of biological factors involved but also of moral and ethical implications.

Makarenko said: "Sex education of the child means primarily developing his social personality and acceptable behavior."* This is the only approach to sex education which seems to be right. Hence, it should be suggested that parents and pedagogues follow it strictly and divert children's and adolescents' attention from questions related to intimacies of life. Only at an older age, when the girl or boy learns to be discreet about some special intimate secrets, does the girl become ready for brief talks with her mother and the boy with his father or with the pedagogue about individual aspects of sex life. Most parents and pedagogues manage this problem well, but many do not live up to it either because of their lack of physiological knowledge or their lack of understanding of the relationship between physiological development and other developmental processes, which deeply influence the behavior of children and of adolescents. Often when something occurs which children do not understand, they pose direct questions to adults or parents or even peers about the most intimate aspects of life, such as where babies come from, the rela-

* A. S. Makarenko, *Book for Parents,* 1951, pp. 413-417.

tionship of parents, their feelings, actions, and so forth. Most educators and parents are tactful, knowledgeable, and experienced. Their influence upon the new generation is very positive, and, when necessary, reactions are always appropriate. They treat the children's questions with respect and give correct and serious replies. These educators wisely satisfy the youngsters' curiosity, though at the same time try tactfully to divert their attention from the topic dealing with the intimate facts of life. Experienced teachers use their biology lessons to influence the formulation of a correct and socially acceptable approach to biological laws.

However, some parents and even educators cannot decide how to react. Some try to avoid a direct confrontation, while others use discouragement as a way of getting out of a situation which is uncomfortable for them. Often they are not able to hide their embarrassment, which increases the children's curiosity or, what is even worse, they attempt to give artificial, distorted, and mysterious answers to simple questions. In this way many parents and educators manifest their helplessness, lack of information, and often plain ignorance.

In other cases educators remain insensitive to children's inner sufferings, which are the natural result of their particular developmental stage. The students, fully aware of this indifference, become deeply affected by it. On the other hand, the educator draws erroneous conclusions about students' progress or their behavior. This anti-educational approach creates unnecessary conflicts between students and teacher and its results are often harmful. The words of A. S. Makarenko fit here especially. He says that the "educational collective has not yet worked out a unified approach." This pertains even more to parents and pedagogues. Obviously, it is difficult to recommend for parents and pedagogues the appropriate handling of all unexpected, unusual, or odd behavior which children display during various stages of development. Neither do we have a prescription for answers to all questions children ask about sex; however, first of all one must suggest that adults always avoid signs of surprise, embarrassment, shock, or pleasure when children venture prematurely into exploration of the facts of life through questions. The behavior of parents and pedagogues must be natural, as usual. The explanations must derive from the laws of nature and be made without distortion. Stories of storks and "buying children in hospitals" only confuse children. Answers must be brief, to the point, and general rather than detailed. When the persistence of children is especially pronounced, examples from nature such as that of flowers, animals, and birds could be drawn upon, but without emphasizing details. In general, the tone and way of reply is more significant than the content.

It is absolutely false to cover the subject of sex with secrecy and avoid any discussion related to it because of created discomfort. People who act in this way are poor educators. Neither should any curiosity about the facts of life be treated as potential sexual indulgence.

Instead of upholding "conspiratorial silence," children and youth must be taught how to develop an ability to control their actions through strong will power. The youngster must begin to learn in early childhood that not all desires can be and should be immediately fulfilled. Lack of self-restraint and the tendency of many parents to satisfy their children's wishes immediately lead to an inability to control one's urges. Under these conditions children and adolescents may begin to fulfill their desire artificially by masturbation and older ones to seek premarital sexual relationship which in adulthood may result in self-indulging family life.

The environmental conditions and the example set by adults have a decisive influence upon the growing generation. M. I. Kalinin said: "To educate means to influence the psychological and moral development of a youngster, namely, to make a man out of him. The example set by the teacher and his relationship to students is the main method of teaching."*

In connection with this, it is necessary to state how important it is for parents to keep their intimate life secret from their children; unfortunately, many parents forget this. They demonstrate their mutual feelings openly through words or action. Sometimes

* M. I. Kalinin, *Communistic Education,* 1947, p. 49.

the parents engage in sexual relations, unaware that the children are awake. Obviously, this will reflect negatively in the children's future behavior.

Some people have a bad habit of frequently using foul language without any embarrassment, regardless of who is around them. Often young people begin to imitate these adults and soon they cannot talk without using vulgar words as cynical adjectives. This in turn leads them to a distorted view of heterosexual relations and finally, in maturity, induces them to violate social morals in the area of family relations. No adult has the right to ignore foul language, especially among young people, and to think it is not "his business." Everyone must participate in the fight to keep our language clean, which is an important part of sex education of the young generation. It is necessary to mobilize public opinion, the authority of the healthy youth collective, all methods of teaching and rearing children, to uproot any manifestation of vulgarity in language and in interpersonal relationships and to imprint, instead, understanding of ethics, of conscience, responsibility, shame, which prevents undesirable social behavior, and nurtures honor, duty, and other positive feelings which all adults must cultivate in youngsters.

Misuse of alcohol, which results in many undesirable family scenes, is inexcusable, especially in the presence of children. The drunkard loses control of his sexual desires. In most cases, young people also under its influence engage in premarital sexual relationships. It is pertinent to mention that the use of large quantities of alcohol results in sexual impotence and general physical decline. Hence the fight against alcoholism is also a fight for a normal sexual life. Parents who teach their children to drink must be strongly reprimanded.

Though in the process of implementing educational tasks the jurisdiction of the law is not decisive, its significance should not be minimized when social morals are violated and serious moral harm or material loss is experienced by individuals and by society at large. In such instances the use of legal restraint is purposeful and socially useful.

Soviet society and its public opinion play a powerful role in the educational process and in the fight to establish favorable conditions for a healthy socialist life. Unfortunately, this strength is not enough to eliminate violations of sexual morality.

The task of explaining the facts of life to young people lies with physicians, educators, parents, and cultural institutions and organizations. Literature and art also provide a great deal of help. The educator is especially helpless with youngsters who begin their sexual life before coming of age and before their sexual maturity. The whole educational process becomes interrupted. The basic task of the educator is to try to prevent youngsters from becoming promiscuous; and the best way to accomplish this is for them to get married and start a family as soon as they mature sexually and become of age.

Young people already of age (eighteen years or older) must be taught by a different method and content. No question should be left to chance. Separate talks should be planned and conducted for young girls and boys by educators and by physicians. The universities and places of work should revise the organization of lectures and discussions so that they include literary topics concerned with relationships between individuals. One of the reasons that sex education is not well integrated in practice is the lack of communication between the departments of health and education.

There is no doubt that we need to broaden sex education propaganda and its real understanding among parents, educators, and the nation at large in order to achieve better results, and that without close cooperation between the departments of health and education this will not be achieved. The "conspiracy of silence" and haphazard ways of teaching must give way to a meaningful approach to sex education and problems related to it.

## § Sexual Maturity

Sexual maturation is a complex process consisting of various psychophysiological phenomena, which are inseparably linked with the environment. An elementary knowledge of biology is essential to facilitate understanding and to provide correct interpretation and guidance in matters related to developmental physical changes which occur in children and in adolescents. This knowledge is also helpful in combatting the prejudice and superstition which interfere with a correct educational approach in this area.

All living organisms develop and multiply in accordance with the established laws of nature related to their species. Among human beings, hormones stimulate growth and development of the organism and play a part in sexual maturation. Visible manifestations of this process, such as beards and mustaches among boys and breast development among girls, should never be a subject for teasing by parents and other adults, because this may prematurely awaken sexual awareness in the youngster.

Experience proves that although first sexual sensations manifest themselves in the age range between five and fourteen, they occur more consciously after fourteen. The subsequent period in which sexual feelings reveal themselves and the whole duration of their development is a drawn-out process which changes with the years. The study of causes which produce early sexual sensations revealed that only a minority of cases under study experienced sexual desires spontaneously. The majority had their sexual awareness awakened by environmental influences exerted by peers, adults, literature, painting, theater, and movies.

Many studies in the area of sexual life indicate the existence of a great age range which reflects the prevailing social conditions of the environment in which the subjects under study were brought up and in which they live. The period in which full sexual maturity takes place depends on many external conditions of development and upon internal characteristics of the organism. This period varies for men and for women. The majority of boys experience it between eighteen and twenty-one years of age, while the girls go through it at an age between sixteen and nineteen years. Naturally, deviations occur often on both sides of the range.

It is apparent that the whole life of children and youth and their exposure to various influences must be under constant, firm supervision of parents, counselors, and teachers. On the other hand, a too close control which stifles their natural development must be avoided by all means. The task of educators and of parents is to eliminate or weaken all negative influences upon the growing organism which foster premature sexual drives.

The problem of onanism, related to the above, is a mechanical stimulation of sexual organs which satisfies the sexual desire. The practice prevails more among boys than among girls.

Many factors such as too tightly fitting garments, habits of holding hands in the pockets or under blankets, stimulating each other by tickling under arms and on the breasts, crawling or lying on the stomach, as well as constipation and full bladder, all encourage masturbation. Other stimuli, such as reading, cynical conversations, observing sex life of animals, inactivity, isolation from the collective life can also produce desire for a sexual outlet through masturbation. Finally, it is important to mention here also an itch resulting from various skin diseases in the area of sexual organs and also the narrowness of boys' foreskin and an accumulation of secretions of the sebaceous gland under the foreskin. Of course, the latter cases need medical attention.

To divert children from preoccupation with sex, they should be encouraged to participate actively in sports, follow a correct daily schedule which would not leave unoccupied time periods, and maintain a healthy diet. At all times, children must sleep on hard beds, never lie on the stomach or keep their hands under the blanket. This becomes especially important in young adults who, in addition to mechanical excitation which takes place in childhood and in adolescence, are stimulated by influences of the environment and of their own psychic responses. Many girls are afraid to ride bicycles in spite of liking it. Though this sport is not harmful, it is recommended that girls sit on the bicycle in such a way that the edge of the saddle should not protrude between the vaginal lips, in order to avoid sexual excitation.

When youngsters are not in the collective, it is advisable to keep an eye on them and at the same time discourage any activities they attend in isolation from others, especially in cases when the parents are aware that their children masturbate.

The experience of physicians indicates that under our social conditions, onanism is on the decline, although of course it has not been completely eliminated.

Masturbation, without doubt, brings about a negative reaction of the nervous system and of the general condition of the organism. Apathy, tiredness, indifference to mental and physical tasks are some of the undesirable results produced. Under the wise supervision of adults, children and adolescents usually quickly outgrow this bad habit and their health becomes restored. In most cases, masturbation stops when the sexual life begins.

Scientists explain the biological and social reasons for masturbation in various ways. The outstanding Russian scientist, I. I. Mechnikov, wrote that the cause of masturbation "depends unquestionably upon disharmony in the human nature, in its premature development of sexual feelings." As a result of his research Mechnikov arrives at the conclusion that there is a "clear discord between sexual maturity and general maturity of the organism." The feeling of love, as well as sexual attraction, "appears at a very early age, long before the organism is ready for reproduction."*

Parents must avoid all actions and movements which irritate the sexual organs of young children. To hold the child with his stomach and perineum directed toward the breast of father or mother, to rub the youngster during a bath, or to lavish kisses and caresses upon young children, especially on areas such as breasts, stomach, etc., are practices which must be discontinued. The sooner these harmful manifestations of primitive parental love disappear, the better for the youngsters affected by them.

Sexual maturation is closely related to all vital functions of the organism. For young people this process is charged with a deep emotional involvement. Continuous biological stimuli together with the environment create complex, not immediately acknowledged, and difficult to identify sensations, which often result in intense inner conflicts. When these occurrences manifest themselves, unfortunately, not all parents and educators respond to them with sensitivity and attentiveness, which is due partly to lack of information regarding the developmental stages and conflicts which take place during the period of adolescence and partly to the lack of awareness of their educational role in this area.

* I. I. Mechnikov, *Studies of Human Nature,* 1904, Chap. 5.

## § Moral Education of Youth

Medical research proved that abstaining from sexual relationships is absolutely harmless not only to young people, who have not started their sexual life yet, but also to adults who for some reason have to interrupt it for a long period of time. On the contrary these people are full of energy and creativity. On the other hand, sexual indulgence results in an early loss of potency and premature aging.

People who violate the established morality by engaging in premarital or clandestine sexual relationships or by premature sexual involvement seriously disturb the basis of our socialist existence. Their old-fashioned, reactionary ideology considers sexual life only as a physiological need to be satisfied. Of course this approach does not correctly reflect the values of a socialist society in which the young people were brought up. Since they never lived under a capitalist system, their undesirable behavior can only be explained by incorrect education and bad influences in the home and in the adult environment.

Luckily, though, these people constitute only an insignificant minority of our society, and sexual life built on the above-mentioned principles is not characteristic of the wide masses of Soviet people and of Soviet youth; but for the sake of our educational goals, these minimal groups, no matter how small, cannot be ignored.

Soviet society, from its inception, fought all reactionary manifestations in various areas of the life of its people, setting high ideals for marriage and family relationships. This struggle to eliminate undesirable sex attitudes is an important element in Communist education.

The development of respect, which begins in early childhood, is a very significant factor in the area of ethical and esthetic upbringing of children, since this respect for others underlines all existing human relationships. The parents teach the youngsters to revere adults, because they have already acquired life experience and are responsible for the children and their well being. Parents who overemphasize their own authority, while downgrading that of others, use negative methods of raising their children. As a result the children become egotists and lose respect for teachers and other authority figures, instead of being taught the necessity for listening to and following the advice of elders.

Some of these factors in the education of youngsters are closely related to our topic and as such deserve special attention. To this category belong relationships among young people who, in order to stress their friendship and under the disguise of pseudo-naturalness, resort to overfamiliarity and vulgarity, which is, needless to say, very harmful. This brings about the loss of human feeling and subsequently, what is even worse, violation of established rules of behavior and of sexual morality. This occurs particularly in heterosexual relationships of young people. For example, it is not permissible to use an embrace or a pat on the shoulder as a spontaneous expression of friendship, while making free cynical remarks or throwing hints. This kind of relationship insults human dignity and the girl's natural shyness. This attitude may result in lack of respect for women.

As soon as an educator detects lack of controls in his students, which is an easy task for an observant teacher or upbringer, he must try to correct this behavior and begin to set limits within which the young people can express their friendship to members of the opposite sex; because not all that is acceptable between boys or between girls can be transferred to girl–boy relationships. The limits are derived from the respect implicit in the natural bashfulness of boys and girls. Any disrespect for this feeling is considered a violation of ethical behavior. To define certain limits of sexual boy–girl relationships and to translate them into practice is one of the most important educational tasks which the parents and teachers face in this area.

The concept of love, on which the successful control of sexual drives rests, is closely related to respect. Though these two feelings must be fostered in children from a very early age, neither of them so far manifest themselves in its higher meaning in daily life. Succeeding in putting the object of love on a pedestal gives strong support to firm sexual controls and adds beauty and happiness to a relationship.

In a socialist society love cannot be separated from other

forms of human relationships. This feeling, and the behavior expressing it, is not a personal matter of one individual since it affects two people—the one who loves and the one who is loved—and therefore is closely related to responsibility and sexual ethics.

Complete human happiness in family life can be achieved only by mutual love, respect, responsibility, common sexual morality and spiritual values.

An individual living in a socialist society must be moral and honest not only in his actions but also in his thoughts, reasons, and feelings.

Ethical and esthetic education is a serious task which rests not only with the home and the school but also with the Komsomol and the Soviet society at large.

The method of severe public condemnation of sexual indulgence and promiscuity together with public praise of those positive qualities which constitute an ethical and moral approach to sex life will produce a change in attitudes and subsequently desirable results.

## § Marriage Hygiene

### *Marriageable Age*

The actual and legal age for marriage in our country, which was arrived at as a result of many historical as well as socio-economic changes, is the most advisable one. Young people in the age group twenty to twenty-four biologically as well as socially ready for marriage are able to accept the responsibility of sexual life as well as to start an independent family life.

Deviation in either age direction is not advisable for various reasons. People in the older group decrease their ability to conceive children and experience a longer period of time for premarital sexual relationships, which in many instances affects the family life tone unfavorably. It may even bring about the danger of contamination by venereal diseases.

Adolescent marriages before the youngster reaches eighteen years are very harmful. Physiologically the organism is not yet ready for pregnancy and childbirth. During the pregnancy period, many miscarriages, stillbirths, and other complications occur. Children of early marriages tend to be listless and their life expectancy is shorter. These early marriages result in an early loss of husband's potency and their premature aging. The First and Second World Wars brought about a disproportionate decrease of male population of our country, which resulted in family disorganization. After the war a strong effort was made gradually to eliminate these troublesome factors of Soviet family life which are foreign to our system and which contradict the nature of the Soviet individual.

*Forming the Family*

Each individual has the undisputed right to choose his mate and to found a family, in which mutual love and attachment play a decisive role. In this complex process of establishing a family the selection of a spouse becomes crucial. There are many unstable marriages where undesirable outside influences produce many additional problems of daily living such as extramarital relationships, broken homes, and conflicts. Among these marriages are those where there is no genuine depth of mutual feeling and common life purpose, where there is a diversified educational background, extreme differences in chronological age, opposing personality characteristics, etc.

When young adults contemplate marriage, a "hands off" policy of the parents is not correct, since the problem is a very serious one, and their children may need advice and help in taking this important step. Obviously, the interference should be tactful and wise. Instead of being negative and despotic, it should be constructive, positive, and guiding. The higher the respect of young people for their parents, the better the results achieved.

Before marriage many problems should be taken into consideration, such as health of both parties contemplating marriage, mutual interest, knowledge of each other, etc.

Since the institution of marriage is, hopefully, usually for life, carefulness rather than thoughtlessness should be the guiding factor. People who consider the family a temporary state break up their family easily and without regrets about their wife or husband and children; they violate the moral and ethical code of our society. This attitude brings about sad results for all members of the family.

Since any marriage under the Soviet system is a union affecting not only the two participants but also the common interests of the society and of the government, the U.S.S.R. established a code which deals with "Marriage, Family and Guardianship" in order to specify and assure the rights and responsibilities of spouses and of all other family members.

When a conflict between feelings and logic comes about, the moral support of parents and other people close to the couple can be very helpful, since this support channels the confused emotions in the direction which would protect the interests of the individuals involved. As A. S. Makarenko said: "One of the most important tasks of education is to develop an ability to control one's own emotions, imagination and the desires resulting from them."

This ability is of particular importance during the period of young adulthood, when heterosexual relationships are being formed and mates are chosen.

*Hygiene of Sex*

One of the first questions posed by newlyweds is what is the normal frequency of sexual relationships in marriage. Neither medicine nor hygiene has established any norms, since there is considerable variation from family to family. The great majority of families arrived at their norm without any outside help.

One of the first principles of sexual hygiene which must be followed is abstinence from sexual relations during menstruation. At this period sexual activities are unhygienic; furthermore, sexual intercourse disrupts the ongoing complex physiological process in the organism of the female and may result in a series of gynecological disorders, while the male can become infected in the urinary canal.

During pregnancy sexual relations should be decreased, while in the last months no intercourse should take place. The nervous and muscular tension in the female during intercourse upsets the pregnancy, which may result in complications. The same is true during the first two months after giving birth, when the female organism is not yet back to normal. Unfortunately, the experience of many physicians indicates that some men do not follow this advice, while others believe it justifiable to engage in extramarital relationships during this period. Obviously this approach is really immoral.

Sometimes, to avoid conception, the sexual act is interrupted and the climax reached outside of the vagina. For the purpose of extending intercourse many people artificially delay the climax through distracting attention just before reaching it. This practice when frequently used may create disorder and stagnation (stasis) of the inner sexual organs in male and female, which subsequently may lead to such malfunction as decrease in potency in the male. These and other deviations may bring about dissatisfaction of one or even both partners, and for these reasons, these practices should not be used. In instances when for various reasons pregnancy is undesirable, it is necessary to resort to preventive measures, among which prophylactics are the most reliable. There are also other means which the woman can use.

A consultation with a physician must definitely precede choice and implementation of prophylactics, since some of them may prove to be harmful and only he is qualified to give advice in this matter.

Abortion, to which women often resort, effects the birth rate greatly and raises deep moral and ethical questions. As a rule, the decision rests solely with the woman, who has a right to make her choice. She is assured of qualified personnel to perform the operation in a regular hospital setting, which prevents her from turning to quacks. The government ruling on this is motivated entirely by the interests of the woman.

On the other hand, government and public opinion in our country severely criticize women who exhibit a thoughtless and lighthearted approach to abortion, which should never be performed without serious, justifiable reasons. To choose abortion out of egotism or unfavorable economical conditions, without careful analysis of the situation, is inexcusable. Young women who abort a first pregnancy deserve a special reprimand, as well as the husband who pushes his wife into an unnecessary abortion.

Women must always remember that abortions are detrimental

to the health, especially when performed frequently. Such women risk becoming barren and prematurely aged, and also may experience gynecological and nervous disorders, increased irritability, and disturbed functioning. In some families where the woman underwent many abortions in order to escape the responsibilities of child rearing, she was unable to conceive by the time she desired to become pregnant.

All the above-mentioned reasons provide sufficient evidence against the desirability of abortion especially among young people without children.

Childlessness is another problem of family life which produces a lot of discord and often ends in the breaking up of a marriage. Sometimes this handicap has anatomical reasons. In most cases infection of the sexual organs, either the wife's or the husband's, has created conditions that inhibit the passage of reproductive genital cells. In such instances, a doctor should be consulted and, if the condition cannot be corrected, the couple should adopt a child or children.

The impotence in men frequently occurs as a result of masturbation, alcoholism, venereal diseases. In other cases this sexual impotence, especially among physically healthy young people is brought about by emotional stress, such as lack of faith in oneself, insecurity, fear of failure and of sickness, etc. A correct medical diagnosis and treatment always helps to restore sexual potency, except in cases when an anatomical change occurs in the sexual organs.

Venereal diseases must be dealt with in greater detail, since they are transferred in most cases during intercourse. The occasions when an infection takes place by way of a nonsexual contact are extremely rare. Of course, syphilis may be transferred to a fetus through the blood system of its mother.

Though in our country there is no social justification for the existence of venereal diseases, and their occurrence has decreased sharply, their absolute elimination has not yet taken place, due to the undesirable behavior of a small segment of our population. In most cases, venereal diseases are contracted during intercourse outside marriage and as a result many innocent marriage partners become contaminated.

In the experience of our specialized medical institutions, there is a general lack of information and plain ignorance of venereal diseases among our people, regardless of education, age, and social position. This ignorance produces many grave problems in family living, especially for the innocent partner who is infected by the spouse. Society must lend support to these people, while the guilty one must be dealt with severely; legal action invoked by the criminal code should be instituted against such offenders.

The code of the U.S.S.R. which deals with "Marriage, Family, and Guardianship" specifies the necessity of obtaining health statements from both prospective marriage partners while registering their marriage. The admission of having had, in the past, venereal diseases, tuberculosis, or mental illness creates serious obstacles to entering into marriage, since the disease may require prolonged hospital treatment. Both parties are forewarned about the legal responsibility facing them in case they submit false information. Since marriage is prohibited only *during* sickness, all individuals who had been sick in the past must present a statement from the physician before attempting marriage registration.

There are more complications when the husband or wife becomes sick with venereal disease after years of married life. Usually in such cases the injured party requests a divorce, but in many cases other considerations prove it to be wise, though difficult, to reinstate the moral unity of the family.

In almost every instance venereal disease becomes a matter of extreme shame, embarrassment, and reproach, which intensifies the conflict within the family; yet any infidelity is in essence the same, whether it be revealed in less obvious ways or not at all.

Physicians often encounter family conflict where the husband or wife decides to break up a marriage after learning of their mate's venereal disease, though he or she is not of better sexual morals and ethics. Such cases can be explained only by hypocritical attitudes toward sex life.

As soon as venereal disease is detected in the family, all preventive measures must be taken to protect other members of the family. The continuous care of a specialist must be secured immediately and all his directions followed to the smallest detail. There are many prophylactic stations which render preventive and rehabilitative services and help.

Only after all the measures undertaken have succeeded should the husband and wife make a decision regarding their future. While engaged in solving this serious problem, they must bear in mind that, when the treatment is correct and diligently followed, the cure is complete which guarantees that the marital relationship can be resumed without risk to the injured party.

Individuals who refuse to be treated voluntarily can be forced by law to undergo treatment. The Marriage, Family, and Guardianship code specifies the legal responsibility of those who deliberately infect others with venereal diseases. This legal responsibility extends also to those who, being sick, endanger others, though an infection has not occurred.

The best way to avoid venereal disease is to abstain from incidental premarital and extramarital sexual relationships. Between 60 and 80 per cent of the cases of gonorrhea and syphilis are the result of accidental sexual intercourse. Hence marital fidelity and the control of premarital sexual drives prove to be the best prophylactics against venereal diseases.

Alcoholism seems to be a concomitant of gonorrhea and syphilis, since one in a drunken state is more apt to engage in fleeting relationships. Though the hygiene of sex includes various important problems which are closely related to the sexual life, its intimate character prevents many people from acquiring the necessary information.

### *Sexual Morals*

Sexual life represents one of the natural forms of man–woman relationships. In a socialist society this relationship is regulated by norms and principles of moral, ethical, and legal nature. Our attitude toward promiscuity and cynicism manifested in sexual relationships as well as toward marital infidelity and irresponsibility toward family obligations and duties differs radically from that of bourgeois society. In other words, after the revolution an entirely new concept of sexual morality came into being in our country. The all-important aspects of life such as love, family, and sexual life are now perceived differently. This process derived its essence and its social significance from the statement by Marx and Engels: "The relationship between man and woman is a natural behavior between two human beings. Consequently it reflects the degree to which the natural human behavior became human."*

The above-indicated principle is the result of the historical progress of our country. We changed from bourgeois monogamy to socialist monogamy, which is built upon the basic idea of equality between men and women and is free from any forms of exploitation. Nevertheless, this new approach which, as Engels said, "became an actuality also for men,"† continuously has to struggle with the old forms of marriage and family relations which remain imbedded in some individuals still not affected by change. This is the reason why, in our society, among the many exemplary, stable families which constitute the foundation of our contemporary socialist community, there are still some unstable ones left.

It is obvious that since the process of change is long and difficult, insufficient time has elapsed to inject all socialist norms and principles into the area of marriage and family life, and to make this formulation final.

The forms of violating sexual morals are varied. They occur among adults who are already socially established, as well as among those without families, or with severed family ties. This amoral behavior deserves not only strong public condemnation but also corresponding legal action.

Unfortunately, these violators of social and sexual morals do not always meet due rebuff, which indicates serious shortcomings in our education. Each of these "heroes" receives silent endorsement of his undesirable sexual behavior, or even active support from individuals in his environment. These people still tolerate immoral sexual behavior in an old-fashioned way and regard it as a "necessity" or a "prank." This thoughtless and

* K. Marx and F. Engels, *Collected Works,* 1930, Vol. III, p. 621.

† F. Engels, *The Origin of Family, of Private Property and of Government,* 1952, p. 77.

lighthearted approach to sexual life is still observed in wide sections of the population.

The stability of the family is the most significant element in the relationship between man and woman. This factor depends to a greater degree than any other upon the moral and legal responsibility of the individuals involved. Though the law and morality of our country under certain circumstances accepts the breaking up of a family unit as a necessity or a possibility, many grave questions are raised in regard to the disposition of each case. There is no doubt that, in spite of all precautions, there is some misuse.

Divorce is a legal form of governmental permission to break up a marriage. This legalized way to regain freedom derives from broadest democratic principles which as V. I. Lenin indicates "does not mean disintegration of family relationships, but on the contrary strengthening it by taking the only recourse possible in a stable, civilized society based on democratic principles."* On the other hand, the law is primarily concerned with the interests of children, and consequently the rights of both spouses must be subordinated to them. This approach increases the responsibility of adults and motivates them to analyze seriously their behavior and their reasons for possible divorce procedures before deciding upon them. In this way, the Soviet legal code of "Marriage, Family, and Guardianship" stabilizes the family and relationships within it.

Of course this does not mean that divorce solves everything. The experience of daily life proves that some thoughtless individuals request divorce for such trivial and insignificant reasons as "character incompatibility," "alienation of affection," "dissatisfaction," etc., while serious reasons do not appear as frequently.

Divorces do not always become officially registered. In many cases the family actually disintegrates when one of the spouses (usually the husband) deserts and begins a family "on the side" or leads a disorganized sex life. Almost always, the reasons for these "divorces" are alcoholism and promiscuity, and in rare cases, groundless or unfounded jealousy.

* V. I. Lenin, *Collected Works,* Vol. 20, p. 393.

Divorce produces great harm in the process of children's upbringing; they suffer most when the family breaks up. Youngsters without a father or mother are well aware of the parental misbehavior. They grow up without parental love and care, which play a very significant role in the formulation of a child's personality.

However, life often creates multiple variations of husband–wife relationships, which produce emotional as well as family conflicts. Frequently a realistic appraisal of these situations is impossible and the individuals involved have great difficulty in determining objectively the most rational course of action. The decision arrived at depends greatly upon individual characteristics such as will power, feeling of duty, of responsibility, degree of egotism, honesty, decency. To reach a satisfactory conclusion is a very difficult task, since the general interests of the society and of family members directly affected by it demand that love should yield to social obligations.

No attempt is made here to minimize the meaning and strength of such love between two people already married and with families. However, it is also important to differentiate between real love and infatuation, conditioned by such negative characteristics of the individual as egotism and self-indulgence.

No one has the right to build his own happiness at the expense of others or to subordinate the interests of the whole society to private and egotistical ends. This is the essence of the basic demands of socialist morals in the area of sexual morals and marriage and family life; it corresponds with the principles of the socialist system under which the interests of society take priority over the personal interests of individuals.

A case of unrequited love, a rather frequent occurrence, becomes amoral only when an effort is made to force the object of love into moral and/or sexual submission. In the process of struggling with this feeling, strong emotions come into play, especially in young people, and sometimes they go so far as to lose their equilibrium. They need a strong will and inner controls to pull themselves together. The sensitivity of others in their environment to their problems proves to be of great help. The ability to control feelings in adverse situations is certainly a positive characteristic, but at the same time this unfortunate love should not be viewed as a tragedy or disaster. In a socialist society one can always recover from private troubles by engaging in the life of the collective or in work.

The struggle against infringements upon social morals is spearheaded by the entire Soviet society. Public opinion, literature, the press, and law, severely condemn all acts of amorality and request punishment for all intentional violations. At the same time, various methods of influencing amoral individuals are implemented in order to bring about desirable change in their attitudes.

## § Conclusions

Sex is one of the factors which Communist education cannot ignore in its struggle to establish sound principles of a healthy socialist life. The approach which suggests ignoring it is a very faulty one. Obviously this area, just like any other sphere of life, changes constantly under the influence of ongoing socioeconomic advances. To study these changes is of special importance to us, and the conclusions of such study, dealing with the sexual life of the population, would become valuable and serious guides for Communist education. Parents and educators pass on their life experience to the growing generation. But unfortunately we cannot forget that the majority of the adult population is not sufficiently knowledgeable in regard to the complex problems of education. In most cases they try to ignore the sex instinct of children and of adolescents, and this avoidance of the issue has a great influence upon the behavior of the individual during his entire life.

"The very powerful sex instinct, when left in its 'primitive' state or when fostered by 'primitive' upbringing may only result in antisocial behavior, while the improved social content of education which fosters unity with other people, discipline, and inhibition of reflexes, channels this instinct into highly ethical behavior which subsequently leads to human happiness. In the family the individual is exposed to his first social experience, and if it proves to be positive and correct his road to success in sexual education is assured."* The school is another equally significant factor in shaping the individual. Consequently, here too sexual education can take place. The basic method of correct education accepts and directs the sexual instinct. It also assures the heterosexual and family relationship according to socialist values, by developing patriotism, respect toward women, elders, and other people, and toward love and family. These attitudes in the spirit of the moral theory of Marxism and of Leninism are formulated as follows by Makarenko. "Social ethics demand that the sexual life of every man and woman should continuously maintain a harmonious relationship to family and to love, and only such sexual life which was based on mutual love and which manifests a twofold goal of happiness and procreation as well as child rearing is accepted as normal and ethically justifiable."†

The problems of marriage hygiene are closely related to the educational process which encompasses the whole life span of an individual.

The art of education demands a positive, critical, and tactful approach to all manifestations of desires and of emotions. Arriving at appropriate methods of sex education is a pedagogical problem. No doubt this area is among the most difficult ones, theoretically as well as practically.

Though most educators and parents succeed in developing in children and in youth, will power, ability to control desires, and respect for problems related to sexual life, there is still a need for further improvement as well as for broadening understanding in the area of sex education. The deeper the comprehension among adults of developmental stages, their tasks and characteristics, the better will be the results.

* A. S. Makarenko, *Collected Works,* 1951, Vol. 4, p. 245.
† *Ibid.,* p. 408.

*Part Two*

# *Family*

Though the role of the family has been changing constantly since the October Revolution—in accordance with the developmental stages the system went through—the heavy emphasis on the responsibility of the parents has remained the same. The prevailing philosophy stresses the importance of "bringing up children as able and true builders of Communism," and there is no doubt that parents are delegated a considerable part of this task and are "held responsible" for its fulfillment.

For the American reader it may be important to comment on the difference in over-all philosophy. For, in a way we, too, would consider it an "important responsibility" for parents to bring up their children well, and we, too, emphasize the importance of youth as the "Future of our Nation." The difference lies mainly in the specific interpretation with which the term "parental responsibility" is being used. In the American philosophy of life, the rearing of the young remains an undisputed task of the family as an entity in its own right. While public authorities—federal, state, and local government—are of course interested in what children develop into, we would not consider it proper for them to interfere, beyond certain obvious limits which are clearly defined by law, in the way parents handle their children. Our public authorities would, of course, intervene in cases of neglect, cruelty, or disobedience against basic laws such as school attendance, but we would not expect public authorities to have any say beyond that. In the Soviet society, in contrast, the family as a unit is considered directly accountable to the larger collective of which it is a part. Parents who do not raise their children in the spirit in which the collective wants them raised are considered failing in their responsibility to the collective. "Wrong" attitudes toward the rearing of the young, therefore, become tantamount to "breaking a law" and are considered an offense against the public authority invested in the collective at large.

It is likely that the recent trends in the direction of the School Internat may bring with it a further shift in the concept of "responsibility delegated to the family." However, this development is still too young to permit concrete predictions about just where the realm of "delegated parental responsibility" versus "direct responsibility of the school collective" will fall.

# 5 *The Family in Soviet Society*

*A. G. Kharchev*

## § Socialistic Upbringing of Children

SINCE THE MAIN ELEMENT of any society is man, the rapid growth of socialist society demands a large increase of the Soviet population. N. S. Khrushchev, addressing a group of young people in Moscow who were leaving for the virgin lands, said: "The population expansion increases the strength of our country. The bourgeois ideologists created a theory about overpopulation and tried to curb its increase. But we, comrades, look at it differently. Even adding a hundred million to two hundred millions of people will still not suffice."

The family plays a very important role in building Communism, because it assures the increase in population which is

A. G. Kharchev, *The Family in Soviet Society,* Lenizdat, 1960, Leningrad, 1960, pp. 84-111.

This reading consists of one chapter from a pamphlet which, though written for general consumption, is directed primarily at youth. All statistics quoted in this chapter refer to data accumulated prior to 1960.

the real strength and richness of our country. The birth rate in the U.S.S.R. is now 25.3 per 1000 of population, while in France it is 18.4, in Japan 17.2, in England 16.5.

Prior to the revolution 273 of every 1000 new-born babies and infants below 12 months of age would die, while in 1957, infant mortality in that age group declined to 45 per 1000.

The role of the family in a socialist society is not limited to biological procreation. It also upholds the spiritual values and safeguards cultural traditions influencing the moral outlook of each family member, especially those of the young generation.

The development of personality begins at a very early age. Therefore, the family becomes the first source of influencing its growth. Mutual love and limitless trust are necessary elements for successfully bringing up children in the family. This love, like the love between man and woman, though basically natural, is social in content.

In a socialist society, providing children with security and correct upbringing is, to a much greater degree than anywhere else, a way of serving the country and fulfilling one's duty to the nation. In 1955 everyone in the U.S.S.R. heard about a famous adoption case; during the war, a blacksmith in Tashkent and his wife adopted fourteen refugee children of various ages. This is not an isolated case.

The realization that family upbringing carries a great social significance increases the parents' responsibility for the future moral make-up of their children, and for the whole process of forming their personality.

Lenin talked many times about stormy, searching youth, underlining the important psychological characteristics of this age group, such as directness, strong emotional reaction, responsiveness, quest for knowledge, striving for truth, justice, and idealism. All of these characteristics define the romantic perception of life which is peculiar to older children and adolescents alike and which expresses itself in dreams about conquests and a fascination with brilliance and it often includes an impatience with daily, ordinary occurrences. Therefore, the family in the process of rearing children must help them to discover the romanticism in their daily life and in "ordinary" work, the greatness of "small deeds"; it must find original ways to acquaint them with their real environment.

Since the romantic thinking of children and adolescents as a rule combines imagination, ideals, and reality, direct visible examples from daily life are helpful in shaping the personality of youngsters.

Children are easily convinced, but just as easily disappointed, especially when what they see contradicts what they are told. Childhood and adolescence are not only times of great hopes but also periods of great doubts which may result in lack of self-assurance, particularly when the child or adolescent does not periodically have an opportunity to experience his own ability to overcome difficulties.

Some believe that upbringing is equivalent to education because they think both are the school's concern. This, of course, is not true. Upbringing means not only the acquisition of academic and practical knowledge in certain areas but also the development of political, esthetic, moral values, formation of character, and the strengthening of will power. "The principles of Communism," said Kalinin, "are in essence as follows: well-rounded education, honesty, love toward socialist fatherland, friendship, camaraderie, humanism, eagerness to participate actively in the building of socialism, and many other high qualities, all very obvious. Upbringing which fosters these virtuous characteristics becomes a very important factor of Communist rearing."

Though the ethics of Marxism and Leninism always emphasize the necessary unity of the spiritual and physical, the intellectual and the emotional in the development of personality, we have seen in our time an additional stress on well-roundedness. The favorable conditions which exist now in the family make it important to perfect those aspects of the educational process which depend directly on the parents, their general cultural level, and their moral maturity.

The influence the family has upon this spiritual make-up of children is determined by what A. S. Makarenko called "general family tone." "The general atmosphere cannot be artificially invented or sustained. Only your personal life and your actual behavior creates and upholds it."*

"General family atmosphere" is the environment in which the child's character is formed and it influences the child regardless of parents' subjective wishes, often in spite of them.

Sometimes the parents try to hide family discords and fights from the children, but they never succeed; the youngster senses the slightest change in mood in the family, the smallest lie. He may not notice it in relationship to other people, but he easily senses it in regard to his parents, because he loves them. When a child loses faith in his parents, he begins to distrust others too, and often lands in trouble.

There is a close relationship between the general atmosphere in the family and the character of the children. A close-knit family brings up straight, valuable, and unaffected young people.

A stable and friendly family is possible only when high morals prevail within it as well as in relationship to the society; the youngster's character depends also on socially conscious behavior traits such as honesty, straightforwardness, upholding of principles, responsiveness, respect toward collectives, etc. The general family tone not only influences the children's behavior but also conditions parents' impact upon youngsters.

In a socialist society children depend on their parents economically as long as they are not able to work productively. This dependence does not affect the parent-child relationship since parental responsibility to support morally and provide for the material needs of children is considered legal, ethical, and social duty rather than a private matter.

Parents influence their children in the following ways:

1. *Parental opinion* is a moral criterion for the youngster. The child is not yet able to judge his action in the light of social demands and morals, to know what in his behavior is good and what is bad. He may perceive as "bravery" and "independence" anti-social types of behavior (regardless of where he picks up the notion—in life or in literature). Parents' interpretation be-

* A. S. Makarenko, *Book for Parents,* 1949, p. 158.

comes a way in which he begins to orient himself in a life not yet fully understood by him.

2. *Imitative behavior* begins with the child's dreams of becoming, when he grows up, a doctor, engineer, worker in a factory, teacher, blacksmith, like his father or mother. He imitates their behavior. Obviously bad habits are as easily absorbed as the good ones. The formation of habits, though in the beginning only an unconscious imitation, later becomes a conscious action and eventually grows into a personality trait.

3. *Parental habits.* An adolescent imitates not only his parents habits but also their ways of thinking, their reasoning, their attitudes toward fulfilling their duty to society, in short, their whole life. The youngsters in this age group no longer imitate blindly. They criticize and judge parental behavior.

"Your own behavior," wrote A. S. Makarenko, addressing the parents, "is the most decisive factor. Do not think you bring up a child only when you talk with him or teach him or direct him. You bring him up during every moment of your life, even when you are not present. The way you dress, the way you talk with other people and about others, how you react to happiness and sorrow, how you behave with your friends and enemies, whom you laugh at and whom you laugh with, what you read—all this means a lot to the child. The youngster immediately detects the slightest change in mood. He perceives all your thoughts and their changes without your being aware of it."*

A. S. Makarenko distinguished the following incorrect ways of asserting parental authority:

1. *Suppressive authority.* Parents use fear as the most frequent means to get their children to conform. Threats and reprimands are also often used to achieve subordination. As a result of this approach children become liars, cowards, rude, and high strung.

Although in special circumstances fear may be a useful and beneficial approach when all other methods fail, it should never be considered *the* educational means of getting results, especially with children.

* A. S. Makarenko, *Collected Pedagogical Works,* Vol. I, 1947, p. 17.

2. *Distant authority.* Parents avoid direct contact with children and delegate their authority to others, such as grandmothers, nannies, and older siblings. This kind of behavior brings about a break between parents and children; the latter withdraw, become introverted and distrustful, and often easily fall under bad influences.

3. *Self-assumed authority.* Parents use every opportunity to convince the children that their parents are superior to their whole environment. Often these parents gossip about neighbors and friends and are rude to their subordinates in the presence of their youngsters. As a result, the children cultivate the same behavior and in the end the parents become the first victims of their egotism and self-conceit.

4. *Preaching authority.* Some parents preach to everyone, do not tolerate differences of opinion, nag at length; all of this prompts youngsters not to take their parents' demands seriously. They try to avoid direct contact with parents, and become estranged. When the parents' preaching clashes with the youngster's strong will, it may result in suppressing his initiative and will power and make him a passive follower. When youngsters discover that a dichotomy exists between parental preaching and behavior, this kind of "authority" may become an excuse for bigotry and hypocrisy.

5. *Bribing* is the most enticing of the wrong methods of asserting authority. Sometimes this method is falsely interpreted as an expression of love. Its main manifestation is too much leniency and compliance and too many rewards for desirable behavior. Parents who devise gratifications (bribes) for good grades change the motivation for learning. Expectation of a reward rather than duty and responsibility become the child's motivation. Subsequently such children learn how to be calculating and self-centered.

Though a great effort is now being made to strengthen the ties between school and home, and between academic education and vocational preparation, some parents still try to "rescue" their children from fulfilling small work assignments in school or in pioneer camps.

For instance, the director of the pioneer camp of the Russian

Academy of Science* in Komarovo tells of a case in which a famous scientist, during an interview, requested that his son, supposedly a talented musician, be relieved from camp duties. In this case his wish was not granted, but there are many instances in which the parents succeed "in their educational program" and bring up their children as useless freeloaders! Even when the child is really talented, it is to his advantage to develop respect for labor and to learn as a young child to strive stubbornly toward his goals.

Parents often attempt to get preferential treatment for their children from the teachers, in preschool, in a secondary school, or even in a university. Sometimes a parent, who, because of his talents has a very good profession, tries to push his child in the same direction in spite of the child's lack of ability. Other parents, mistaking such behavior for love, indulge their children, spoil them, support their parasitic existence and delinquent behavior (the last two are closely related). Mothers and fathers will blame their son's friends and companions for his misbehavior, not realizing that they themselves are the culprits. Their overindulgence and leniency made their child the way he is.

Certainly there is no objection to healthy parental love and kindness which fosters rather than hampers the process of maturation by setting consistent standards and demands. Without this, parental love is amoral and antisocial. A parent who really loves his child, will strengthen his character, prepare him to overcome difficulties, work on his weaknesses, among the worst of which is unwillingness and inability to work.

Finally, there is one more manifestation of parental irresponsibility, namely, the complete lack of concern that results in child neglect.

Families which bring up children incorrectly, or do not really take care of them are following an antiquated bourgeois tradition rather than that of a new socialist morality.

The analysis of delinquent acts committed by persons up to twenty-five years of age proves that in the majority of cases the

* Each industry, agency, and professional organization supports a camp for the children of *their* staff. So, for example, the Academy of Science maintains a camp for the children of all employees of this institution.

blame for the youth's antisocial behavior lies with the family. The following case may be cited as an example:

In June of 1959, a university student (member of a youth patrol) in the city of Gorky was accosted by thugs and severely beaten. When the attackers were brought to trial, it became apparent that one of the gang members was an only son of an overindulging mother, who did not know how to set limits or how to bring him up as a well-disciplined, socially useful human being.

The reason why, in our socialist society, there are still young people leading the parasitic existence of thieves, murderers, and grafters is a very simple one: we still have irresponsible parents and families neglecting their youngsters and their future, who, in spite of socialist surroundings still manage to give their children a bourgeois ideological training, not realizing its harmfulness to society and to themselves.

A genuinely socialist family upbringing always contains education for labor, real parental love, high demands, friendship, trust, high principles, and justice.

Larger families seem to be more able to establish a firm order and to maintain better harmony. Somehow everything falls into place at the right time, everybody taking part in daily routines and important plans.

The parents who are concerned only with the physical needs of children, neglecting the development of traits such as honesty, bravery, and love and respect for labor cannot be helped by any pedagogical method, no matter how wonderful it is. Attention to the whole life of a child, not to isolated instances, is needed to bring up children successfully. All positive characteristics must become a norm, not a means to earn favors. When, during childhood, proper measures of restraint are exerted and limits clearly defined, the maturation process brings positive results, and the parents have reason to rejoice.

There is a lot of proof supporting one of the most important of Makarenko's theories regarding "correct Soviet upbringing." He says it is impossible to visualize raising children in a socialist society without the fundamental emphasis on education for labor.*

* A. S. Makarenko, *Lectures About Upbringing of Children,* 1947, p. 57.

Only jointly with governmental and social agencies and organizations can the socialist family accomplish its task of successfully educating their children. Soviet society and government assume a considerable amount of educational expenses. As an example, the cost for one student in school or at the university is about 33,000 rubles.*

Each year the number of creches and preschools grows. During the years 1951–1957 the government built creches for 442,200 children. In the same period of time the kolchozes at their own expense established creches for 325,200 children and preschools for 64,100 youngsters.

School Internats established by Decree of the XXth Congress of the Central Committee of the Communist Party are growing well. "We should take action now to build school internats so that in the future all children of school age will have an opportunity for a free-of-cost upbringing in them," said N. S. Khrushchev. "Until the revolution only aristocrats could send their children to boarding schools, while children of the working class were growing up in the 'street's internats.' The time is not far away when, by parental agreement, all children will be brought up in school internats."†

The important economic role played by the government in assuring the education of children in creches, preschools, and school internats is illustrated in a table compiled by V. B. Olshansky (from available local data) in Leningrad in 1959.

| COST OF EDUCATING ONE CHILD | GOVERNMENT'S SHARE | SHARE OF PARENTS EARNING | |
|---|---|---|---|
| | | *Up to 400 r.* | *Up to 1000 r.* |
| Creches | 420 | 30-38 | 65-81 |
| Preschool | 300 | 50 | 106 |
| School Internat (12 month) | 560 | 60-80 | 270 |
| Schools (9 month) | 3000 | — | — |

* All amounts cited in this chapter refer to the ruble before the money reform of January 1961.

† *Pravda,* May 9, 1959.

This government participation in the raising of children is not only material but also moral. It expresses itself in exerting coercion upon parents who do not fulfill their obligations or incorrectly perceive their duties, and this influence is legal as well as moral. In an article appearing in *Smena* in 1959 under a headline: "Can He Be Called a Father?" the behavior of the father (drunkenness, abusiveness, fighting) was criticized severely because it was setting a bad example for the children. As a result of this article, the father was reprimanded publicly at work, and under this pressure he was forced to change his behavior. Of course, not all such cases come to public notice so that something can be done about them.

Now in connection with the natural growth of society's influence in the many economic, political, and moral aspects of Soviet life, industrial and social collectives feel responsible to a greater degree not only for work attitudes and quality but also for the family life pattern of their members.

Often the collective renders direct help in taking care of and bringing up children. When a mother gets sick and must be hospitalized, co-workers or neighbors take turns in caring for the children in the family, watching over their physical needs, and also seeing that homework and school duties are not neglected.

Society also places great emphasis upon helping families in their recreational activities, the organization of which, depending on content, may produce either positive or harmful results for the working or social collective. Youth leisure-time activities not thoughtfully planned bring about great moral harm, because boredom and lack of purposeful activities may lead the adolescent to drinking and hooliganism.

Noticeable progress has been made lately in planning recreational activities for children and families. Trade union clubs organize more frequent family evening activities and meetings and have revitalized sports activities. In housing developments children's clubs and playgrounds are being organized. People living in the developments are used as recreation leaders, such as retirees, housewives, and students. Such a club begins frequently as a small voluntary group in which parents also take part. They make excursions to museums, theaters, movies, exhibitions, trips to the country, and other places of interest to the children.

The main goal and purpose of these clubs is to give children's collectives a strong, healthy moral foundation and to tie them closer together by using veterans of labor who contribute their own experience in helping to bring up children as deserving citizens of a socialist society.

Family upbringing in the U.S.S.R. is in content a socialist rearing of children for two reasons: First, its components are socialist consciousness, ideals of collectivism, awareness of one's duty to serve the country, and second, the society and government render great material and moral help. But in spite of this, even now, conflicts arise between the community and the family. This happens when the family rejects the aims and demands of society.

When ignorant parents at home speak disrespectfully of teachers and of school in the presence of the youngster, they create trouble for their child and for themselves. When the authority of the school is not supported in the family, students' behavior becomes rude not only in school but also at home. Sometimes conflicts between society and family become aggravated by the incorrect position of the parents toward institutions of public education. Of course, teachers in schools, preschools, and creches are not infallible, but to emphasize their mistakes to the child and, even worse, to criticize the teacher or the teaching collective destructively means to negate the whole educational process. These parents think that they improve and strengthen their authority in the eyes of their children when they criticize the teachers, but in the child's mind there is a very close relationship between parental and public authority. As soon as one source of authority is discredited, the other also begins to be doubted, because of the youngster's constant inner struggle between his dependence on adults and his striving for independence. Parents probably would make fewer mistakes in the process of bringing up their children if they more often recalled their own thoughts and feelings during childhood and adolescence.

All contradictions existing between the family and community upbringing in a socialist society are of a subjective rather than an objective nature, such as the inadequate moral tone of some families or of their individual adult members. The most decisive means of fighting all outdated and wrong child rearing practices which still remain from the past is to elevate the general cultural and moral level of the population.

The main social purpose of the Soviet family is to secure successors who will further develop the physical, cultural, and moral aspects of the Soviet socialist society, and who will be ready to take part in life as active and conscientious builders of communism.

Bringing up a child—developing his point of view, his ideals, his feelings—is a very difficult and gravely responsible task, which demands from parents moral maturity, seriousness, and real "know how."

Society has the right to judge what values the family teaches and how it brings up the young generation.

## § The Building of Communism and the Future of the Family in It

The entrance of the U.S.S.R. into a period of extensive building of communism will create for the Soviet family the necessary conditions for developing and enriching new socialist aspects of marriage and of family relationships. Also, in this period of transition Soviet family life is affected by the higher economic as well as cultural level of the population.

The main characteristic of the future will be the transition from individual households to communal living and the task of caring for and bringing up children will become an easier one, because many new nursery schools and school internats will facilitate the proper upbringing of children outside the family.

After the successful elimination of feudal, bourgeois ideals, Communist morals will triumphantly prevail between man and woman and parents and children.

Already the fulfillment of the seven-year plan to develop the national economy of U.S.S.R. sharply enlarges the role of governmental social agencies in providing economic support for the family and in educating the young generation.

The production of necessary equipment to lighten women's domestic chores will be doubled by 1965.

The number of public eating places is steadily increasing, not only in urban, but in rural communities. The increased prosperity of collective and state farms is gradually helping to eliminate individual orchards and livestock of farmers, thereby relieving the woman of added home chores.

The continuing growth of natural production and its gradual transition to a period in which everyone will receive according to his needs will make household economics in its present sense unnecessary. This of course does not mean that the family must necessarily lose individuality of tastes, nor that the communal living will bring about the lowering of standards. In other words, one cannot visualize Communist living as a poorly run rest home with a uniform menu.

Communism anticipates a great variety of individual requests. Of course, communal living does not mean that families will not be able to eat their meals together or share other "family activities," so long as they do not interfere with the work schedule, with social activities individual members are engaged in, or with the family's need for rest.

Abundance of material goods and the solution of the housing problem will alleviate if not eliminate objective reasons for family discord and conflict. Everybody will have an opportunity to retain his youth and physical beauty longer. Nervousness and irritability which our generation acquired during the war years will disappear. The difficulties which the people will have to overcome in the Communistic future will be a different set of challenges, such as fighting nature, developing production, perfecting moral values, surmounting problems of creating rather than of destroying. Thus, living conditions in the Communist society will strengthen and improve the marriage and family relationships.

The change to Communism will also mean intensifying the role of society in bringing up children.

By 1965 the number of creches and nursery schools will double, and the number of school internats will increase fourteen times. What is more, the collective farms are in the process of building, and plan to continue to increase the number of children's establishments and school internats. As the chairman of one collective stated: "Beginning in 1962 all children in our collective farm will be fully supported by us from the day they are born until they finish their secondary schooling. They will receive their education in a boarding school setting, starting in the creche as infants, then continuing into nursery school and finally to a secondary school internat. This would not mean that the parents and other members of the collective would forfeit their educational function in relation to the youngsters. Parents will be able to take their children home for a night during the child's day off, as well as at other times. The Party and the governing body of the collective farm does not permit any encroachment upon parental rights."*

Besides the creation of individual school internats in cities, in workers' settlements, as well as in state farms, a compound school internat for children will be developed in the process of the building of Communism. There the youngsters will be brought up from infancy to late adolescence fully supported by public funds. One such compound internat is already in existence in the region of Smolensk, not far from Safanovo. It is a children's town in which the youngsters benefit from all the comforts of contemporary life and cultural enrichment. The creche, nursery school, secondary school and two dormitories are located in the center of the town. There is a dining hall with a capacity of 450. Their recreational facilities include a stadium, playgrounds, solariums, a zoological corner, a greenhouse, and a large waterfront with a watchtower, boats, swimming pool and a beach. For extracurricular activities they have a library, three pianos, two televisions, a radio station and a movie theater. For practical experience they have an experimental farm, workshops to get acquainted with the new methods in industry, and this is where the youngsters learn about their future chosen fields. The

* *Pravda,* September 6, 1959.

teachers in this compound school internat are skillful and experienced. Everything here is geared toward providing a well-rounded education and correct upbringing of the young generation.

The main purpose in creating and developing school internats in urban as well as rural communities is to help the family, mainly the mother, in the process of rearing children. At no time is the intent to take away from the family the task and the responsibility connected with the bringing up of the new generation. Parental authority and supervision are recognized by the school internat as two of the most important factors in raising children, and the school draws heavily from the experience of the parents. As a result, their moral influence upon their children remains unchanged.

The collective of peers is another very significant factor in the process of shaping the child's personality. Many families, especially urban, have only one child. This tends to foster egotism, self-centeredness, and despotism. Even families with few children have encountered difficulties while trying to avoid these pitfalls. When parental experience is combined with the "know-how" of professional educators, and parental love with the sensitivity and objectivity of the collective, the effectiveness of the educational methods used grows considerably.

It should be remembered that, as a result of war, the number of unwed mothers increased considerably. Thousands of children grew up fatherless. Though in principle the morals of Communism are opposed to illicit relationships between men and women, these women cannot be judged harshly, since in the majority of cases their action did not stem from personal moral inadequacies but was a result of the tremendous decrease of male population during the war years in our country. Many unwed mothers are in great need of moral as well as economic support, which the community must give them. School internats for their children become one of the most important forms of help extended to them.

School internats have another very significant role to play. They strengthen the equality of women, who have a greater opportunity to utilize their creativity in industry as well as to devote themselves to the sociopolitical life of our country with the knowledge that their children are well taken care of.

In order to transfer to the community various functions and duties which are at the present time performed by the family, it is necessary to create favorable conditions in agencies serving the families. At present, many of them leave a lot to be desired.

The shortening of the working day in the U.S.S.R. will result in great changes in the established Soviet family life pattern.

"A great deal has already been accomplished in this regard," N. S. Khrushchev said in his speech during the Fifth Session of the Supreme Council (Soviet) of U.S.S.R. "During the last two years the workers in the coal and metallurgical industry have had their work hours shortened, while workers in chemical plants and many others have had pay increases." By a Decree of April 1, 1960, 16 million people already had their working day shortened to seven and six hours. By the end of 1960, all working people in the U.S.S.R. will have shorter working hours. The Communist Party and government are planning to institute a shorter week in all agencies and offices during 1963. And there is a plan to start shortening the working day to five and six hours beginning in 1964. This will give the family more time together, and it will make the meaning of leisure in the life of the family more important. It will also leave more time for parents to raise and supervise their children in the home situation. More free time increases the opportunity for the cultural development of adults, and for the cultivation of their spiritual needs. Consequently, the quality of recreational activities of the family should improve. As the recreational agencies give better services, the bond between family life and recreational resources of the community becomes closer. Engaging in available leisure-time recreational activities does not destroy the "specific" character of each family; it only broadens and enriches their interests.

As was mentioned above, Communism plans to root out fully all bourgeois and feudal remnants in marriage and family relationships.

The cultural, moral, and aesthetic values of Communist society will increasingly reflect themselves in the relationships between man and woman, parents and children, reinforcing marital ties, fidelity and family happiness. The meaning of duty, conscience, honor, and human dignity will deepen.

There is a growing trend, especially among youth, to recreate the national traditions and to develop new Soviet customs, to celebrate maturity rituals, weddings, births of children, and other important family events. For example, in Leningrad, the Komsomol weddings are simple, beautiful ceremonies, and their meaningful rituals are very popular. The opening of the Palace of Marriages increased the significance of the ceremony and made it more beautiful. In a region of the Latvian Republic one special day a year was designated to celebrate new births, another the coming of age, and one to commemorate the dead. In Suguld the young girls wear white gowns and the boys dark suits during their "maturity rites," which now are celebrated there once every year. On the designated day, before dawn, the young people arrive at the regional Palace of Culture. The girls are in snow white attire and lead the festive procession four abreast. The parade marches through the whole city toward the castle. There the participants listen to speeches, after which they receive autograph books inscribed as follows: "Be proud that you live in a country where a Communist society is being built. Your great life calls upon you to find your place among active fighters for a brighter future. Do not squander your strength in vain; fill every day with meaningful activities. Do not be afraid to dream about heroism in labor and in life; fight to make your dreams come true."* Friends shower them with flowers and parents with gifts. The festivities continue all day. In the evening the girls and boys return home where they continue to celebrate with family and friends.

A few months before the festivities take place, the youth meet with old revolutionaries and soldiers with whom they discuss work, proper behavior, "secrets" of growing, and practical topics pertaining to daily life.

These festivities are not only enjoyable, but also morally

* *Izvestia,* June 8, 1959.

significant; they create in the youth a sense of responsibility for their own future, and at the same time emphasize the continuity of life.

The ethical and aesthetic growth of the family and of the whole society brings about a change from regulating family relations by law and sanction to moral means of public influence. This process can already be observed in action. In many cases public opinion or fear of it influences people who violate social codes of behavior more effectively than can the law.

The fact that the collective has an opportunity not only to disapprove and reprimand already committed acts but also to prevent and help to correct mistakes makes its moral role more powerful in marriage and family life. Sometimes when a marriage is near the breaking point, the collective uses its influence to maintain the unity of the family; and often successfully.

Broadening the role of public opinion in regulating marriage and family relationships will gradually lead to a narrowing of the need for legal action; eventually, we will see the establishment of a code of behavior which is upheld by deeply ingrained moral values.

Though socialist law and Communist morality both fight for the same goals, sometimes moral standards respond with a greater sensitivity to the economic and social development of society and meet various needs and demands of daily life better than does the law. Therefore, one of the most important tasks of a socialist society is to merge the legal and moral laws affecting family life.

Currently, Soviet society is planning to review some of the official positions taken by the Supreme Soviet of U.S.S.R. in its Decree of June 8, 1944. According to this Decree only an officially registered marriage imposes legal rights and responsibilities on spouses; divorce can be obtained only through court procedures, after first publicly announcing this intention in the newspapers.

Though this Decree played an important role in correcting thoughtless attitudes toward marriage, it had negative results as well. For example, many critics of this Decree feel it is imperative to eliminate differences existing between birth certificates issued to legitimate children and to those born out of wedlock. They also feel strongly that the divorce procedure, should be simplified and the father's legal and financial responsibility to a child born out of wedlock should be established. Obviously, now, when Soviet society is living through a period of rapid economic and spiritual growth, the law of the land cannot remain static; it must develop and perfect itself.

This regulation of marriage and family relations by means of society's moral pressures will not weaken family ties. On the contrary, as the people's consciousness of their responsibilities increases it will be impossible for temporary, accidental, and thoughtless relationships between man and woman to develop. Since marriage will actually be synonymous with love, its stability will be safeguarded. This does not mean that a marriage in Communist society will be indissoluble, and that there will be no conflicts in the family. In some rare cases love may fade away and a new one may begin. But the number of such cases will probably diminish, because in a Communist society people will not only inherit but also develop further all that is good and noble and toward which we now strive as an ideal. As a result the higher phase of Communism will become a period of marital fullfilment, where there will be no need for divorce and a second try.

6

# *Reward and Punishment of Children in the Family*

*I. A. Petchernikova*

## § Introduction

THIS PAMPHLET is the result of direct experience acquired from dealing with problems of discipline in many Soviet families. Though this booklet does not discuss all of the problems inherent in the upbringing of children, an attempt was made to bring a fair sampling to the attention of the reader. The illustrations included in the text stress concrete situations of daily life rather than general theory.

If this pamphlet proves to be of any help to parents in choosing the right method of bringing up their children, and if they succeed in developing in them consciousness, independence, initiative, and respect for the principles of socialistic life, the task of this pamphlet will be accomplished.

I. A. Petchernikova, *Reward and Punishment of Children in the Family*, Uchpedgiz, Moscow, 1959, pp. 3-87.

## § How to Help the Child Become Idealistic, Highly Motivated, and Industrious

The main goal of both the Soviet school and the family is to raise communistically conscious and highly motivated children who set high standards for themselves. The whole educational system in Soviet Russia is geared to bringing up a well-rounded and well-educated man, prepared for life and its challenging tasks, who is capable of taking an active part in building Communism.

Soviet children, almost as a rule, dream of becoming forefront factory workers, scholars, actors, pedagogues, social workers, artists, as well as people creative in other fields of socialist endeavor. To achieve this goal one has to develop a conscientious attitude toward learning, an ability to subject oneself to strict discipline, a persistent desire to develop high motivation as well as industriousness.

There are quite a few parents who believe that the establishment of conscious discipline in children requires that parents be very strict with the youngsters by exerting controls from without. This point of view is incorrect; conscious discipline refers to self-discipline, which requires that the future Soviet citizen accept not only the authority of his educators but also responsibility for his own actions. A. S. Makarenko wrote: "Only by inclusion of various positive factors in his upbringing can the young Soviet citizen successfully acquire discipline. Among these positive factors a broad political and sound general education, productive work, and recreation occupy an important place. The interaction of these influences produces well-rounded, genuine, disciplined citizens of a socialist society."

There are many special methods which help to develop desirable controls from within. Soviet parents generally are concerned with the various methods of child-rearing in the family, and particularly with ways of administering reward and punishment to children. In parents' meetings they frequently ask: "Is it permissible to spank children?" "How does encouraging a child differ from pampering him?" "If a disobedient child is dealt with by encouragement won't it harm him?"

An attempt will be made here to answer some of these questions. But first, two very important issues will be examined: (1) How to prevent manifestations of unruliness among school-age children. (2) Why parents should use an educationally correct approach to modify their children's behavior.

## § How To Forestall Unruliness in Children

Often unruly behavior arises when parents fail to recognize particular character traits of the child's personality as reasons for his "bad" behavior. In such instances the school authorities can come to their aid. Parents should visit the home-room teacher at least twice a month, to seek advice about different problems at home and to inquire about the progress of their children in school. This practice allows the teacher to receive equally vital information from parents. Nothing should be kept secret. When youngsters discover that the teachers know about misbehavior at home, they tend to improve quickly.

Each school child lives a complicated and diversified life. His personality, his particular character traits, show up clearly, particularly in a collective group situation. Thus parents must be informed not only about his scholastic achievement, but also about his relationships with his peers in the classroom and in the pioneer group, and his participation in the children's collective.

Unfortunately, parents are not always in close touch with the school and the Pioneer and Komsomol organizations. At times they come to school only when their presence is requested by the homeroom teacher. There is nothing more apt to interfere with the correct upbringing of children than inconsistencies between school and home regarding the behavior expected from the child. Such inconsistency often creates misconceptions in the children's minds, and as a result produces behavior disorders and discipline problems.

Since it is not always possible to remove undesirable family influences which reflect a viewpoint about bringing up children different from that of the school, active members of the parents' committee as well as the teachers must try to attract all parents to school and strive to get them to attend regularly parents' meetings, where the basic philosophy concerning the goals of Communist upbringing is often discussed.

Unfortunately in some schools the parents' meetings are still poorly organized. As a rule the attendance at such meetings is better in the lower grades and worse in the intermediate and higher grades. This could be explained by the fact that many parents rely too much on the assumption that in older age groups the children have already developed self-discipline; the parents then relax their control, satisfied with a superficial checking of school records, and ask few questions.

Of course, this is not characteristic of all parents. The situation is significantly better where the school faculty and parents' committee work closely with the family.

In practice the parents' meetings are attended predominantly by mothers, although all family members in one way or another participate in the shaping of the child's personality.

An editorial in *Pravda* (August, 1954) states as follows: "The combined effort of school and home is an indispensible factor in achieving positive results in bringing up children. But unfortunately many teachers and parents do not find a common language and act in contradiction to each other, which affects the children negatively. There are parents who do not react wisely to teacher's comments about their children. They defend idleness, unruliness, and even criticize the teacher's action in the presence of their children. This is not permissible, because it seriously damages the authority of the school, and this becomes detrimental to the task of upbringing. On the other hand, teachers should also listen more sympathetically to the advice of parents directly interested in the school."

The thoughts expressed in this article are just as relevant today as they were in 1954. The maintenance and the strengthening of the teacher's authority as well as the development of a consistent discipline at home and in school are very significant. When parents are doubtful about the teacher's approach to the behavior of their children, they should resolve their doubts in a talk with the teacher or the school director, or during a parent-teacher meeting. But in all instances the authority of the teacher should be carefully safeguarded.

Firm support of the school and of the Pioneer and Komsomol organizations, strengthening of good working habits developed by the teacher, consistency in demands at home and at school, daily emphasis of teacher's authority, will help the parents to make the children well-organized and disciplined.

Sometimes, when parents demand that the children improve their performance, the children submit to this demand for a while. Unless this demand is consistently made, however, the child's performance will relapse. Permissiveness and inconsistency tend to undermine parents' authority in the eyes of their children and to encourage lack of discipline.

Often parents set demands too difficult for the children to meet. This is most apt to occur when the child is very young or is not used to self-discipline. In some families, parents will for a long time disregard the disorganized behavior of their children, but then suddenly clamp down on them with a flood of demands. Naturally, the child cannot change his behavior at once. As a result, conflict arises between him and his parents.

The positive example of parental behavior plays a great part in the process of building up in children a sense of order and obedience. When the parents are sloppy, disorganized, and rude, it is extremely difficult for them to instill in the children a feeling for discipline and courtesy.

While younger children usually do not particularly notice the faults and weaknesses of their parents' daily behavior, the older ones begin to observe carefully what goes on around them, which at times can create tragic misunderstandings.

Unfortunately, few parents achieve a close relationship with their children, though it remains one of the most effective measures for preventing discipline problems. Some parents try to obtain the love of their children by catering senselessly to their whims, by forgiving everything and not demanding anything. This kind of parental "love" can produce nothing but harm. Other parents who try to justify indulging their children offer excuses such as: "The golden years of childhood are the time for a child to be spoiled." "In school they are dealt with firmly; let the home be the place in which they enjoy freedom." "To spoil children means to empathize with them and to be affectionate." But these arguments do not make sense. As a result the children develop into egotistic despots, accustomed to a life of idleness and loafing. In vain the parents hope that the spoiled children will appreciate their love and care and will treat their parents with gratitude. These children do not respect their parents; at times they even ridicule them.

As a result of this the youngsters are ostracized in the children's collective. When realizing it, they try to change, with the help of their teachers. But they face a very difficult task. Of course, it is the parents who are really to blame.

## § The What, How, and When of Corrective Measures

Many parents manage to bring up children without using any special measure of coercion, particularly that of punishment. When the child's behavior is wrong, the parents, using a sound educational approach, help the child to realize the error of his deed and give him incentive to correct it.

Problems in child-rearing often develop when the parents want to achieve desirable results but lose patience too soon. Of course, it is easier to yell, get angry, and to reprimand than to use psychological insight and find a way to make the child think and reconsider. To achieve this, one needs not only patience and self-control but also a certain amount of sensitivity.

The development of a child's personality is a complex and delicate matter. It demands a lot of attention, thoughtful reflection, pedagogical knowledge, and constant searching for the proper approach. In many instances one has to take into serious consideration the child's inner state and his feelings. For example, a first grader is restless and stubborn, creating a problem because she is not yet used to the school routine. Her nervous system is not yet adapted to the new environment. There are also cases when children who are already good readers upon entering the first grade become bored with studying the alphabet and refuse to return to school. Their parents, instead of finding the reasons, punish them, which in turn traumatizes the children. Subsequently, their increased restlessness creates a discipline problem in the classroom.

By paying attention to the daily experiences of the child as well as to his feelings, one may discover the reason for any unusual behavior. It is very important to learn to listen to children when they talk, even if at times what they confide to a parent cannot be approved of. Yelling at them in these situations, as some parents do, will not alter the situation.

Great sensitivity and delicacy of parental approach is especially necessary with small children. It is very disturbing to see adults who shout at small children, spank them, or preach long sermons. Obviously, only inexperienced parents who do not know much about the skills needed for raising children will act this way. Preschool children can change their behavior relatively easily when an educationally sound approach is used.

## § Methods of Encouragement

Children respond to praise, since they appreciate it when their accomplishments and their self-improvement are noticed and acknowledged by parents and teachers. Encouragement develops in children a belief in their worthiness and in their own strength. This encouragement fosters sensitivity and enthusiasm as well as discipline. Even a very tardy child, when encouraged, may gladly fulfill any given task which awakens in him a healthy feeling of self-reliance and dignity. Parents who think that the method of encouragement is not successful with all children are very mistaken. They claim that though some children perform better when encouraged, there are still children who react only to strictness, and that even the smallest encouragement has an undesirable effect upon them. There are no children who would not respond favorably to encouragement if it is used wisely. There are no children who do not smile contentedly when the parents praise them after a successful achievement.

Hence, it is especially important to praise the children who, having been previously in trouble, have changed their behavior pattern under the positive influence of some successful pedagogical method. In such cases, many pedagogues and parents find it helpful to utilize trust and respect as means to produce favorable changes in behavior. As we well know, A. S. Makarenko achieved excellent results in his work colonies by employing these techniques. This method proved to be especially successful in dealing with pre-adolescents as well as adolescents.

Often parents use gifts and spending money as means to encourage children. Needless to say, this is an obvious misconception. To produce a gift for a child each time he is praised by teacher or gets a good grade diminishes his excitement and brings him no special pleasure. The duty of each student is to behave and to take studying seriously. Parents occasionally may buy books and toys for children, but under no circumstances should it be implied that the gift is a reward for something. While giving to a child, one should say, "Take this new book or new toy. This will prove to be useful to you."

Books and toys play an important role in the development of children, since they enrich and stimulate a child's life. But parents should explain to their children that gifts as such are an expression of love and should always be well taken care of. On the other hand, it is clear to the children that they are expected to reciprocate with good behavior, conscientious study, and help other members of the family, when needed.

On rare occasions the parents may use a gift as a real prize for something very special, such as improvement in behavior, mastery in new subject matter, or as a reward for a socially significant deed. These special gifts may be given the child at the end of the school year, but never should they be promised in advance. Other special occasions, such as family celebrations and festive days (first of May, Woman's day, Anniversary of the October revolution, and New Year's day) should also be a time to use encouragement, since prior to those special days even the most unruly children become less of a problem.

To reward children with money, however, is not permissible under any circumstances. Money should be given only for a specific purpose, such as to purchase a book, notepaper or lunch. One should not reward the child with money for good grades or for household chores. Studying and helping at home should be considered an essential duty of the child and fulfillment of these duties should be acknowledged only by simple praise.

## § Under What Conditions Encouragement Brings About Desirable Results

While using encouragement to bring about desirable results, one has to keep in mind the necessary conditions for successful application of the method. First of all, parents should praise their child only as much as is needed to stimulate his improvement in learning, in behavior, and in developing character. When the child is praised too much, the opposite is achieved. Unfortunately, some parents do not think about the consequences when they indiscriminately and constantly praise a child to others within his earshot. If this pattern continues, he finally becomes a self-centered egotist who tyrannizes the family. Only then do the parents panic and turn to the teachers and upbringers for help.

Praise and encouragement, in order to be a successful educational technique, should not be overdone. They must correspond to the child's merits.

It is very important to encourage a child when he shows signs of improvement. He should be praised and his self-assurance should be supported. This will help him to believe in himself and to realize that if he wants to he can achieve even better results.

Consistent demands in relation to the child should follow

encouragement, and they should not be modified under any conditions, even if he starts to improve. Furthermore, new demands should be set for the child after his improvement has been acknowledged.

It is very important to notice and to praise any positive personality characteristics of the child and to recognize any of his genuine deeds. When the child is polite, good, brave, gay, clever, conscientious at fulfilling any task, patient, persevering, resourceful, and attentive to people around him, he deserves praise not only to create assurance in him that he behaves himself well but also to motivate his striving for perfect behavior.

In watching the development of positive characteristics of personality and in supporting them in the child by encouragement, one should not overpraise; instead, it is advisable to draw the child's attention toward elimination of shortcomings.

Some adult family members make the error of praising children only for their ability. When a student is gifted in some area, his success should be viewed as a natural occurrence. The gifted children should be praised very cautiously when their performance is up to their capacity. It is also important to praise them in cases when they exhibit initiative in voluntarily fulfilling extra tasks. One has to remember to encourage and praise children not for their natural talents but primarily for their efforts to develop good study habits, to accomplish conscientiously any given task, and to correct shortcomings in their personality.

## § Punishment—For What and How?

Pedagogically correct methods of punishment are just as important as those of encouragement in bringing up children.

The outstanding youth educator, Felix Dzerzhinsky, wrote: "Extreme severity, paddling, and other kinds of physical punishment cannot effectively reach the child's heart or conscience. Children perceive physical punishment as an overpowering force, and resentment produces stubborness even when the child acknowledges his wrongdoing and fault."

Children will lie, cheat, and cease to be frank with their

parents in order to avoid physical punishment. It may even deeply traumatize the child.

Maxim Gorky, in his memoirs, recalls vividly how his grandfather used a rod to get him in line. He remembers that after the spanking he felt as if "someone tore the skin off his heart." In the city of Gorky (his birthplace), the cottage where his grandfather lived was converted into a museum. Standing near the same old bench on which his grandfather cruelly spanked the little Maxim, is a pail filled with twigs, which were then used instead of a paddle.

Corporal punishment evokes not only physical but also psychological suffering. It is a loathsome remnant of the gruesome past.

Now the Soviet school and family are bringing up a self-reliant, brave, and vivacious man, the future builder of Communism. He must be industrious, full of initiative, and always able to subordinate himself to the collective. Hence, from a very early age he must learn to discipline himself.

Finally, physical punishment can create a health problem because of the aggravation of the nervous system. In short, physical punishment does a lot of harm to children and is absolutely against the principles of Soviet education.

Makarenko, in one of his talks with parents, says: "When you spank your child, he perceives it as an act of your indifference to him, under which he suffers cruelly. And a mature citizen, mistreating the weak, still growing, delicate body of the child is indeed a very comical sight. If it weren't for pity for the child, one could laugh watching this barbarism."

Some parents punish their children by humiliating their human dignity, thereby killing their trust in their own strength and possibilities. Children will then lose hope and stop trying.

If a child is listless because of some sickness or trauma, or if he is acting out some of his difficulties, it is important not to humiliate him, but to support him by manifesting faith in him. These children should be told repeatedly that with perseverance and belief in their own strength they can achieve as much as their friends, provided they do not give up trying.

It is definitely not permissible to use fear as a means of

bringing about desirable results. Many parents frighten little children by telling them that an old man or witch or a bear will come and take away those who misbehave. Dzerzhinsky commented, "Fear brings out only cowardliness, meanness, depravity and hypocrisy. Fear does not help children to differentiate between right and wrong, good and bad."

Some mothers, when they cannot control children, will say, "When father comes he will punish you. I will tell him to spank you." Frightening the child in this way is wrong. If the father is indeed a sensitive, solicitous man, who generally wants to come closer to his children and take part in their education, he cannot because such threats will create an estrangement between them. In such circumstances, a firm and reserved man may be seen by his children as cruel and dangerous. The father cannot then have any influence upon them.

The main responsibility of parenthood is to create in children a respect and love for work which would exert a positive influence upon their personality development. This in turn will help to foster characteristics peculiar to the new man in a socialist society. If work or chores are used as a form of punishment, they may develop a hatred toward labor. This deplorable attitude would have grave consequences.

The main goal of schools and parents' committees is to lead all Soviet people in a fight against incorrect methods of rearing children. Nobody can afford to remain indifferent when at times the inner self of the child becomes deformed, harming his psychological and physical development. Unfortunately, one still hears quite often, "One should not interfere in somebody's family life. Parents can do with the child whatever they please. They will do the best they can." This point of view is against the communist moral principles governing the relationship between people in a socialist society, which is built on mutual help and solidarity. When parents resort to methods of rearing children which are not pedagogically sound, they must be stopped immediately, and then a very intensive effort should be made to re-educate them.

In recent years pedagogical education has gained great momentum in our country. Hundreds of thousands of parents attended and successfully finished a course of study especially designed for them.

Though the basis of improving our prevailing child-rearing practices rests with educating or re-educating parents, efforts are not always made to attract parents who cannot correctly bring up children, and their need for enlightenment remains unfulfilled. It is the responsibility of the better informed parents to change the child-rearing practices of backward families through constructive criticism and sound advice, since all of our children have an equal right to grow up physically as well as mentally healthy.

While opposing harmful measures of punishment, the parents should also be warned against the other extreme of permissiveness. There is a pedagogical point of view which believes in the so-called method of trial and error, rejecting any kind of punishment. For example, if the child wants to touch the hot samovar, one should not try to stop him. He will burn himself and discover his error. Consequently he will learn not to touch the hot samovar again. This point of view is fallacious. One shouldn't leave the upbringing of the younger generation to accidents. The risk is too great. The school and parent must guide the children, take all measures to prevent unruliness of children, fight disorganization with a pedagogically sound approach, and undertake measures of reward or punishment as needed.

Since measures of punishment are measures of force, some parents wonder if it is permissible to use coercion to achieve results which would be in accordance with the goals of Soviet child-rearing. Explaining and convincing are important methods of Soviet upbringing, but they do not preclude coercion to produce positive results when the interests of the family collective or of the child demand it. This tends to increase the responsibility of children for their own behavior. It forces them to set higher standards for themselves, inspires them toward more desirable goals, and teaches them to subordinate personal gains to those of society.

The first step of punishment is reprimand. When refusal to correct misbehavior becomes apparent, stronger measures must be undertaken. In serious instances, such as rudeness to grownups, refusal to do homework, abuse of younger siblings, carelessness toward clothes and books, especially textbooks, etc., a firm rebuke and reproval should be used. At no time should the reprimand be delivered in the form of constant nagging, since this does not produce the desired effect. The great physiologist Pavlov showed that when the very same stimulus constantly hits upon the same brain cells, they are no longer irritated, and cease to react.

When a child misbehaves, reprimand him briefly, explain the undesirability of the behavior, and express dismay. This should not be followed up with overfriendliness even when the parent feels that the child genuinely regrets his misbehavior. One should for some time withhold affection so as to demonstrate to the child that his behavior upsets adults. This approach has proved to be a very strong incentive not to repeat the offense, and hence the result achieved is a desirable one.

## § In What Way Does Punishment Help to Develop Well-Motivated Children?

Usually parents view punishment only as a way to prevent undesirable behavior, though actually its implications are much broader. Deviating behavior of children manifests itself in various ways: acting up, sulking, rudeness, abuse of younger siblings, truancy, listlessness, and idleness. The last two cannot be classified as undisciplined behavior. Often these children are well behaved and obedient in school and at home. Even though they are not troublesome, their behavior and character development must become a matter of serious concern. Strong action must be taken to pull them out of their listless and aimless existence.

Some parents justify this kind of behavior as a hereditary trait and as a peculiarity of the nervous system. They do not understand Pavlov's theory concerning the flexibility of the nervous system and its ability to change under environmental influences. Pavlov claimed that the development of personality is determined much more by education and upbringing in the broadest sense than by the individual's inherent biological characteristics. Favorable conditions in the environment and a purposeful upbringing with a goal in view may bring about changes in the way the nervous system responds.

Since things we cherish most are always achieved by stubborn, consistent striving and by ability and by persistence in overcoming obstacles, the task of the Soviet family is to develop in children initiative, the desire for action, and strong will-power. Hence it is imperative to draw the passive child into the life of the children's collective and help him establish friendly relationships with his peers.

Often parents complain that their children eat, dress, and do their homework slowly. When all means prove to be of no avail, punishment should be employed to produce desirable results. When the child is deliberately and stubbornly slow, parents should openly express their disapproval and show the child that they consider it serious misbehavior which must be changed, since not only he but also his collective will suffer because of his tardiness. When the child attempts to overcome his slowness, he should be encouraged by praise and by belief in his ability to overcome these weaknesses.

## § Measures of Punishment and the Task of Moral Upbringing

Moral upbringing of the growing generation in the spirit of Communism combines trust, encouragement, and punishment as valuable methods to achieve its goal. There are children who on the surface seem to function well, but close scrutiny of their behavior will immediately reveal negative characteristics and habits.

Parents should not be satisfied with superficially good behavior. They should pay equal attention to the inner world of the child and carefully watch all influences upon him. Often faults detected in a child's behavior can be traced to an adult family member whom the child imitates. In that event the adult should change his behavior for the sake of the child. Sometimes the tolerance of parents who do not pay attention to so-called "minor things" and try to justify them, is the reason for such behavior.

Frequently the family situation explains the lack of moral stamina in the children. When parents give children money but do not check on how it is spent, the children waste it in various ways. There is certainly no reason why an adult should leave a party for adolescents unsupervised. When the amusement is healthy and well planned, nothing can disturb it. This, of course, does not preclude children's initiative and independence; let them prepare and organize games and amuse themselves as much as they want to. But some games are not suitable for parties of Soviet youth.

During the 13th meeting of the Komsomol, Nikita S. Khrushchev called for a renewed struggle against drinking among youth. "To prevent fire it is easier to extinguish sparks before they develop into a big flame."

Special attention should also be given to the problem of smoking, since it has ill effects upon the organism. A very firm stand should be taken immediately. One has to start by reprimanding and reasoning with the offender, and finally, in the absence of improvement, deprive him of privileges. Until satisfactory results are achieved it is imperative that demands remain consistent.

It is equally important to react immediately to foul language. Not a single instance should go without punishment. There is no need for explanation because school-age children understand how disgusting this behavior is. Firm measures should be undertaken, and the student should not be forgiven until his changed behavior becomes firmly imbedded.

During its 13th meeting the Komsomol discussed at length the necessity of developing high moral standards among our youth. Parents must never forget that raising the young generation in the spirit of Communism is their sacred duty. To fulfill it various pedagogical educational methods, among them punishment, should be utilized.

## § Under What Conditions Punishment Fosters Positive Trends in a Child's Personality

The best way to help to correct misbehavior is by clarifying to the child the reason for his punishment. However, some parents believe reasoning is possible only with older children, and therefore they expect the younger ones to submit unconditionally to adults and their demands. Of course this point of view is erroneous. The interpretation of children's behavior should start at a very young age, since they are perfectly capable of understanding the issues involved as long as they are reasoned with at the level of their comprehension.

Since any punishment used too often may lose its effect and fail to produce positive behavior, any routine approach to utilizing punishment should be avoided. Each misbehavior should be the determining factor of the kind of punishment evoked.

Fairness plays an important part in establishing good relationships between children and parents. It helps to produce desirable results when problems of discipline arise. The children who trust their parents' judgment accept the punishment without bitterness and the close relationship between parents and children is not impaired.

Decisions of punishment should not be made hastily. Many parents react to undisciplined behavior with anger, which prevents them from analyzing the situation. Immediately they proceed to punish the culprits, and even when they later realize their error of judgment, they remain at a loss as to how to correct it. As a result of such conflicts, some children become traumatized. They lose faith and trust in adults, which has bad effects on their upbringing.

When a disciplinary problem arises, the task of the parent is to make the child understand why, in a particular situation, his behavior was an infringement of discipline. Then after a careful analysis, one may proceed calmly with the decided-upon punishment.

The parent should never threaten in haste, nor should his

word be inconsistent with his action. When parents repeatedly threaten but do not follow through with punishment, children ignore their demands completely. Obviously, this approach is not a pedagogically sound one. Every warning to the child about his disciplinary infringement should be succeeded by the next step—punishment—because otherwise the threat would be empty. Each disciplinary problem must be dealt with as soon as it occurs.

When administering punishment it is necessary to keep in mind the children's stage of development. Primary grade youngsters are in better control of their behavior than preschool children. The older children have learned to subordinate themselves to school rules, to demands of the class collective and of the teacher. To allow a child of this age group to exhibit emotions without restraint may create ill after-effects in the development of his will power.

Parents have to begin to develop self-control in children at a very early age. However, this has to be done carefully, exercising sensitivity, consistency and persistency. When little infringements of discipline result from an excess of high spirits in this age group, discretion instead of punishment should be used to divert their attention in a positive direction. Children of primary grades should be punished only when they fully understand their bad behavior and then make no attempt to correct it. Depriving them of pleasures is a very acceptable form of punishment, though this should not be misused, because play and reading of fairy tales is an organic need for them, since the young ones can hardly live without toys and stories.

Young children react strongly when as a punishment parents deprive them temporarily of their affection and warm attention. Usually children are frightened when they notice the parents' changed attitude toward them.

Boys and girls twelve to fifteen years of age demand a special approach. They are full of vitality while their bodies undergo rapid changes. Their muscular strength grows and energy develops. This energy must be channeled in the right direction, such as sports and socially useful tasks and work. This should be taken into consideration especially during summer and winter school vacations when daily routines are changed completely and they find themselves with a lot of free time on their hands. When the parents neglect them during this period, they may begin to display undesirable behavior.

Adolescence is a period of maturation during which youngsters no longer consider themselves children and strive for independence of thought and action. When parents insist upon ignoring this developmental stage and do not change their approach, the youngsters rebel. The crux of the problem lies in adults' lack of respect for adolescents as individuals in their attempts to curb the independence of these "almost grownups." Teenagers do not respond well to too much warmth and affection, but as long as these are combined with reasonable demands, they can take it.

Since teenagers react strongly to unfair treatment by parents and resort to boycott of all demands, it is advisable to analyze misbehavior calmly. Then when the necessity for punishment becomes clear the parent must explain patiently and at length why this action had to be taken. The experience of many has proved that better results are achieved in dealing with disciplinary problems by a positive approach than by a negative one.

This does not mean one has to give up guiding and disciplining the adolescent. It only means one must proceed with caution and tact, because teenagers are really almost adults. They live a rich inner life and maintain a variety of relationships in the collective. Many of them have their ideals already shaped. They strive seriously to improve their character and to strengthen their will power. They raise tentative questions about their future professions and dream about personal lives of happiness and fulfillment.

Encouragement and faith in their strength and abilities is an important factor in supporting the youngster's dreams and positive strivings. Firm demands and well developed self-discipline foster their creativeness and help them in socially meaningful activities. Some introverted youngsters live in seclusion in their inner world and, although they carefully observe everything around them, they never voice an opinion or share their thoughts with anyone.

To gain their confidence, great patience, understanding and tact are needed. Parents should analyze their own behavior critically and set an example by being genuine, broadminded, and honest. No pressure should be exerted upon youngsters to share any of the experiences of their inner life, nor their relationship with classmates and friends. However, it is very important that parents show interest in their children's school, in the Komsomol and in their achievements in learning, in sports, and in socially meaningful activities. Even very introverted youngsters enjoy talking about these things. These talks and discussions help parents and children to come closer to each other.

Though some confidential communications by adolescents do not warrant encouragement, the frank and trustful expression of their concern helps parents to find ways to alleviate them.

However, this does not mean one should not point out his mistakes to an adolescent. The best way to express one's opinion about misbehavior is to discuss it abstractly. Insensitive, tactless parents gradually lose the confidence of their children, who become reluctant to communicate fully with them.

Parents' critical judgments, expressed seriously and tactfully, usually make a strong impression and sometimes influence the adolescents to change their thinking as well as their behavior. In their relationship with undisciplined adolescents, some parents feel helpless and hopeless. They believe that it is too late to change them now, and that those youngsters will not become motivated to change their behavior until they encounter great difficulties as adults. This is a mistake. These parents do not accept their full responsibility for bringing up their children. However the school is also to blame for not exerting the necessary and proper influence.

Parents of undisciplined adolescents never visit the school, nor do they come for consultation, nor do they attend parent meetings. When the teachers finally reach the parents at their place of work, it is then much too late. When teachers, parents, and the school collective make a concerted effort every misbehaving adolescent can be helped to improve successfully.

As soon as the adolescent begins to improve, encouragement should reinforce his efforts. This will give him additional strength to continue his self improvement, the goal of which would be regaining respect of family, teachers, and the school collective.

## § Fostering the Well-Rounded Development of Children Through Reward and Punishment

Though the task of the Soviet school and of the family is to raise well-rounded youngsters, there are many instances when too-heavy emphasis is placed upon school achievements and discipline while other areas of development are neglected.

There are many school children who constantly get good marks and whose behavior is excellent, but who are physically underdeveloped. Their interests in art are limited and they are not enthusiastic about socially meaningful work. These youngsters cannot grow up as valuable, cultured, well-rounded people with inexhaustible initiative and inspired creativeness. In spite of their honesty and knowledge, they are dull and colorless. Never a part of the collective, unpopular and unloved, they lead a lonely existence.

The goal of the school is not only to prepare the students for their future profession but also to broaden their various interests, which would enable them to visualize wider perspectives inherent in their work and inspire imaginative execution of their tasks. The intellectual and mental tasks in which he is engaged during his learning in school and home are of great significance in developing a youngster's personality.

Parents often ask if they should punish children for bad grades. The teachers take appropriate measures when youngsters fail in school; the parents usually assume these to be punishment.

The bad grade, which is usually accompanied by teacher's reprimand and by the criticism of the collective, is a punishment in itself. It is unfair to use more than one punitive measure for the same misbehavior. Overreacting to poor grades intensifies a student's negative approach to learning. Furthermore, the reasons for the failing marks are often very complex. Since parents do not always understand them, they have no sound basis for punishment.

Obviously a good, experienced teacher creates an opportunity for all children to study with equal interest. Unfortunately, not all teachers are equally good at motivating the learning process in their students. It is not right for the parents to punish the child for the mistakes and inadequacy of a teacher.

Sometimes pupils receive poor grades when new material is not clearly explained or when the teacher, not planning his time wisely, becomes excited and overinvolved in his presentation. The bell interrupts the lesson, the homework, hastily assigned, is not understood by all the children, but the teacher has no time left to answer their questions. The youngsters are then subsequently punished at home.

However, this does not necessarily mean that parents should not react at all to the bad marks. The responsibility of the family is to cooperate with teachers and the class collective to raise the achievements of the students. Repeating a year, which still happens in our schools, brings about great harm to the Soviet state and reflects negatively on the upbringing of the younger generation.

Parents should react not only to a bad mark but to any mark which is below the pupil's average. When a student who usually receives excellent or very good grades suddenly gets only a passing one, this should create serious anxiety in the family. One should discuss this with the student and find out from the teachers the reason for the bad grade. If it becomes apparent that lack of attention, disorganization, bad study habits, or laziness are responsible, firm controls should be set up in the home. Sometimes adolescents will object to strict supervision. They feel it is beneath their dignity to be treated like children and they believe that they can correct the mark without the interference of parents. But here one should stick to consistency of demand and expect them to report systematically their assignments, explaining that this is necessary until they are able to restore parental trust. In these instances the expression of distrust, which in itself serves as a special measure of punishment, is sufficient.

Stronger measures should be left for other occasions when greater misbehavior, such as falsifying marks or cheating, occurs. When parents react too strongly to low grades, children sometimes resort to cheating, since they cannot immediately fulfill the demand to improve the grade.

Lowering of children's achievement may be due to many different factors, such as poor health, exhaustion, incorrect scheduling of work and rest, overinvolvement in sports, a very heavy load of household chores, or too much time spent on socially meaningful work. It is important to find out the reasons in order to take measures which would eliminate the obstacles. Consultation with the teacher and the school doctor may bring about a faster change.

As soon as the student begins to improve as a result of the combined watchfulness at home, at school, and in the collective, he should be encouraged immediately with kind words, praise, and affection. The parents' task is to support his efforts, especially when these efforts are apparent even before the teacher notices the improvement.

Some parents are inclined to think that once their children begin to work independently in industry, they do not need help. In reality they still need advice on how to fulfill theoretical as well as practical tasks, and especially in how to overcome various difficulties they run into.

Parents' praise and approval extended at the right time becomes a great incentive in the pursuit of new accomplishments. To encourage students in intellectual interests is also of importance. They should get used to reading literature, Pioneer, and Komsomol news at an early age, and be well informed in current, national, and international events. When youngsters analyze well the material they have read, one should praise them.

Since books play an important role in the intellectual development of students, reading should be encouraged. Time should be found to discuss with children the books they read, in order to help them not only to interpret but also to retain the content. Skimming through books thoughtlessly should be discouraged firmly among both older and younger students.

To deprive youngsters of books for which they are not ready

is very difficult. Even a serious conflict should not deter the parents from guiding the reading selections of their children. In case the youngster stubbornly refuses to obey, resort to disciplinary measures.

Sometimes the student becomes much too involved in reading; he reads instead of working on his assignments, reads while eating, and stays up very late to read. This should be categorically forbidden. When such a student refuses to obey adults in the family, he must be punished.

Many parents hope their children will develop creative abilities in science, technical fields, arts, or literature. Unfortunately, they often simply dream and do little else to foster those gifts and abilities in their children. The reason for the discrepancy which exists between the parents' dreams and reality is twofold. Either the behavior of youngsters does not suggest the existence of talents and interests, or the parents have no time or patience to nourish them.

Few parents know how to make demands on gifted children which would encourage them to fulfill difficult and complex tasks. They believe talents develop by themselves without special help. Very often special abilities of youngsters get lost because of this parental passivity. It is sad to encounter children who have not utilized their gifts because their families failed to give them the necessary encouragement and guidance.

Generally, Soviet youth is creative. Its talent thrives under the favorable conditions and under active support by school teachers and by parents. The earlier one creates favorable conditions and the earlier one gives necessary support, the better are the results.

Ability and talent develop only through continuous effort and by overcoming difficulties through persistent practice. When parents genuinely desire their children to grow up as creative people, they must assist in developing their gifts and follow up by encouragement and punishment when the need for it arises.

Some parents complain about lack of interest of their children toward any kind of creative activity. These youngsters should not be left alone; the parents must stimulate the children and awaken their intellectual curiosity.

Interests and inclinations form quickly when parents purposely draw the attention of the youngsters to the excitement of being creative. Friends to whom the adolescent responds readily can exert positive influence, which should be reinforced by making it possible for them to work together.

Parents, as a rule, see that the children do not miss school, show concern about their children's school achievements, and consult with teachers; however, they do not consider extracurricular activities to be of any importance. Many parents of school age children who are engaged in special activities do not know anything about their children's creative accomplishments and have never met the leader of the extracurricular group. When it turns out that a student has signed up for a group but often misses the meetings and does not fulfill his tasks, he should know that his parents are not indifferent to his inconsistency and laziness. Parental demands will force him to fulfill his tasks and also to compete with his peers.

Extracurricular groups not operated by schools are poorly attended. The participants frequently change groups or belong to two or three different ones and do not show special interest in any. This persists as a result of lack of parental supervision and of punishment.

Frequently parents wonder why children should not be punished for not fulfilling their household chores whereas a superficial attitude toward creativeness should elicit a strong disciplinary measure. Children's household chores are neither interesting nor complex. To get the youngsters to do their work is relatively easy. A simple demonstration and consistent demands can do the trick, but to have children fulfill them with pleasure is another matter. These chores are usually related to the youngster's duty toward family and encouragement proves to be the most successful means of achieving it.

However, the youngster's creativity develops according to his desire and interest. Punishment forces children to give up their superficial attitude toward a chosen task. It prevents them from indulging in idle dreams which pull them away from reality. It brings them back to the activities they seem to enjoy engaging in; it stimulates them to develop their potentialities and creative imagination; and finally, it induces them to practice their newly acquired skills systematically. Though this may seem strange, it is a fact that pedagogically justified measures of punishment do not diminish, but on the contrary strengthen, the interest of students in creative work and force them to concentrate in order to achieve results and to progress at a steady pace. For, as a rule, success reinforces creativeness.

Many parents anxiously wonder whether they should encourage children's interests even though they do not show any talent. Any interest in creativity should be supported and encouraged, since children find it very difficult to accept discouragement. There is no need to traumatize these youngsters. In some instances talent may suddenly begin to develop as a result of encouragement and consistent practice. The student's creative achievement, no matter how small, is very helpful in fostering will power, which gives incentive for furthering progress.

In many instances children with great musical talent have wasted their promise because of neglect, while others with limited abilities, because of encouragement, won musical competitions. Pavlov maintains that the flexible function of the human nervous system is affected by change in environmental conditions. Probably there is a relationship between this physiological law and the stimulation of creativity in children.

Sometimes youngsters' yearnings lie in one area while the parents try to foster interests in another. Often, the parents in order to promote their choice force the child to abandon his interest, but this fails to produce any results. Instead of suppressing youngsters' interests, one should help them to plan their schedule carefully, leaving time for both kinds of creative work and for rest. When parents do not restrict the child's creative activity, he will in gratitude fulfill his family's other demands with great zest and later will be able to choose the area that satisfies and excites him most. In any case, whatever the decision, the two interest areas will be instrumental in broadening him as an individual.

Physical education is a part of the well-rounded development of youngsters. Usually the family pays attention to it when the children are smaller and their daily routine is firmly followed. Later, the parents become less concerned, reasoning that adolescents especially should be able to follow their schedule without supervision, although they openly admit to having difficulties with getting them to attend to their personal hygiene and health needs.

Adolescence is a period of physical and sexual growth, during which great changes in the youngsters' organisms take place. Many teenagers are increasingly tense and irritable. Unpleasant occurrences connected with changes in the adolescents during this period can be minimized or even eliminated when they follow a strict daily routine, get systematic physical exercises, and actively participate in sports. These health matters should be of importance to the youngsters who must begin to prepare themselves for their role as future parents.

One should encourage children to engage in sports, which foster will power, perseverance, bravery, and decisiveness. As a result the youngsters' health and general mood will improve. When students devote too much of their time to sports at the expense of homework and other activities, however, a warning should be issued, but when neither a warning nor reasoning helps, disciplinary measures should be undertaken to calm down exaggerated enthusiasm and re-establish self control.

To be effective, punishment or reward must take into consideration not only the chronological differences but also individual differences existing among youngsters. Some react better to punishment, others to kindness, reasoning, and encouragement. Observing the children, getting to know and to understand them helps to find the best pedagogical approach to them. Following this course even under difficult conditions brings about better results.

When there is only one parent to bring up children, it is important for that parent to follow the teacher's advice, to begin to teach the children from very early years how to work well and help each other, and to set reasonable, consistent demands while not losing sight of their individual differences.

Since parents often encounter difficulties in distinguishing various developmental stages and in recognizing chronological as well as individual differences, the school and home should together work out the best way of bringing up youngsters.

Each parent-teacher conference offers an opportunity to get to know the youngster better and to find the most effective way of dealing with his problems.

Bringing up children correctly demands great perseverance, patience, and a mastery of a pedagogically sound approach. In order to achieve the objective, it is necessary for parents to acquaint themselves with the existing literature in the field of child rearing practices and family living.

There is no doubt that the joint efforts of parents, school, Pioneer, and Komsomol will succeed in bringing up youngsters as idealistic, conscientious, industrious, cultured, and self-disciplined builders of Communist society.

# 7 *Fathers and Children*

*L. Kovaleva*

## § Building the Family

MANY PEOPLE invest manual labor and creative thinking in building a new factory, housing development, or offices. Obviously the same investment is necessary in the creation of a family.

Unfortunately, many persons still consider family life a simple and primitive procedure. They say that in order to create a strong family, firm subordination is needed—namely, absolute authority on one side and perfect obedience on the other.

Sasha is very afraid of his father, who substitutes the belt for various prohibitions, which give him the illusion of parental authority. "When I say no—I mean no! My son must always obey."

"Father, may I go to the movie?"

"No."

"But today is Saturday and the movie is for children."

"When I say no, I mean no!" repeats the father, who does not really know why he said "no." But now it is too late to

L. Kovaleva, *Fathers and Children,* XI Series. Pedagogika Izd-vo "Znanye," Moscow, 1963, pp. 3-39.

change it, even when it does not make sense. One has to guard parental authority!

The false idea that obedience is the main virtue of the child still exists in the minds of many fathers. Striving for submission while supporting their authority with decisive but unreasonable measures, they sometimes lose their sons at this point, when their sons could become their helpers and genuine friends. When senseless despotism poisons the natural filial feelings and the son leaves home, the father complains bitterly.

There are other instances when the son grows up to be a timid man without initiative, who easily compromises and accommodates himself. Of course, here too the family is very surprised and hurt.

Many fathers assume that any working family without "drunkenness and fights" is a good and healthy one. Unfortunately, it is not that simple.

There are honest, knowledgeable workers, respected by everyone, who treat their family problems thoughtlessly and wish to spend their leisure time away from the family. They would rather work overtime than be with their children. This is not accidental, since a walk with youngsters, or reading to them, or even going to a movie means an effort. Children do not only learn physics and mathematics; they learn to live. Curious about their surrounding, they lavish questions upon their parents who are not always able to supply the answers. This is one of the reasons why fathers try to avoid direct leisure contact with their youngsters. As a result, the children, bored at home, gradually separate themselves from the family. When this becomes obvious the parents ask themselves the sad question, "Whom do they take after?"

## § The Street Takes Over

The word "street" may have different meanings; not only pleasant ones such as warm memories of the place where we grew up and of the friends we had; but also sad ones reverberating with the cry of hurt children, cursing, police whistles, and the sound of running feet.

We no longer have *bezprizornye*—children without legal guardians. Even the word itself has died out and lost its tragic meaning; but while these children were among us, the street was their home, and sometimes its spontaneous force pushed them into most inappropriate situations.

Though children who are called *beznadzora*—without supervision—as a rule have a roof over their heads, beds to sleep in, and food to eat, this, for some deep personal reasons, is not enough to keep them off the streets and out of trouble. Sometimes the father is to blame for being a drunkard and turning his home into a bar. In other instances it is the mother who is at fault, because of her quarrelsome character or thoughtlessness.

There are also cases when both parents do not want to, or cannot, straighten out their relationship, and their fights make the home unbearable to their youngsters.

Sometimes sickness, death, or other tragic circumstances affect family life and the children begin to avoid the home, preferring to be in the street or hall or yard. They find themselves with a lot of free time on their hands—the same time which other children devote to homework, house chores, reading, and recreation. In order to "kill time" they play cards. They begin to need money, and to get it they use many dubious ways which often produce "unexpected," undesirable, and dangerous results.

## § Walk on Tiptoe

Since most people comprehend at an early age the difficulties inherent in the teaching profession, many children are anxious to show their teachers their love and appreciation. Even those who play pranks in the classroom are fully capable of showing gratitude along with feelings of guilt. This acknowledgment expresses itself in the form of a gift, one of the most obvious ways to manifest love.

It is sad when children do not acquire in their childhood the ability to sacrifice their own pleasure for the sake of somebody else. To anticipate the wishes of the ones near and the desire to fulfill them, no matter how small and insignificant the gifts seem to be, is a characteristic to be treasured dearly. People who have not experienced the joy of giving are indeed very poor, since they are deprived of the simplest and most human happiness.

As a rule, the feelings of children are beautiful and pure and so are their small token gifts. Unfortunately, this genuine giving changes as soon as adults begin to interfere and to take away the initiative from the youngsters. It is now the mothers who collect the money, with those better off setting the tone. Other parents, who are really in no position to do so, try to match their donations, which in many cases represents great hardship for them. It is the mothers who present the gift to the teacher who finds herself in an embarrassing situation, since in most cases the item chosen is rather an expensive one. Obviously the interference of adults is absolutely uncalled for. To replace the children's genuine intentions by adult ideas is a sad mistake.

Children do not exist only to be educated; they also live, love, hate, and worry. Their feelings are distinguished not only by naivete and directness but also by intensity, strength, and passion, which adults may envy, but which in any case they must respect.

There is no excuse for exchanging these vivid, bright, and pure feelings of children for "measures" which some adults consider proper.

## § Don't Lose Those Smiles!

The wonderful Polish writer and educator Janush Korchak, who in the Warsaw Ghetto in 1943 gave his life for the love of the children placed in his care, wrote in his book *When I Become Little Again:*

"Children tire us out, not because we have to bend down to them, but because we have to elevate ourselves to their feelings so that we do not offend them."

Children reply in different ways when asked what good manners are. Some say it is being polite, others, being respectful to elders, others again, being well-behaved. Though all of these answers contain a degree of truth, there is certainly more to it. Good breeding reflects the inner self; it implies a smile and an ever present desire not to disturb, and when possible to help others, the people one spends one's life with, and those one encounters briefly. Let all of them be grateful for something.

Chekhov, famous for his sensitivity, gentleness, and restraint, believed anyone can acquire good manners and educate himself. He inserted a lot of meaning in the word "breeding." Chekhov wrote to his older brother, Nicolai, whose behavior was of great concern to him: "You are good, generous, not an egotist. You would share your last penny. Feelings of envy and hate are foreign to you. You are trusting, open-hearted; you pity people and animals; you are neither venomous nor rancorous, and above all, you have a talent. You have only one weakness—your ill breeding. Please forgive me for saying it, but truth has a priority over friendship."

People who are well bred respect the individuality of others and therefore are always tolerant, gentle, polite, and compliant. Minor annoyances do not disturb them. They are frank, unwilling to lie in any circumstances. Chekhov considered good breeding and vulgarity to be two opposing extremes.

Since children develop their first impressions of marriage and family life in their own home, they learn from the relationships they witness. Realizing that children hear and see everything, parents must show consideration for each other, be attentive and sensitive, and, above all, restrain themselves from reproaches, since their example sets the future attitudes of their children.

When an individual is brought up in a warm, friendly atmosphere, full of smiles, laughter, and mutual respect, he will accumulate these wonderful feelings to bestow them later in life upon others with whom he will be in contact.

On the other hand, when family life conditions do not provide love, warmth, and reasons for smiling, or a desire to help others, the individual becomes an introvert, secluded, morbid, and always lonesome. Only very good friends and an active, buoyant collective outside the family can effect a favorable change in such an individual. Sometimes parents who foolishly wasted their whole lives on mutual recriminations and petty quarrels, after realizing how much harm they inflicted upon their children, come to the sad conclusion that they should have educated themselves before attempting to educate their children.

## § Look Into Yourselves, Fathers!

Tanya, aware that her mother agrees to everything the girl wants as soon as she sees tears in her daughter's eyes, often uses this method to get her own way, although her father and her sixteen-year-old sister, Shura, object to this "educational" approach.

In her mother's absence, Shura raises Tanya differently. Unmoved by tears, she demands that her little sister fulfill her tasks independently, and Tanya, without her mother's support, must apply herself.

One day the little girl told Shura how her friend mistreated a kitten, throwing it in the air and kicking it. When it became apparent that Tanya had felt no compassion for the kitten, but stood by laughing, Shura proceeded to drop Tanya's favorite doll, throwing it in the air and kicking it with her foot. The doll landed on the floor, with a crack on its forehead. When Tanya, crying, reproached her older sister, saying the doll was hurt, Shura drew an analogy. She tried to make her little sister aware of the pain the kitten felt, reprimanded her for not defending it, and explained to her why she was just as guilty as her friend.

In the evening Tanya related the incident to her mother. The mother scolded Shura for using such a cruel method to explain instead of just talking to her about it, but Shura insisted that the more successful way to fight cruelty is with a cruel method of action instead of by preaching.

Yes, in bringing up children it is important to analyze the details of each incident, and obviously preaching will not always produce desirable results. For example, a father explained at length to his son reasons why one should not tattle, but when the boy returned home with a bloody nose, he immediately, without examining the circumstances, demanded the name of the culprit. In the process of raising children, this discrepancy between preaching and practice can never bring about worthwhile results.

All parents demand honesty and truthfulness from their children. Their monologues about these virtues fall into two main categories:

1. Do not take anything which does not belong to you without asking.

2. Do not hide your bad school marks.

While parents preach on one of these favorite topics, they overlook the mockery in their children's eyes. While the youngsters have grown from seven-year-old boys into seventeen-year-old adolescents, the content of the sermons has not changed. For example—a son listened politely to his father's speech, and then suddenly asked him whether he thought Evtuchenko's poem, printed in *Komsomolskaya Pravda,* reflected genuine feelings. Then he proceeded to defend the poem while his friend Vitya attacked it. The perplexed father was silent; he had not read the poem, although his son had placed the paper before him. Even if he had read it, he would not have analyzed it. After all, to him honesty means only, "Do not steal," while the son, who is concerned with honesty on all levels, including that of sincerity in art, views this concept as rather primitive.

Our time is complex, and so are our children. As a rule, they read and think a lot. They try to understand what they see around them, as well as what they experience through books. It is sad that their mothers and fathers, who have been educated under the Soviet system, which means that with very few exceptions they finished secondary schools, quickly lose the ability to influence the development of their children, to give them advice and leadership, to share in their interests. Consequently, they place the responsibility for the ethical and spiritual development of their children upon the shoulders of the teachers, which is convenient from all points of view, since it frees them from moral responsibility: "Daughter spends so much time in school, let the school bring her up. I am not a specialist in education." Also, there is little effort to keep up with them intellectually on the level of their concerns: "Let the school and Komsomol worry about it, I have no time."

As a result, fathers lag behind their children so much that they cease to understand them. They seem to be one family, even a friendly one, as long as they deal with daily concerns such as buying a newspaper, waxing the floor, meeting a relative at the railroad station; but as soon as the discussion begins to involve spiritual values, tastes, the strivings of sons and their attitudes toward the future, communication between parents and children stops.

As one of our talented writers stated: "Is not the 'father-son' conflict rooted in the efforts of fathers, even the best of them, to pass on to the children accumulated values, while the children long to search for new ones? Is not the basis for this cleavage the fathers' attempt to develop their children even while they themselves have lost this precious ability?"—Look into yourselves, fathers!

## § Remain True to Yourself

Alex asked his father's advice about an essay he was writing; should he write the essay in a way to please the teacher and get a good mark, or express his genuine beliefs at the risk of angering the teacher and perhaps getting a bad grade? Alex followed his father's suggestion that he remain true to himself and voice his real feelings and opinions. The boy had the father's assurance that in case of a problem, he would clarify it with the teacher.

When the teacher returned the composition, the note on it said that in spite of good grammar and style, he got an "F" because of unorthodox ideas, which contradicted the conventional ones accepted by all.

The father, while visiting the school, attempted to point out to the teacher that Alex was punished for sincerity and the originality of his beliefs, although his unusual approach to a work of literature proved his deep thinking. The father maintained that the teacher's attitude pushed his students to hypocrisy. Instead of encouraging the students to think creatively and independently, he was training them to repeat what the teacher said, or what they thought he would like to hear. Obviously, the grades he gave them became automatic and meaningless in the absence of a genuine, positive, learning experience. After the conference the teacher thought for a long time about the conversation.

## § But What If This Is Not Love?

During adolescence many youngsters develop attachments which they mistake for love. There are many instances when the parents would like to interfere, but it is best to let the youngsters work it out by themselves. Sometimes parental objections will push youngsters toward instead of away from each other. Parents must exercise restraint and patience, since this developmental stage of adolescence is a long and drawnout process. In this area, only when the youngsters arrive at conclusions and decisions independently, do they retain their meaning and provide a valuable learning experience for the future.

## § What Is Hiding Behind "Instructions"?

Not long ago some children brought me a very amusing typewritten document. The heading of this paper was "Instructions." It outlined behavior for boys and girls when they decide to "go together." Though this vulgar "document," written by an adult, was laughed at by the young people for whom it was written, some youngster might have taken it seriously and perhaps even followed the specified rules.

This kind of trash almost always reaches children through adults. And its vulgarity kills genuine feelings and creates hypocrisy and fear.

Friendship between girls and boys is a relationship that must reflect a genuine and simple camaraderie, free of malicious smiles and hints and suspicions by peers or adults. Sometimes, family members without sensitivity or delicacy tease a youngster about a "girl friend" or "boy friend," which is absolutely uncalled for. Often this occurs because the parents do not believe in the seriousness of children's feelings, considering them to be unreal, playlike emotions which do not measure up to adult standards. This is definitely false!

The tremendous capacity for love that children have encompasses everything. It is a crime to cheat this kind of love! Children's hate is sharp, fierce, and direct. This directness of judgment and action is a result of the intensity of their feelings!

When love and hate have to be limited by some regulations, it must be done by tactful, inconspicuous, and sensitive measures that do not insult the vulnerable and helpless pride of children.

## § Where There Is No Understanding

Parents react to any offense by their children with an immediate feeling of indignition and desire to punish, without investigating the circumstances. The mother or father who, without getting unduly excited, makes an honest attempt to understand the situation before reacting with punitive measures, inspires genuine trust in the child. This trust that he will find understanding is very important to a youngster, since parents are the most significant persons in the lives of their children.

Volodya, after many attempts, finally succeeded in constructing a beautiful kite. While in the park flying it, he accidentally bumped into an approaching neighbor whom he had not noticed. The man became very angry and after returning home complained to Volodya's father. As a punishment, to "teach" his son "respect" for adults, the father broke the precious toy, without bothering to investigate the incident. This violence had deep effects on Volodya, who would have preferred being spanked. But that was out of the question, since his father took great pride in "never laying a finger on the boy." From then on, Volodya never shared any thoughts or explained any of his actions to his father, anticipating he would be misunderstood most of the time.

Now Volodya is sixteen years old. The father visits the school frequently to find out how he is doing. He often complains that the boy keeps to himself and that he has lost touch with his son. One day, when the students of Volodya's class were asked what books should reflect about the lives of children, Volodya suggested "When there is no understanding between parents and their children." All of his peers supported this idea strongly. Needless to say this is one of the most real and painful problems of adolescence.

## § Spiritual Nourishment

As usual, Lena and her girl friends, full of anticipation, went to a club dance. At midnight, Lena returned home. The mother, as always, awaited her daughter, since they both enjoyed discussing the still-vivid events of the evening. While Lena described them she was startled to have her mother ask what they talked about. Rather defensively the girl replied, "But, Mother, why should I talk while dancing?"

When they retired, neither could sleep. The girl was feeling blue, although she could not pinpoint the reason, and the mother was recalling her own youth—her hopes, exciting discussions, and heated arguments. She was feeling sorry for Lena, who was missing something precious; at the same time, she was blaming herself for failing her daughter. Though she was constantly concerned about Lena's schoolwork, her study habits, and her health, she nevertheless neglected other needs just as vital. She did not implant habits of spiritual recreation, which would bring a different kind of joy and satisfaction. No education can be complete without a well-developed appreciation of beauty, but too often adults try to influence only the minds of children while neglecting their feelings.

It is relatively easy to strike the "right chord" in the youngster during his childhood and adolescence with lasting results. Perhaps these "responding chords" bring about the so-called "harmonious development of personality" we strive hopefully to nurture in our children when we visualize their future.

## § Dreams

Dreams provide individuals with great strength to materialize in reality very difficult tasks. The ability to dream beautifies life; it helps us endure dark moments and adds joy to happy occasions.

There are different kinds of dreams, and their variations supply significant clues to the personality of an individual. He may be an egotist with petty bourgeois aspirations, who above all cherishes his "I" and materialistic greed overpowers spiritual dreams in him.

When the family does not strive for goals above materialistic wants, it is natural that the children's dreams will not rise above this primitive area of utilitarian desires. They will remain indifferent to revolution in Cuba, festival in Helsinki, or the fate of James Meredith, since all these topics lie way beyond their meager and limited scope of interests. Of course there are other dreams, too. They reflect entirely different values. There are families who dream about future human endeavors; while such dreams seem to surpass our wildest imagination, they may still become quite probable in the near future.

While our working hours become shorter, our intellectual activities during our leisure time widen and consequently our esthetic needs become greater. Unfortunately, often the adults of the family, deeply involved in their tasks, gradually drift away from their growing children; suddenly they discover that they cannot guide them any longer, since they do not understand their children's needs or life experience and lack empathy with their ideas. As a result, parents will get angry with their children instead of trying to understand them. It is impossible to raise children without knowing them. No educational method is foolproof for all. Though there is one suited for each child, a thorough knowledge of the youngster is needed in order to select the right one.

As a rule, the dreams of children are a continuation of parental desires, often appearing in a purer, improved form. It is good when parents can recognize their dreams behind the superficial skepticism which often accompanies the maturation process of adolescence. It is wise not to challenge or doubt the moral character of their sons just because they prefer tight trousers to wide ones and because they speak laconically instead of using more elaborate phrases. These are transitory phenomena; they need fatherly patience and indulgence.

Most important, the sons must become good people, real humanists, able to give up their own comfort, support a friend in need, defend their opinions and beliefs when they are sure they are fair. The main task of our education is to develop such honesty and civil bravery in children.

Not long ago we thought and wrote a lot about education for work. Since the school has taken it over, this problem is no longer the most important one to cope with in the family.

Now life poses new tasks for us: to raise children who are interested in and care for everything—family plans, the fate of James Meredith who in the other hemisphere risks his life to prove his right to study in the university for white students, the flights of astronauts. These growing and ever changing interests of children should be fostered and broadened in the family, while their feelings are improved and trained. A good, friendly family, from a Communist point of view, is a source of goodness, warmth, and humanity.

There are many important characteristics the individual acquires and develops in the family situation which later are reflected in his relationship with fellow workers and other people whose paths he crosses; concern for others, gentleness, sensitivity, and the ability to curtail his own desires for the sake of others. Makarenko had such a "genuine" man in mind when he wrote in his "Pedagogical Poem" that the beauty and strength of an individual derives from his goals; the broader the aims of the collective which are absorbed by the individual as his own, the more beautiful and strong is his personality.

Let's raise our children as such genuine, strong, and harmoniously developed people.

*Part Three*

# *The School*

A few words should be said about two very significant Soviet educators, theoreticians as well as practitioners, whose influences are felt in the Soviet educational system up to the present time—A. S. Makarenko (1888-1939) and S. T. Shatzky (1878-1934).

Shatzky is of special interest here, since as early as 1911 he organized a summer working colony for children chosen out of the children's clubs which he helped to establish in Moscow. The basic task of the colony was to create conditions for a children's collective which would foster their talents and at the same time create in them habits of social living based on work. Shatzky viewed upbringing as a complex task which included physical development, work, recreation, arts, intellectual activity, and active participation in the life of the community. He considered work, necessary for the benefit of the collective, to be the most important educational force, and the combined work and study curriculum to be a significant factor in implementing theoretical knowledge and practice in the educational process.

In order to improve the quality of learning he suggested working out a system of independent study for the students. This he maintained would foster the development of their initiative and energy. Shatzky devoted a great deal of attention to children's ability to fulfil socially meaningful work. He also claimed that each teacher, in order to be successful, must develop in himself a quest for knowledge.

Makarenko's writings are well known not only in the U.S.S.R.

but also in many other countries.* As one of the initiators of the Marxist-Leninist system of education and upbringing, he regarded all educational problems from the philosophical standpoint of dialectical materialism. "Pedagogical logic is determined by educational goals which change as society changes." This was one of his main premises. He always stressed that there was no Makarenko system, only a Soviet system of educating the young generation.

The Soviet system created by Makarenko has among its most important characteristics the following:

1. *Demands*—He advocated a combination of most exacting demands upon the youngster with utmost respect for his individuality.

2. *Discipline*—He proposed that children require the discipline of combatting and surmounting difficulties.

3. *Character Building*—Makarenko felt that the first two elements play an important role in the character building process.

4. *Family Role in Upbringing*—He stressed the importance of correct family upbringing and gave many instructions to parents (lectures on child education).

5. *Collective*—He was the first one to elaborate in detail the educational significance of the collective.

6. *Perspectives*—Makarenko said, "Man must have something joyful ahead of him to live for . . . this joy has to be organized, brought to life, and converted into a possibility. Primitive sources of satisfaction must be steadily converted into more complex and humanly significant joys. . . ."

In his foreword to Makarenko's book *The Road to Life*, Professor Y. Medinsky, of the Academy of Pedagogical Sciences,

* He was appointed head of the Colony for Delinquents by the Department of Public Education: the Gorky Labor Colony 1920-1928 (near Poltava, Ukraine), and the Dzerzhinsky Labor Commune 1928-1935 (near Kharkov, Ukraine).

Among his writings are *Road to Life, Learning to Live* (1938), *1930 Marches On, Book for Parents* (1937), *Lectures on Child Education.* Posthumous works: *Selected Pedagogical Writings,* 2 volumes, *Complete Works,* 7 volumes.

commented: "When properly applied by the educator, the system of perspective keeps the collective in a buoyant, joyful mood, holds a clear-cut purpose before the youngsters, strengthens their confidence in their powers, and spurs them to strive for ever-greater achievements."

# 8 *Problems Inherent in Soviet School Education*

*A. S. Makarenko*

## § Educational Methods

I INTEND to approach the discussion of educational methods as an educational practitioner. Without hesitation I take the liberty of presenting here my practical experience as well as the conclusions derived from it. I assume that the practitioner influences and contributes to theory just as much as a theoretician to prevailing practices.

Though many believe I am primarily a specialist in working with delinquents, actually out of my thirty-two years of working as a pedagogue, sixteen were devoted to work in school situations and sixteen with delinquents. However, my work in schools always took place under special conditions—in factory trade schools, where the influence of the working collective, as well as that of the party, was ever present.

Precisely in the same way my work with delinquents was

A. S. Makarenko, *Problems Inherent in Soviet School Education* (Lectures), Uchpedgiz, Moscow, 1963, pp. 20-103.

by no means specialized. From the beginning I established that there is no need to use special methods with delinquents, and I succeeded after a very short while in bringing the delinquents up to an accepted standard, and then proceeded to work with them as with normal children. During the last period of my work in the Dzerzhinsky commune I had a normal collective, and a ten-year school which set standard goals toward which any other school would strive. Children in this collective, although once delinquents, actually lost all the peculiar characteristics which would distinguish them from normal youngsters. Furthermore, the continuing and consistent effect of a working collective in which they lived created many additional positive educational influences, not always present in the family situation.

Therefore, my practical conclusions may also be relevant to any collective of children and consequently to any educator in this word's broadest definition.

Now I would like to say something about my practical, pedagogical logic. I arrived at some conclusions not without painful doubts and mistakes, which may strike some of you as rather odd, but which I can support unhesitatingly with sufficient evidence. Some of them, theoretical in character, I will outline in brief prior to discussing my personal experience.

I disagree with our contemporary pedagogical theoreticians who claim that there is no need for a special method of rearing children, since subject teaching should also include upbringing techniques. I believe that in some instances there is a need for differentiation between methods of teaching and those of upbringing. In the Soviet Union children as well as adults are continuously exposed to the process of education, either in its organized forms or by the general influence of social demands. All our goals are inseparable from educational tasks. As an example one could cite the Red Army, which not only teaches the soldiers military science and techniques but also effects deep changes in their character and attitudes. The Soviet educational task is unique in its goals as well as in its form. By now, the educational method successfully used during the twenty years of Soviet government in various institutions of learning and upbringing is ready to be summarized.

In my task of re-educating the so-called delinquents, I had to stress the upbringing task as the most important one and concentrate upon character change, since the girls and boys given into my care exhibited dangerous and striking character traits.

In the beginning it seemed to be a special educational task, particularly that of educating for labor. This extreme position I did not maintain for long, although some of my colleagues in the commune held onto it much longer. School attendance was absolutely voluntary, an approach which at that time seemed rather implausible, since virtually no one attended classes. Any failure in school could prompt a student to skip lessons, which was his legal right.

Soon I became convinced that in the system of work colonies the school is a very powerful educational tool. Recently I have heavily advocated the regular ten-year school and I am deeply convinced that completely successful re-education and rehabilitation are possible only with its help and support, though I still maintain that the method of upbringing has a separate logic, relatively detached from that of education. Though both of them constitute more or less independent departments of pedagogical science, they must relate organically. Hence, any educational work in a classroom is also upbringing. However, I think that fusing them is impossible. Later I will discuss this question in more detail.

I am convinced that the methods of upbringing must not be derived from the hypotheses of other sciences. No matter how well developed they may be, such as psychology and biology, especially after Pavlov, we have no right to apply their findings directly. These sciences must be of tremendous significance in educational work—not as basis for our methods but as controls for the testing of our practical achievements.

I also think that experience is the only way to arrive at educational means which are checked subsequently by the findings of related sciences.

Pedagogy, especially the theory of upbringing, is geared primarily toward a practical goal, that of a clearly defined political aim which derives from our social needs and strivings. Naturally, its formulation can stem neither from biology nor from psychology. Only when the two sciences can precisely describe the development of personality and behavior will we be able to lean more upon their findings. The relationship of the social needs and the goals of socialist upbringing to the theories and research in these two fields must always remain flexible, perhaps changing toward their greater participation in the process of rearing our children, youth, and adults.

Deductive reasoning, ethical fetishism, and detached isolation are the three distinctive types of errors pedagogical theory remains guilty of. Time and time again I have had to fight these fallacies. For example, a new teaching technique is recommended as a means of bringing about positive results. The only verification of it is the mere assumption that since the technique employed is infallible, it can only produce desirable results, no matter how deeply hidden they remain.

Ethical fetishism did not fare any better. Let's examine, for instance, education for work. In this respect I too fell prey in the beginning to its stereotyped conception, consisting of pursuing it as self-service, a simple, aimless exercise for using up accumulated physical energy. Subsequently, my experience as well as that of my colleagues proved that there are various ways of introducing work, but it must always be viewed as a part of the on-going process of upbringing. Without it we lose its educational value. It remains a neutral factor, and hence produces no positive results.

As for the third pedagogical error, no means can be viewed as good or bad in detached isolation from the whole system of upbringing. For example, the infliction of punishment may in some instances develop a slave while in others it will create a fine, proud, and independent man. I succeeded in bringing out human dignity and pride in my pupils by way of punishment. Obviously such results can be achieved only in an environment conducive to it and at a certain stage of development. Any pedagogical coercion, reasoning, or social pressure can sometimes be unsuccessful. No technique should be viewed in isolation, and no means should be recommended as "the only" continuous system of action. Any Soviet school in the hands of an experienced, well-trained pedagogical collective will change considerably over a twenty-year period, and in the process produce a system of upbringing deviating greatly from the one of its beginning stage.

In general my belief is that pedagogy is a very dialectical, flexible, complex and diversified science. This is the basis of my pedagogical credo. However, I do not attempt to imply that I tested everything by experience or that I clarified all existing pedagogical problems and aims.

I conceive of the goal of upbringing as a combined effort to encompass the development of the total personality: its character traits, overt behavior, attitudes, beliefs, as well as political and academic education. Only a blending of the individual approach while setting and upholding group standards can bring about positive results. Of course, this delineation is of a very delicate nature, and requires great skill on the part of a pedagogue. I often ask myself, where do I set legitimate limits while guiding my pupils? How much advice is desirable, and when does it change to coercion? The right of the pedagogue and his good intentions alone do not qualify him for this task. He has to have tact and sensitivity in dealing with each case individually. Only then will he produce the most satisfying results.

There is no doubt that the collective is the most important factor in the process of Soviet upbringing. Hence the correct way would be to use the entire school as a basis of a strong, unifying collective, exerting powerful influence, instead of supporting many smaller ones, with occasional conflicts resulting from tasks which either duplicate or contradict each other. The school must be the only collective which unifies all the processes of upbringing. Each member must realize his dependence on it, subordinate his personal interests to those of the collective. There are many schools which do not have any extracurricular activities, claiming they do not want to interfere with the work of the Pioneers. I believe the school collective must organize and unify the whole process of upbringing.

The Pioneer movement may work side by side with the school; however, its organization as well as the responsibility for it must belong to the school, since decentralized leadership and split responsibility cannot produce positive results.

Though I fully realize that such a unified, excellently equipped children's collective is obviously more expensive, this streamlining may in the end prove to be more economical.

There is no feasible way to organize a collective without having a goal in view; the common aim is the strongest unifying force, and therefore it must be set by an entire school, not just by a classroom.

There are many ways by which an aggregation can change into a unified collective. No artificial means can accomplish it, nor is there a shortcut, since efforts to speed up the process always prove to be disastrous. On the other hand, a collective in which the child remains eight to ten years, when well organized, may prove to be a gratifying and valuable instrument of upbringing. The longer the collective exists, the stronger its influence becomes; but a large turnover in leadership may make the collective fall apart.

There is no stronger tie which reinforces its continuity than tradition. To build up traditions and safeguard them is especially important in the task of upbringing. Obviously, a Soviet school without tradition cannot be a good school, because a correct Soviet upbringing can only be achieved through a powerful collective, one that respects its dignity and has an awareness of its collective image.

Among traditions I especially cherish the militarization games, though without any limitation or repetition of the laws governing a military unit. I disapprove strongly of using marching as a transition point from one activity to another (marching to the dining room, to work). This is absolutely uncalled for. However, my collective was militarized to a certain degree. Our terminology, taken out of military life, included such words as "unit commander" and "guard." We also incorporated its rituals, such as banners, drills, uniforms, guard duty and roll calls. Consequently, all of these became of great significance in the children's collective, since they have a special talent for glorifying "militarization" and making it more enticing. I find it necessary to perpetuate this trend since it reinforces the life of the collective and adds beauty to it.

## § Discipline, Routine, Punishment, and Reward

I am absolutely convinced that creating a special "abnormal" pedagogy to deal with delinquents tends to foster deviation in youngsters, while on the other hand a positive, purposeful approach to them transforms their collective very quickly into a normal one.

Since there are no "born" criminals or innate delinquent character trends, our discussion can very well apply to "normal" children and youth.

I consider routine to be a specific system of methods which help to bring up children, and discipline to be the result of the whole process.

Until the revolution, discipline was a rather narrow superficial concept which, for the sake of convenience and order, meant absolute subordination. Although our society emphasizes the ethical and political aspects of discipline, I had opportunities to observe teachers who still subscribe to the antiquated view when no breach of discipline was treated as an immoral or antisocial act. In the pre-revolutionary school, the teachers thought it to be, if not an heroic exploit, then at least a witty and humorous one which expressed character, vitality, or strong revolutionary tendencies.

Now every Soviet educator must consider infringement of discipline in a much broader perspective, but this is possible only when discipline is accepted not as a means, but as a direct result, of the whole upbringing process. Consequently, Soviet discipline must be conscious. In the twenties, when the permissive upbringing of children, or at least a trend in this direction, was very popular, the conception of conscious discipline became broadened, considering that discipline must ensue from awareness of behavior. In my early experience I discovered the fallacy of the approach which conveys that it is sufficient to fall back on disciplinary regulations in order to achieve conscious discipline. One cannot obtain any positive results exclusively by preaching and explaining.

In the process of reasoning, I encountered verbal and stubborn opponents who ably defended their own point of view and thereby succeeded in turning this method into continuous arguments. However, I insist that our discipline, ethical and political in character, must be accompanied by a full understanding of its purpose and goals. I firmly believe that our conscious discipline must encompass such areas as academic learning, political and physical education, character and body development, conflicts as well as their solutions, friendship, trust, relationships, all of which constitute the totality of the process of upbringing.

In order to achieve our conscious discipline we must teach morals; although the contemporary school curriculum does not include this as a subject, there are still many opportunities in extracurricular activities which could be utilized by the leaders to incorporate such teaching.

In the old school system, it was through religion, a compulsory subject, that moral standards were set. But the idea of morality rested upon faith and conviction—which were not revered either by priests or by pupils.

I'm sure that eventually we will incorporate theoretical teaching of morals in our schools. I achieved very positive results, of course much better than those of the old-fashioned school, by utilizing this method (among others) in the curriculum I created for my colonies. For example, in discussing stealing, many theoretical aspects such as honesty, respect for government or somebody else's property, and attitudes toward it may be brought up. Of course, the emphasis used here differs greatly from that old logic, "Thou shalt not steal."

Also, the theory of correct behavior and relationships in Soviet society may be taught without effort since the vast accumulated experience may be used successfully as examples and each member of a collective will set compulsory limits for himself.

The importance of morals is affirmed in conscious discipline, which cannot be obtained by outside controls only. Each member of the collective must be convinced that discipline is the best and only means to achieve the goal of the collective. This logic constitutes the first step toward establishing a specific theory of desirable behavior, namely, that of morals.

The logic of our discipline places each individual in a position of greater security and freedom. This paradox is easily understood by children, who find it verified in every step of their experience. Discipline in the collective is a full guarantee of the rights and potentials of each individual.

Obviously, in our society and history we can find rich evidence to substantiate this assertion. The very goal of our revolution was to free the individual, though the pattern of our society is discipline.

These socially moral demands which the children's collective must meet, help the person in charge to cope with any conflict which may arise. When a pupil exhibits undisciplined behavior, he is accused by the whole collective of infringing upon the interests of all other members of the collective by depriving them of their rightful freedom. Perhaps this might occur when delinquents, who previously lived in an undisciplined children's collective, fell prey to gang leaders who exploited them by sending the weaker, smaller children to steal and to commit acts of hooliganism. For these youngsters, discipline appears to be their only rescue, a condition of real necessity for their future development as valuable members of Soviet society.

Another very important theoretical moral assertion a collective must bear in mind is that its interests always have priority over that of an individual. Though Soviet citizens should understand this premise very well by now, it is amazing how many intelligent, educated, and cultured people, even those who are socially minded, in reality do not comprehend it.

I am inclined to believe now that the best and only way to educate the collective as well as the individual is to set the interests of the collective above those of the individual and to proceed by all available means to fulfill the premise regardless of how merciless decisions may seem. However, while employing techniques alloting undisputed priority to the interests of the collective, precautions must be taken to limit ruthlessness in order to safeguard the individual from disastrous consequences.

By way of illustration: when the youngster who was a commander in charge of the collective for the day was caught stealing a radio, the general assembly voted to expell him from the colony, and no amount of persuasion could change its decision. The representatives of the NKVD, under whose jurisdiction the Dzerzhinsky colony was, had no better luck in swaying the vote. The colonists maintained that only strict discipline will scare others. They wished to reject the culprit completely not only because he stole but because in doing so while he was their elected representative in a position of trust, he let the entire collective down. Hence they no longer cared what happened to him. After twelve hours of deliberation, the decision remained the same, and the boy was expelled. He was secretly assigned to another colony collective. When, after six months, my colony discovered that I had made these arrangements, I was reprimanded for disobeying the resolutions of the general assembly.

Another very pertinent theory is that discipline enhances the atmosphere and morale of the collective. How to make it enticing is simply a problem of finding the correct pedagogical technique to set it into practice. Of course, one should be continuously watchful not to turn it into a superficial process only.

When the collective achieves true discipline in its highest form, and when demands are increased accordingly, the upbringing process achieves its desired ends. I would like to say finally that real discipline means the individual can fulfill an unpleasant task with pleasure.

All of the above-mentioned theories must stress the political meaning of discipline as its most significant and basic element. In essence, Soviet discipline places many demands upon the individual, while concomitantly maintaining great respect for him.

Children always respond positively to firm, consistent demands, when these two qualities are utilized as a workable synchronized unit. Inconsistency and faltering never bring about desirable results. Only when it became apparent to me as well as to my pupils that I was absolutely correct, and when the issue involved was clearly understood by the youngsters, were demands imposed dictatorially; the children then accepted them unconditionally. For example, I disagree with pedagogues who maintain that children must run, shout, and break objects around them. Contrary to this belief, I became convinced that the children's collective can successfully inhibit such behavior by inducing in its members respect for one's neighbor as well as for public property. Order must reign in a commune; otherwise the collective cannot exist.

It is not difficult to achieve this in schools. I would simply define and set patterns of behavior firmly without much theorizing, because this could only complicate the issue.

Each collective must start by enforcing rules and limits without permitting anyone to contradict or question them. However, in a later stage a nucleus of pupils who want to establish conscious discipline in the collective will lend their support, until finally the whole collective will grow to enforce them. During the last period in my colony I had to defend the individual member many times from too great demands placed upon him by the collective. The transition from dictatorial demands by the leader to those upheld by the entire collective is a basic learning process in the development of the children's collective.

During the last years of the existence of my commune, petty stealing, rudeness, and other bad habits not yet unlearned were not punished, since these behaviors were considered symptoms of sickness, or a result of lack of control or of political and ethical ignorance. However, firm measures should be taken when a member of the collective who is a fully aware individual acts against the collective, until he acknowledges his subordination to the collective.

As for punishment, we must admit that our methods do not always produce desirable results, although we agree that this technique is a necessary and useful one. Many pedagogues feel that resorting to punishment reflects badly upon the quality of the pedagogues even if it is permissible to do so. I believe that punishment is not only a right but a duty when the necessity for its use arises. The pedagogue must follow his conscience and judgment, and not shy away from this responsibility. It must be executed in a natural and simple manner, just like any other method.

Our approach to punishment is not the Christian one—that of necessary evil. The Soviet upbringer should not have any qualms, since he uses it as a last resort only. We must consider it a way to solve a given conflict while avoiding creating new ones. Our punishment must never contain either physical or emotional suffering. First of all the guilty individual must understand and regret his mistake, and then proceed to correct it. Of course there is no purpose in punishing without the agreement of the collective, because such punishment would get no moral support. Though each punishment must be geared toward the individual, there are nevertheless some general rules and forms which limit the right to punish. I cannot imagine a healthy collective in which ten people have the power to execute punishment, since they could not maintain uniformity of approach.

In our commune we had a law which gave me the right to punish the "freshmen" by depriving them of allowances, the right to work, etc. But as soon as they graduated into the ranks of commands, confinement was the only means to punish them. This lasted from one to ten consecutive hours. This system proved to be very effective with the youngsters. Everyone was anxious to join the command ranks. It is important to mention here that I had no right of pardon. I was deprived of it by the general assembly in 1933. The culprit usually devoted the period of his "arrest" in my office to study. I was the only one permitted to converse with him. Of course, the topic of the action which precipitated the arrest was taboo, since it was considered vulgar and indecent to touch upon it.

When the collective is united and trusts its members, the general assembly's methods of punishment are original and interesting and provide a good learning experience. However, in my experience, I leaned mainly upon individual discussion rather than punishment.

## § Pedagogy of the Individual Approach

During the early years of my experience, I wrongly perceived the existing relationship between the collective and the individual. I thought that influences upon the collective should take priority over those exerted upon the individual. However, later

I became deeply convinced that there is no direct transition from one to the other, only a gradual one through the nucleus collective, established solely for specific pedagogical goals.

I think the theory of pedagogy will in the future devote special attention to the concept of the nucleus collective. That is a collective in which the members are united by continuous amicable living and working relationship as well as by a common ideology.

This role in a school situation is played by the classroom. But its shortcoming in fulfilling it manifests itself in its inability to become the connecting link between the individual and the general collective of the school. In some schools I observed that the classroom became an end in itself, disregarding the general school collective. There were even instances where the latter was almost nonexistent.

Although the situation in which I worked was conducive to fostering common interests and goals, in the beginning I did not have classrooms as natural nucleus collectives. When we began to operate a full ten-year school, I decided against creating them, because I came to the conclusion that a too-closely knit nucleus collective becomes isolated and hence detrimental to the interests of the general collective of the school. A well-rounded political upbringing can be achieved only in a collective which encompasses all the broad values of Soviet society. To achieve this goal I created in my colony heterogeneous age units, though many pedagogues who believe in homogeneity in grouping would not agree with me. In the later years these units were based on "voluntary selection." Though in the beginning I myself was rather frightened by it, this principle helped to establish a most healthy, natural environment for primary collectives. The general assembly had to choose and distribute among all units those youngsters not selected by any group. While on one hand this process of selection is very drawn out, at the same time it gave me an opportunity to recognize the most difficult members of our collective.

To support the functioning of these primary collective units, we established in the Dzerzhinsky colony the technique of so-called parallel pedagogical action. This method implies that officially neither I, as central figure of the commune, nor any official organs of the commune, nor the Komsomol, had any relationship with the individual; we dealt only with the unit. In reality this method was geared to influence the individual, but by a parallel, indirect means, that of the primary collective. We wanted to convey to the individual that he is a human being, not merely an object of various upbringing processes which are aimed at producing positive results in the future. To achieve this, very complex techniques had to be established and implemented for the nucleus collective.

Since I always consider the unit an entity, each time it earned praise, the entire nucleus collective was rewarded, while in cases when disciplinary action was necessary, only the leader of the unit was punished because I held him responsible for the action and behavior of both the entire nucleus collective and its individuals. The role of the individual member in earning merits or demerits was of no interest to me. I felt it was the task of the leader and of the nucleus collective to bring him back in line.

I believe this method proved to be the best one to achieve the main objective of the nucleus collective, namely, instigating and carrying out action which would achieve socially significant goals related closely to real life experience.

However, the nucleus collective should not hamper the development of the general collective; neither should it try to substitute for it. It must remain a basic means for influencing the individual.

In the beginning I concentrated upon working with individuals who were acting out their antisocial behavior. Later I discovered that it is more pertinent to work with those youngsters who are inconspicuously hiding. These I began to regard as the most dangerous ones. As it later became apparent, the "acting out" ones became better members of the Soviet society than the latter group.

Subsequently, I arrived at the conclusion that my main objective is to bring up active, brave, industrious Soviet citizens. To achieve this, I must raise every one of my charges correctly, not just set a few hooligans straight.

Though in bringing up children the role of the individual

pedagogue is very important, for the best results the whole pedagogical collective must design a continuous, synchronized action which would derive from uniformity of philosophy and purpose. Obviously we need talented and sensitive people with desirable character attributes. To select the outstanding ones remains a difficult task, although many people still believe that anybody can bring up children.

No matter how talented the pedagogue is, he has no right to act on his own. It is better to have five weak pedagogues united into a collective than ten outstanding ones working individually. The pedagogue who works as an individualist may produce role distortions. For example, a popular pedagogue who thinks the love of his students places him above others, may be unable to work in a collective. I consider it criminal to strive for the love of youngsters, since in most cases this is prompted by the pedagogue's desire to meet his own needs. Perhaps some of my charges love me, but on the whole I consider it irrelevant to the accomplishments of my initial task.

It is important to mention here another factor which contributes greatly to the quality of the pedagogical collective and the strength of its influence upon the student body; namely, staff stability. I firmly believe the average length of the upbringer's stay in school must be equivalent to that of his students. For example, when youngsters attend the school for eight to ten years, the pedagogue must consider remaining in the same school for the same period of time. How else can he hope to exert his influence?

I firmly believe that an upbringer and teacher should not have the right to punish. In our colony they could not even reprimand the youngsters, since I think that the right to punish should be centralized in one person in order to avoid confusion and contradiction.

Many an upbringer teacher believes that authority is either innate or artificially built up, and thinks a reprimand delivered to him in the presence of youngsters diminishes his authority in their eyes. But I insist that authority derives exclusively from responsibility, and that each individual must at all times be responsible for his own behavior and actions.

The work of the pedagogue should always be closely related to the nucleus collective. In instances where a member breaks rules or exhibits antisocial behavior, the primary task of the pedagogue is to arouse the nucleus collective to instigate action against the erring member, since his primary role is to motivate the unit to make demands upon its individual members.

When the pedagogue is sensitive, he can sense when it is right to express his feelings and when it is better to remain silent. Though there are many instances when speaking is least helpful, there is never a need to hide or smooth things over artificially.

Among various methods of individual work, those indicated by the youngster himself are of most importance, and usually these are expressions of friendliness.

In some rare cases, when the whole collective is against an individual, I have to use a different approach, since the individual is defenseless and might even break.

As an illustration, the following example may be cited. A girl, a former prostitute, was accused of stealing fifty rubles. All indications were against her, but since there was no conclusive evidence, I defended her, saying I was convinced she did not do it. Finally, after a long fight the collective relented, and she was not thrown out. When she came to my office the next day to thank me for defending her, I told her in no uncertain terms that I knew she was guilty. Taken by surprise, the girl broke down, crying, and admitted it.

Yes, I lied to the general assembly, but there was no other way. She would have been expelled and would have gone back to the street. I am against this sort of solution and fully aware of the danger involved, but it was a necessity. The girl understood that I lied to save her, and this secret, which only we two shared, became a pedagogical means by which I could reach her thereafter to effect a favorable change in her.

# 9 *Decree Regarding Parents' Committee*

## § I. Aims and Purposes of Parents' Committees

1. The responsibility to bring up the new man of Communist society which the Soviet school is now facing may be accomplished successfully only when the parents of the student body collaborate closely with the teachers.

2. The relationship between school and parents should be reinforced by general school as well as classroom parents' committees. Rural schools do not require individual classroom committees.

3. The parents' committee in school and in classrooms is elected during the first quarter of each school year for the duration of one year.

4. Each classroom parents' committee elects from three to five people as their representatives during their classroom parents' meeting. The parents' committee of the whole school is elected during the general parents' assembly: the number of members

Akademiya Pedagogicheskich Nauk, RSFSR, edited by E. I. Volkova, *Parents and Children,* Izd-vo APN, RSFSR, Moscow, 1961, pp. 416-420.
Verified by the Minister of Education, E. Afanasenko, August 24, 1960.

elected by the general parents' assembly differs in accordance with the needs of each school, but always includes representatives of every classroom collective in the school.

The general parents' meeting may decide to form parents' committees solely from representatives of the classroom committees.

The director of the school and a representative from the main regional industry or other dominant enterprise, such as a kolchoz or a sovchoz, automatically become members of the parents' committee.

5. To work concurrently and to fulfill the daily task of leadership in classroom and in school committees, the following steps are undertaken:

a. Large regular school and eight-year schools elect a presidium consisting of one chairman, one or two vice-chairmen and a secretary, and three to five members.

b. Small grade schools and small eight-year schools elect one chairman, one vice-chairman and one secretary.

c. One and two room schools elect a chairman. The school director is a permanent member of the presidium.

6. Under the leadership of elected participants of parents' committees and of parents who are active participants, each school may set up permanent or temporary subcommittees dealing with various areas of concern such as curriculum, educational propaganda, child rearing, polytechnical and vocational education, professional preparation, community work and relationships, parents' education, housekeeping, health and others. The number of these committees as well as their areas of concern is defined by the parents' committee and by the needs as well as the limits of the school situation.

7. In their daily work the classroom and school parents' committees establish relationships with parents in housing developments in order to help the school and home to bring up children, implement compulsory school attendance, provide supervision during youngsters' leisure time by organizing and carrying out educational activities for them.

8. The school parents' committee and parents who actively

participate help the school through its temporary and permanent subcommittees:

a. To establish control over the general conditions of bringing up children in the family and over their study habits at home; to unify the educational goals of school and home; to achieve parents' participation in implementing various educational measures in extracurricular activities as well as in pioneer and komsomol organizations.

b. To watch over compulsory school attendance, to motivate school interests, to safeguard normal life conditions for youngsters: (transportation, hot lunches, clothes), to help daily in extracurricular and play group activities, to assist and support the drive for compulsory school attendance.

c. To organize the intake of students in grades 9 to 11 in view of their preference toward various professions.

d. To organize socially meaningful activities; to bring about proper attitudes toward work through students' direct experience with it; to draw parents into leadership of different aspects of socially useful work such as self-service, practical training of students; to emphasize the importance of vocational education to parents and to watch that the family responds to it.

e. To provide vocational education and training for high school students by pulling together and utilizing community resources such as industry, agriculture; to enlist public agencies and parents for joint decision-making regarding the above; to establish in industry controls for safety and sanitation and to guard against overwork of youngsters.

f. To pre-orient older students toward job possibilities by visits to industrial plants, meetings with parents representing various professions, by discussions of the significance of various branches of industry and culture in our country, etc.

g. To carry out educational propaganda among parents and in the population at large through interpretation of the fundamentals of child rearing practices in school and home, through speeches, lectures, through conferences where experiences of bringing up children in the family are exchanged, through organizing open school days.

h. To watch that the students obey "Rules for Students" in and out of school.

i. To strengthen the existing educational and housekeeping resources and to create comfortable and sanitary conditions in the school.

j. To organize physical and cultural activities during school vacations.

9. Each parents' committee has to prepare (on a half-yearly or yearly basis) a realistic plan for action which is determined by local conditions and problems affecting the given school.

10. The homeroom and school parents' committees meet not less than once during a school year quarter to discuss current issues; presidium of the parents' school committee meets when need arises, but not less than two times during the school quarter.

The school parents' committee, its presidium and homeroom parents' committees carry a motion by not less than two-thirds of regular members present at the meeting.

The representatives of homeroom parents' committees may be invited to the meeting of the general school parents' committee.

11. To decide most vital issues arising in school and in parents' committees, parents' meetings are held (homeroom meetings not less than four times during the school year, general school assembly not less than twice in a school year).

During the homeroom parents' meeting, the homeroom teacher must be present, while the whole teaching staff of the school must attend the general parents' assembly (the school director, and homeroom and all other teachers).

12. Schools with a large student body may substitute for an entire school parents' assembly a parents' conference to which delegates are chosen during parents' homeroom meeting.

In case a rural consolidated school serves a few outlying districts, it is recommended that general parents' assembly be held periodically in each of them.

13. The minutes of parents' committees and general parents' assemblies kept in school files are turned in legally at the end of the school year with the expiration of the office term.

Each parents' committee periodically reports to the parents' assembly about the implementation of previously voted upon decisions.

14. The parents' committee is subordinated to the general school parents' assembly; the homeroom committee is subordinated to the homeroom assembly. The parents' committee of the school reports to the general parents' assembly once during the school year, when the election of new representatives takes place. The reports of classroom committees take place before the homeroom parents' assembly on the day of election of new officers and also at the beginning of the second half of the school year; a majority of parents may request additional reports of parents' committee.

15. The director consents to the decisions of the parents' committees or of its presidium when they are adopted and no special additional verification is required.

16. A difference of opinion between the director of the school and the majority of a parents' committee is discussed during the joint meeting of teachers, advisory council, and the parents' committee; in case no agreement is reached, the final decision rests with the regional director of the office of education.

17. The inspectors of the office of education acquaint themselves with the work of general parents' committees and render them help when it is needed.

## § II. The Rights of Parents' Committees

18. The general parents' committee has the following rights:

a. To present to the director and to the teachers' council justifiable suggestions on how to alleviate any problems of learning, of education, of school maintenance, of improving the collaboration between the teaching collective and the parents. The director and the teaching council must carefully examine suggestions of the parents' committee and inform them about measures taken.

b. Review the homeroom committee's report and make decisions regarding help extended to them in order to improve their work.

c. Hold conferences with individual parents regarding child-rearing practices in their family.

d. Make home visits in order to acquaint themselves with the home environment of students and their upbringing in the family.

e. Praise parents for bringing up their children correctly and reprimand them for shortcomings in their child-rearing practices at home.

f. Periodically attend the director's reports about the present situation of the school and perspectives of its educational work, and also listen to his interpretation of individual problems of parents.

g. Call parents meetings and conferences.

h. Make decisions regarding help to students in economic need.

i. Induce parents to conduct various educational, extracurricular activities, to provide leadership in practical experience for use in industry during the summer, and to help in the realization of vocational and industrial education of youngsters.

j. To establish contact with governmental agencies, industry, and other dominant enterprises in the school's region, such as *kolkhozes and sovkhozes,* in order to help the school accomplish the educational and vocational teaching task, to reinforce the school's economic foundations, and to influence attitudes of parents toward child rearing.

19. The homeroom parents' committees have the right to suggest improvements in teaching, in education, in vocational guidance, and in parent-teacher relationships. But always they have to give the homeroom teacher a chance to explain and clarify his point of view. They also listen to parents' reports regarding bringing up children in the family. They call homeroom parents' meetings, assign parents for duty in the school.

20. The chairman of the parents' committee is a permanent member of the school's teachers' council. Upon the invitation of the school director, members of the parents' committee may also attend meetings of the teachers' council.

Chairmen of the parents' committee not only may be present during meetings of the teachers' council and of the director but also may take part in local industrial committee conferences and in teachers' regional and municipal meetings.

# 10 *Decree* Regarding School Internats*

## § I. Aims and Tasks of School Internats

1. The school internat, a newly established institution of general learning, was created to elevate the level of preparation of builders of Communism.

2. The school internat must create the most favorable conditions to foster a well-rounded secondary education which would include the fulfillment of intellectual as well as vocational tasks, high moral qualities, physical and esthetic development, and preparation for practical work in various branches of the national economy.

3. To achieve these goals the school internat must consistently translate into reality Lenin's demand for a unity between school and life and between intellectual pursuits and practical work experiences.

## § II. Procedures for Setting School Internats into Operation

4. At the joint recommendation of the ministries of education of the autonomous Soviet republics, the regional and district

* Approved by the Council of Ministers, RSFSR, April 13, 1957; No. 209.

N. I. Alpatov, N. A. Myaskovskaya, L. F. Spiryn, and A. Y. Shagova, *School Internat*, Uchpedgigy, Moscow, 1958, pp. 217-223.

departments of education, and the executive committee of the Congress of Deputies, the Ministry of Education of RSFSR establishes the pre-planned school internat system within the existing situational limits.

5. Each school internat is under the jurisdiction of the Ministry of Education of the autonomous republic in which it is located, and also under the authority of the regional, district, and local departments of education. The regional departments of education help school internats to choose qualified personnel and establish curriculum, and provide help in other areas of organization and living. In Moscow and Leningrad the school internats are subordinated to local departments of education.

6. The school internat consists of first to tenth grades.* The student body consists of both sexes, ages seven to eighteen.

At the school internat's opening, children will be accepted for grades one to nine inclusive, with the tenth grade to be organized later.

The school internat may open with first to seventh grades or first to eighth grades, with a gradual increase of older grades. At the start, not less than 120 boarding students should be enrolled, as a rule. All school internats, even those which do not have grades eight to ten, are secondary schools.

7. Each school internat should be located in an environment favorable to health, and it should include school buildings with laboratories and workshops, library and other necessary facilities, living quarters consisting of dormitories, dining rooms, recreational facilities, visiting room, faculty quarters, playground, experimental agricultural acreage, and a housekeeping unit.

8. The school internat may include a kindergarten or a kindergarten and a creche.

## § III. Priority of Admission

9. Parents or guardians enroll the children in school internats entirely voluntarily.

* At the present time all secondary schools have eleven grades. The curriculum of grades nine to eleven consists not only of academic subjects but also of vocational education. The additional year of schooling was added to compensate for time devoted to practical work experience.

10. Priority of entry is given to children of fatherless families, of war and work invalids, to orphans, and to youngsters whose families do not provide the necessary environment to foster positive development.

Tuition is paid in accordance with parents' earnings by an established scale.

Full government scholarships are provided for parentless children or those whose parents support many children. Cases in the second group are decided upon individually by the regional or City Council of Deputies (in the place of parents' residence).

11. Day students also may attend school internats.

12. Applications are accepted between June 1 and August 1. Applications submitted are judged August 1 through 10. Acceptance of students takes place between August 25 and 30.

13. All students in a school internat are admitted to the school internat by a special commission which consists of representatives of departments of education and of health on either a national level or on the level of the autonomous republic, the director of the school internat, and representatives of community organizations. Pupils are admitted according to rules set forth by the Ministry of Education and by the Ministry of Health of the RSFSR.

The creation of an admission committee may be delegated to an executive committee of district and local agencies in accordance with the decision of the Council of Ministries of the autonomous republic and of the executive committee of the regional and district agencies.

14. Parents who place their children in school internats must cooperate with the educational collective by raising the child in a correct way while he is in the family. Parents visit their children during days designated by the director.

At the request of parents or guardians, the director of the school permits the students home visits on Sundays, holidays, and during vacations.

## § IV. Organization of the Curriculum in a School Internat

15. The school internat provides secondary education which prepares for higher educational pursuits as well as for practical work in various branches of the national economy.

The curriculum of the school internat is geared to prepare children to become well-educated and well-developed builders of Communism, who are raised in the spirit of patriotism, dedication, and friendship toward other nations.

16. The basis for the curriculum of a school internat is the combination of intellectual pursuits and practical work experience beginning with household chores, self-service, and school workshops, leading into agricultural and industrial experience in kolkhozes, factories, and plants, always at the readiness level of the youngster.

17. The teaching is done in the native language of students according to plans and programs approved by the Ministry of Education of the RSFSR.

18. The number of students in a class and youngsters in a group should not exceed thirty individuals. Each class of twenty and more pupils should be divided into two groups, for practical work experience, for vocational training, and for foreign language teaching.

19. The school internat attaches itself by agreement with local organizations to certain industrial and agricultural enterprises in order to facilitate practical work experience for the students.

20. Various methods of teaching are utilized to assure conscientious and firm absorption of learning material, which would stimulate the intellectual capabilities and activities of students, and would develop in them the habit of independent work and the ability to implement the learned theory in practice. Besides the lesson periods, which are the basic form of instruction, other means such as trips, practical work experiences in shops, in the experimental school acreage, in industrial enterprises, in agriculture, are also used as teaching devices.

21. Physical education in school internats is achieved by adherence to correct daily planning, well-balanced diet, good personal hygiene, daily physical exercise followed by showers, and a systematic toughening of the organism, with time devoted to sport as a recreation and as a competition, taking part in hikes, etc.

22. Esthetic education of students takes place both in the classroom when teaching the native language, its development, and literature and in extracurricular activities when engaging in exploring various kinds of arts, vocal or instrumental music, or painting, etc.

23. Special attention is given to the development of individual abilities and gifts of students in the curricular and extracurricular activities.

24. The director of the school internat establishes the rules and daily routines, which correctly balance study, work and rest periods.

25. School internats use the methods of reward and punishment, when it is necessary, which were established by the Ministry of Education for all secondary schools of RSFSR.

26. The school year begins September 1 and ends at the same time as all other schools, as specified by the Ministry of Education of RSFSR.

27. During summer vacation the school internat organizes work for students in the school practice lot, in its housekeeping unit, in agriculture, combining it with rest in Pioneer, Komsomol and other youth camps. The rest of the summer the pupils may visit their parents for a period of time not exceeding four weeks. The youngsters who cannot go home have their vacation organized by the school internats.

28. The graduates of school internats receive a diploma, which specifies not only the student's academic achievements but also his vocational training.

The graduates of school internats are sent by the executive committee of the local council of deputies to work in industry, agriculture, cultural and educational agencies in technical and other professional schools in accordance with existing needs of national economy and of the students' practical training, taking into consideration their preferences and abilities. Graduates who wish to continue their education in institutions of higher learning or of particular specializations after complying with general rules of admission may do so.

## § V. The Collective of Students in the School Internat

29. All pupils in the school internat comprise the only collective which takes an active part in all aspects of the whole life of the school internat.

Participation in various socially useful activities, such as athletics and others, are built upon the initiative and independence of students and upon widely used methods of socialist competition.

Collectives in school internats are established in homerooms, living quarters, places of work and in groups of extracurricular activities. These nucleus collectives merge into a general school collective, which elects an all-school council of the student collective during a general assembly meeting.

30. The Komsomol is organized and works according to the rules set by the National Association of Communist Youth. The Pioneer squad is organized and works according to the rules defined in the manual dealing with the Communist organization for children, the Young Pioneers.

## § VI. Personnel of School Internats

31. The positions and salaries of the staff are defined in accordance with existing categories and wage scales.

32. The administrative director of the institutions is selected from among outstanding educators, who have organizational abilities, have earned higher degrees in the field of education and had not less than five years of administrative experience.

The administrative director is responsible for: the whole curriculum, academic as well as vocational, theoretical as well as practical, the pupils' safety and health, the housekeeping of the school, and the functioning of the school internat.

The administrative director as the head of the institution exerts general leadership in all activities of the school internat, in which he receives the support of all school social organizations. All workers must obey the orders of the administrative director.

The administrative director has the right to change duties of workers in the institution without enlarging the staff and without increasing the pay.

The administrative director may teach in the school internat for not more than six hours per week.

33. The educational director must have a higher degree in education and not less than five years' experience; he must be a good organizer and be well versed in various pedagogical methods.

The educational director is in charge of the academic curriculum and of methodology employed in the school internat and he is responsible to the administrative director for its functioning.

The educational director may teach for not more than six hours a week.

34. Outstanding teachers and upbringers must be chosen. They must know child psychology, and combine love for youngsters with an ability to make reasonable demands upon them. They must use personal example as a positive influence upon general and work education of children.

35. The teacher must have higher pedagogical or secondary education for teaching primary grades. The teacher is responsible for the quality of his instruction and for the rearing of his charges, for fulfilling the study plan on time, as well as for the extracurricular duties delegated to him.

36. The head upbringer must be a graduate of a higher institute of pedagogy in his field, and have not less than five years' experience. He is responsible for the school's task to raise the pupils, to follow the daily schedule, routines, and rules, for childrens' safety and their health.

37. The upbringer must be a graduate of a higher pedagogical institute or of a professional school on a secondary level for primary grades.

Each upbringer chosen must exhibit proficiency in a different extracurricular activity (physical education, music, arts and crafts, etc.).

The task of the upbringer is to take care of daily needs and problems of children in all areas of child rearing, organize children in groups to study independently and to fulfill school assignments, and encourage active participation of students in extracurricular activities, guide them when needed, watch the students' adherence to order, to daily schedules, and to routines, guard their health, teach them respect for equipment and other valuables. The upbringer may teach not more than six hours per week.

38. The assistant to the director in charge of household management is responsible for the household of the school internat, for diets and menus, permanent equipment and teaching materials, upkeep and repair of buildings, their sanitary conditions and correct usage of transport.

39. A doctor and nurse are appointed and released by health agencies to which the school internat is subordinate. The doctor is in charge of all health needs of children, preventive as well as rehabilitative. Each child gets a general thorough examination not less than twice a year. When necessary, the doctor hospitalizes sick students, continuously follows the physical development and physical needs of all pupils. He conducts a health education program among students and among personnel of the school internat.

40. The person in charge of the school's experimental acreage secures its favorable work conditions, organizes the practical experience in agriculture for pupils, follows all safety rules, and is responsible for all equipment and materials.

41. The head of vocational training (in internats which have five lower and some upper grades) organizes the practical work program in shops, follows safety rules, leads extracurricular activity in the area of his specialization, and is responsible for the equipment and tools in the shops.

42. The director delegates the responsibility for laboratories to the most experienced teachers in their particular field of specialization. They are responsible for programing their work correctly.

43. The Pioneer leader is assigned by a corresponding department of national education, depending upon whether the internat is subordinate to a regional, district, or city committee of VLKSM [Leninist Young Communist League of the Soviet Union], by persons who have educational training and experience in Pioneer work.

The Pioneer leader is in charge of the Pioneer squad and its program, which follows the outline submitted by the educational collective of the school internat.

44. The librarian is responsible for the continuing growth of the necessary book supply for the students and educational personnel, takes part in extracurricular activities such as literary clubs, etc., and is responsible for the book budget and stocks.

45. The bookkeeper is as responsible as the director for the correct budget and its accounting.

46. The educational director and educational personnel in school internats are appointed by the ministry of education of the autonomous republic, by the chief of the regional, district, or local department of education upon the recommendation of the administrative director of the school internat; the rest of the staff by the administrative director himself.

## § VII. Education Council of a School Internat

47. Each school internat organizes an educational council composed of: the administrative director (chairman), the educational director, the teachers, the pioneer leader, the head upbringer, upbringers, vocational teachers, housekeeping assistant to the director, librarian, doctor, and chairman of the parents' committee.

The decisions of the committee become effective immediately after the director affirms them.

## § VIII. Committees of Parents and of Community Organizations

48. In order to establish close links between the school internat and the parents of pupils, a parents' committee is elected during a parents' meeting. The members of the committee elect a chairman from among the group. The parents' committee enlists parents' active participation in all aspects of school internat's life—academic, vocational, and extracurricular.

49. A committee of community organizations is established in order to create close links with the community, which would enlist their help in creating necessary conditions to improve the work of school internats. Its members are representatives of: the district or city council of deputies, of party, of Komsomol, of professional organizations, and of industrial and agricultural enterprises.

## § IX. Finances and Accounting

50. The school internat is financed by the autonomous republic through the regional, district, or city budgets, in accordance with the affirmed estimate.

School internats in Moscow and in Leningrad are financed by the district budgets.

The students' tuition is considered a part of the budget which finances the school.

Income received for the work of the students in workshops, in agricultural and industrial enterprises as well as in other places of employment, comprises a special fund. In accordance with an estimate established by the Ministry of Education of the autonomous republic or by the corresponding departments of national education and registered in the finance agencies, this fund may be assigned for the improvement of food or for additional life comforts, or for cultural purposes, or to enlarge workshops and the experimental agricultural station, and also to reward the students.

51. The school internat has legal rights, a government emblem of RSFSR, and an identification stamp.

# 11 School Internat

## N. I. Alpatov, N. A. Myaskovskaya, L. F. Spiryn, and A. Y. Shagova

### § Preface

THE INTENTION OF THIS BOOK is to popularize the experience gained by school internats. These institutions of learning were created in our country by the decision of the Twentieth Congress of the Communist Party of the U.S.S.R.

This book is devoted to the description and discussion of attempted solutions to many educational and child-rearing problems. These institutions represent the nucleus of the new Soviet system of education.

The authors followed up the work of some school internats in Moscow, in Chelabinsk and in its region. They observed teachers, upbringers, and students. They participated actively in the pedagogical collective, by discussing many problems during seminars and meetings.

While writing this book minutes of various meetings were utilized.

A limitation of this book is that the authors were unable to throw light on all the problems which are of interest to

N. I. Alpatov, N. A. Myaskovskaya, L. F. Spiryn, and A. Y. Shagova, *School Internat,* Uchpedgiz, Moscow, 1958, pp. 3-50, 217-223.

pedagogical collectives of internats. Special attention was given to problems in the area of upbringing.

The chapters "Historical Background" and "Problems Related to the Organization of School Internats" were written by N. I. Alpatov.

## § Historical Background

The opening of school internats in 1956 brought about a marked change in the cultural life of our country. These institutions were established to raise the standards of teaching and upbringing of youth and to provide an opportunity for developing a new system of raising children which would meet the tasks and demands set for the school in the period of building the Communist society. Within the last forty years, our country has developed economically and culturally at a tremendous pace.

The Soviet youth, brought up in the spirit of Communist morals, had proven to be highly productive in factories, in plants, in agriculture (in *kolkhoz,* in *sovkhoz*), in conquering virgin lands and reclaiming wastelands, as well as in building new cities, hydrostations, and industrial enterprises. Our young people distinguish themselves by being brave and buoyant. Convinced that the Communist society is the highest ideal of humanity, they gladly contribute all their strength and knowledge to further its development.

Though it is known that the school successfully promotes general education, the Twentieth Congress of the Communist Party of the U.S.S.R. drew attention to some serious shortcomings of the school curriculum. The most important weakness in the role the school plays in our society is that it sets apart its teaching from life and gives students insufficient preparation toward practical work. Students receive neither necessary theory nor actual experience, nor are they acquainted with the most important branches of contemporary industry and agriculture. The content of the school curriculum has weak links with the industrial training of youngsters and does not stimulate youth sufficiently for work in industry and in agriculture.

For the last twenty-five years the Soviet secondary school has been striving to educate young people for universities and other institutions of higher learning. During this time the school was seriously engaged in alleviating the shortcomings pointed out by the Central Committee of the Party on September 5, 1931; namely, the inadequate general education and preparation for further studies given in the schools. This effort resulted in a considerable elevation of the preparation level of young people. Professionally well-rounded and erudite youth began to join the ranks of Soviet intelligentia and to contribute considerably to the development of the national economy.

But the continuous cultural and economic growth of our country created new tasks for the school, in the light of which the separation of general education from work training became very apparent. During the last years, industry and agriculture made great strides technically; further development of this technology is one of the major requirements for further progress and increased production in the national economy. Now, more than ever, the need is very great for people who can master the new technology quickly and move it ahead. The country needs educated individuals who would be ready for productive mental and physical work in their chosen field.

A one-sided education cannot in this stage of national development meet the needs of our society. Now the school has to fulfill the new tasks decided upon by the Twentieth Congress of the Communist Party. Our children must develop a Communist attitude toward work, and the entire process of education and upbringing in school must be raised further.

The ministry of education, RSFSR, together with the Academy of Pedagogical Sciences, developed and put into practice a new curriculum which placed equal emphasis on practical subjects, such as "Fundamentals of Industry," and on academic subjects. The time spent in shops as well as in actual experience in industry and agriculture was increased considerably.

The preparation for life must be improved on a basic level. As N. S. Khrushchev pointed out during the Thirteenth Congress of Komsomol, "The main task of our school must be to increase the readiness of our growing generation to engage in useful work and to develop in them a deep respect toward principles of the socialist society. . . . The school must create well-rounded individuals with a good basic knowledge and with an ability to work systematically and be useful to the society through active participation in invaluable national endeavors."*

The Soviet school must also solve many other problems; for example, eliminate the overloading of students with content and home assignments, improve the quality of teaching and create a unified entity out of isolated parts of the curriculum.

The growing youth of our country has great moral fiber. Through the party and the Komsomol, the school and the family has already accomplished a lot in bringing up children; nevertheless, some serious shortcomings remain in the practical implementation of educational measures. The content taught is not sufficiently utilized to fashion the moral beliefs and viewpoints of children. In extracurricular activities, in the work of school Pioneer and Komsomol organizations, they are saturated with formality and conventionalism. Our moral education leans more on words than deeds, and we use too few opportunities for socially meaningful work. The educational work of school and of home remains too inconsistent and disconnected.

Khrushchev said: "As a result of the war, our many widows have the complicated task of bringing up children by themselves. Also, many of our families where both parents work can only devote themselves to educating their children on a part-time basis. As a result, many children are left in the care of other people, neighbors or relatives, or often are left without adequate adult supervision, which frequently leads to sad consequences."†

It cannot be denied that among our hardworking and good youth there are some individuals who pay only lip service to our Communist morals, but violate them easily in life situations. Most often these are adolescents who in their childhood lacked a normal family influence.

In our country, education is widespread. All children begin to attend school at seven years of age. A large number of preschool

* N. S. Khrushchev, Speech, Thirteenth Congress of Komsomol, April 18, 1958, "Young Guard," 1958, p. 14.

† N. S. Khrushchev, Twentieth Congress of the Communist Party, 1956.

age children are enrolled in creches, nursery schools, and kindergartens. Though the nation spares neither money nor effort to widen the existing facilities, we cannot accomplish the educational task without the help of the family. Only improvements in cooperation between them and increased mutual help will create satisfactory results.

The creation of school internats is an important task which will be fulfilled with the support rendered by the Soviet society. The school internats must work out a system to teach and to bring up children in full accord with the manifold tasks inherent in the building of the Communist society.

School internats must create conditions fostering full mental and physical development of students, high moral values, and readiness and willingness to do socially useful and meaningful labor. The slogan of Lenin, "Let work and life be united," must be their motto.

Now, as the school internats are getting their first experience, accumulated evidence proves that this change in the educational system of our country was a correct one.

Keeping in mind the tasks inherent in the Communist upbringing of children, it is necessary to utilize the evidence of practical experience through careful analysis and evaluation of the methods employed and results produced.

Each historical period designs its own educational system which promotes the interests of the ruling classes.

Khrushchev notes, "In the recent past, the ruling classes used a way other than the general school to bring up the younger generation in accordance with principles reflecting the existing social order and its prevailing spirit. The government formed special institutions of learning for children, such as page and cadet schools, and girls' schools. In these boarding schools, the children of the ruling class received their aristocratic education."*

In the eighteenth century Tsarist Russia established boarding schools for children of the nobility. Such military, college preparatory and general boarding schools in which the privileged class

* N. S. Khrushchev, Lecture, Central Committee of the Communist Party of the U.S.S.R., Twentieth Congress, 1956, p. 95.

of the society raises and educates their younger generation are known in England, the United States, France, and other countries.

Though our intention is not to discuss the history of this selective educational system, we will note that Peter the Great created the first Naval Academy in Petersburg in order to educate naval officers, and in 1731 the first Cadet Academy was opened in Petersburg. By 1917 there were twenty-nine such schools and their total enrollment was about ten thousand. These academies were very popular among the sons of Russian nobility. The government provided full scholarships for all cadets. Since the military service was a privilege extended to the nobility, the school curriculum included military training. By 1863, these schools officially became preparatory for military academies.

Obviously, this aristocratic education is the opposite of the task of the Soviet school, which sets as its goals the well-rounded development of the individual and his active participation in the building process of the Communist society. Lenin pointed out the necessity of utilizing all the experience of the old Tsarist school system which could become of value to the new Soviet school. There are some valuable cues in the experience of the aristocratic boarding school which could prove to be of use to us, such as daily schedule, curriculum content, and some of the educational methods and measures they employed.

N. K. Krupskaya said, "Though these schools are very wisely organized from a pedagogical point of view, their aim and spirit satisfies only the needs of a small selected class in a bourgeois society. The workers' democracy, though it utilizes the pedagogical experience of the bourgeois boarding school education system, shapes its own different educational system to meet the particular needs of its changed society."*

The health, education, and welfare of the Soviet children became the ongoing concern of the Soviet government from the time of its inception. After the October Revolution, for the first time in history a socialist school was established. The task was to create a school with an entirely different premise, using as a basis the already accumulated experience of the old system, and

* N. K. Krupskaya, *Pedagogical Works,* Vol. I, 1957, p. 348.

then to modify the content and method to fit the new needs of the changed society.

This was a difficult time. Hundreds of thousands of children, frozen, covered with vermin, roamed through the city streets, railroad stations, trains, ships, looking for food and shelter. Childrens' homes, working colonies, and receiving centers operated above their capacity. It seemed there was no end to misfortune and sorrow which the First World War and then the Civil War brought upon our children and youth. But the party not only retained its power; it also saved from death many children and youth who later helped actively to build the first socialist state in the world.

Lenin initiated a special national commission under the leadership of Dzerzhinsky to solve the problem of neglected dependent youngsters. He, together with the National Ministry of Education, created a network of children's institutions in the Soviet Union.

In 1918 institutions were establishments for experimental demonstrations. This development played a very important role in the life of the Soviet school, and greatly influenced the theoretical and practical implementation of teaching and upbringing methods.

These institutions were started by some pedagogical groups to help them solve some problems related to the establishment of the new school. Later these institutions became integrated into the National Ministry of Education. The school commune was one of the first new types introduced into the Soviet educational system, where the students and teachers created a working and living community. The pupils were orphans and neglected children.

Lunacharsky, the first Commissar of the Commissariat of National Education, maintained that the character of these school communes should be mainly rural, which at that time was unavoidable. The experience of these schools helped to crystallize and solve many problems closely related to the Communist upbringing of children and youth. Of special interest is the students' practical educational experience in agriculture and in industrial workshops. Not of least importance is the experience the school communes gained by continuously scrutinizing and improving their curriculum, self-government, and organization of the collective. Other educational enterprises such as working colonies, recreational centers, and children's playgrounds also helped to establish the core of Soviet pedagogy, its theory and practice.

The experiments and findings of two working colonies for youth, "Gorky" and "Dzerzhinsky," organized by Makarenko, were of special value to Soviet educators and schools, who at that time desperately needed a redirection of their goals and new ways by which to achieve them. The old scholastic education was exclusively subject-matter oriented and, as Lenin maintained, provided the student with infinite knowledge, most of it useless, the rest distorted. Although the school was completely isolated from life, it was impossible to eliminate the whole curriculum indiscriminately, since some parts might prove to be of help in to the building of the Soviet school.

Among the first institutions which came into being shortly after the establishment of the Soviet government were the school communes. In most cases they were located in rural communities, where the securing of provisions was easier. These institutions, regardless of their location, had to emphasize agricultural work, since the food problem, especially acute during the Civil War, was to be self-contained. The city institutions were engaged in industrial work on a much wider scale than the rural school commune. In urban school communes, after securing the doctor's permission, adolescents of fourteen and fifteen years of age were assigned to shops according to their choice, where they worked two hours a day, four times a week, from the middle of October to the beginning of April.

"The whole work experience was divided into three periods: In the first period, the pupil learned to operate his machine and to work independently. In the last week he compared his output with that of other workers. In most cases, the pupil's production was in the range of 70 to 90 per cent of the regular adult quota.

"In the second period, the student worked independently and at the same time learned the theory appropriate to the work he was doing.

"In the third period, machine work stopped. Theory was coordinated with other related facets of life of the industrial plant. At the end of this period there was a final conference and work exhibit."*

The work in the plant or factory was more or less tied to classroom curriculum in the areas of mathematics, physics, chemistry, and biology. The working out of topics related to industry brought about a deeper understanding of the industrial process, machine construction, work organization, and knowledge of special characteristics of manufactured materials. This was all related to polytechnical training.

This vocational education which successfully combined physical and mental work also deserves a great deal of attention. Unfortunately not all city school communes were in direct contact with industry. In most cases, students spent the winter in the city attending school, and the summer working in rural communities. The experience of living in a school commune was very successful. The children learned to live in and for a collective and to appreciate the results of their labor.

The pedagogical collective, consisting of teachers, upbringers, and vocational instructors, organized the day in a way which provided an opportunity for an academic and a vocational curriculum, as well as practical experience in agriculture during the summer and in shops during the winter. The initiative of the children's collective developed greatly. The children's student government dealt with many problems, such as work schedules, celebrations of holidays, behavior of members. In the beginning the economic conditions of the school commune were very difficult.

The role of self-government was very important. Krupskaya and others stress that self-government teaches pupils to appraise their strength and possibilities realistically, to evaluate the meaning and results of their labor, all of which provides them with real life experiences.

Though this is all correct, we should not attempt to substitute

* R. M. Michelson, from "Experience of Vocational Education in the P. N. Lepishinsky School Commune," *Soviet Pedagogue,* 1956, No. 9.

this student school organization for the Pioneer and Komsomol. This great development of self-government in school communes came at the time when the Pioneer and Komsomol movement was still weak.

Makarenko was successful in organizing children in the "Gorky" and "Dzerzhinsky" colonies which were under his leadership. There the collectives were organized on various bases, such as class, chronological age, type of work engaged in. Makarenko suggests that before the collective is well developed, it is advisable to divide the children into small groups of the same chronological age. In exceptional cases younger children may be admitted into older units, "but each case must be individually evaluated before a final decision: under what influence will the youngster find himself, will he be accepted, who is personally responsible for his life and work in the group, and who will take special care of him."*

The primary collectives in the "Dzerzhinsky" commune were composed of heterogeneous groups of youngsters; this was educationally important, since the older boys looked after the younger ones, helping them to assimilate school tradition and good habits in work and life. At the same time the group of older adolescents learned to be attentive to and to take care of others, and they learned "the know how" of setting demands to fulfill collective tasks. This practice took hold in school internats, although in most cases at the beginning the collectives were formed in accordance with assigned sleeping quarters, where, as a rule, a chronologically homogeneous group lived. Later, as the number of older grade pupils grew, the collectives became heterogeneous.

It was important to keep the primary collectives stable, since frequent shifts disrupted the unity among group members and among individual units.

Makarenko was very correct when he wrote: "Because sleeping quarters in a boarding institution offer another situation which can be used to educate for work, housekeeping, and political understanding, they should never be viewed only as dormitories. A group of youngsters sharing a bedroom must be

* A. S. Makarenko, *Collected Works,* Vol. V, 1951, p. 10.

united in: study and work, in progress or failure, in the struggle to achieve goals, in coping with unpleasant occurrences in daily life, and in the growth and success of the whole collective."*

The experience acquired by previous internats, children's homes, and the newly established school internats supports these comments. Collectives based on dormitory and classroom groups proved to be a failure; those created with a common social purpose—such as collectives of carpenters, gardeners, seamstresses—quickly became unified and meaningful.

Makarenko said: "Each action of a pupil, his every success or failure, should be judged as a reflection of the common work quality of the entire collective. . . ."

From the outset, Makarenko always made all tasks very clear to the youngsters, who tried to accomplish them jointly. As a result, the discipline of the youngster became more pronounced, and the responsibility of each individual pupil and the collective continued to grow.

A great deal of attention was given to self-government. At the beginning the commanders of units in the colony were appointed, but later they were elected.

The Komsomol, the pedagogical collective, and the council of the unit leaders participated actively in the nomination, evaluation, and election of a candidate, for a six-month period. It was felt that a longer term was not advisable because of the burden of duties. Also, it was considered important that all pupils have the opportunity for this valuable experience.

Among other duties, the unit leader was a liaison person between the members of the group, the work instructor, and the adult work foreman. Together with the Komsomol leader and physical instructor, he watched the boys in his group follow daily routines, do their school assignment, participate in common work projects, fight negative behavior of individuals in his units, etc. The higher organ of self-government was the general assembly of all pupils which met not less than once a month to discuss problems related to the institutional life: discipline, production, upkeep, cost. Its authority was supported by the administration

* *Ibid.*, p. 12.

and, when wrong decisions were made, the assembly had to repeat its debate. Makarenko wrote: "The leadership of an educational institution must always bear in mind that incorrect decisions arrived at by the general assembly are the direct result of faulty leadership. Factors such as lack of, or too much, concern for the pupils, staff carelessness, negligence, and insufficient preparation beforehand for dealing with the problem are to blame and not the general assembly and quality of its members."*

The council of unit leaders was the central organ of self-government in colonies under Makarenko's supervision. The membership of this governing body included, in addition, chairmen of all committees, the director of the institution, some teachers, the doctor, and the school director. The secretary of Komsomol and the Pioneer leader had the right to be present and to vote on issues under discussion.

The questions of discipline and of reward and punishment are of great importance in the life of school internats. Sometimes the problems are solved incorrectly. Although bourgeois pedagogical discipline is often viewed either as a form of suppression (Herbart) or as a form of natural consequences (Jean Jacques Rousseau), the principle of suffering underlies any punishment. Our Soviet pedagogy solves problems of discipline in a different way. We try to bring about conscious discipline, the significance of which was underlined by Lenin.

In spite of this, we still observe in practice many instances when the school achieves discipline by external means rather than attempting to produce it as an internal choice, which usually is achieved only as a result of a total educational process, first of all by the peer collective in all phases of life. Makarenko said that in the Soviet society discipline is an ethical and political phenomenon. A demand should be placed on the individual to refrain from egotistical behavior harmful to others. Order is the first step in achieving self-discipline; then comes the ability to overcome hindrances and accomplish difficult tasks. Discipline must be placed above all individual interests and be the pride of the collective.

* *Ibid.*, p. 23.

Punishment in the Dzerzhinsky colony had only an educational aim, and therefore was administered exclusively when necessary, meaningful, and when the collective was in favor of it.

The experience of school communes and colonies pointed up the importance work assumed in the life of children and in the task of bringing them up in the Communist spirit. Our school internats must utilize this valuable experience to develop in children the necessary understanding of how meaningful and important work is for the nation and for the building of a Communist society. Long ago it was noticed that in some school internats pupils manifested dependency and demands. Although this was characteristic of the prerevolutionary boarding schools for wealthy children, it may also come about in our school internats when we have not stressed and organized the youngsters' participation in physical labor. This exposure to work is not merely a preparation for life but also a means to develop positive moral attitudes. The sooner the school begins to include children and youth in the real work, the better the chance that they will not develop the negative attitudes and patterns of misbehavior which still plague some of our youth. Although educators made many mistakes, their theory for fostering children's independence and initiative proved to be correct and successful.

On the whole, our schools are making progress in the right direction, but in practice some still are overprotecting the children, and in some cases this practice was transferred to school internats.

The communes and colonies of the Makarenko period accumulated a great deal of experience in many areas of teaching and bringing up children. Our newly created school internats must absorb and utilize this experience, while looking for new ways and methods to meet the changing needs of our society.

## § Problems Related to the Organization of School Internats

When our first school internats were established, the local Soviet agencies had a great deal of initiative in determining their structure. This approach was advisable, since in each case the local agencies established an organization which was most acceptable to them. School internats could be opened not only with lower but also with higher grades. The recommendation stated that creches and kindergartens should also be included in the system of school internats, because it is important that the preschoolers and school age children are brought up together. Most schools which opened in 1956 consisted of the first through the fifth grades.

Although it is too early to draw any final conclusions, the evidence accumulated thus far suggests that new school internats should begin with grades one through seven. An institution exclusively with young children limits its educational work, and does not offer enough opportunities to organize a harmonious working and studying collective.

Of course, it is desirable to take in first of all the young school children, who need and can profit from a carefully planned program, and who, left without supervision, quickly develop bad studying habits, eat and sleep irregularly and, as a result, develop poorly. Also, working parents are more concerned with small children left at home than with older ones. This in part explains why an extended school day for some groups of youngsters is gratefully accepted by parents.

Most school internats have between two and three hundred boarding students and only a few day students, which produces an isolation and exclusivity which is difficult to overcome by executive measures or by combined evenings with other schools. Experience proves that the day students are a positive influence in the school internat collective. Also, offering day school services makes it possible to extend the internat system to a wider regional radius, since in many cases lack of appropriate buildings hampered the spreading of this new educational system.

In practice, the usual population of school internats varies between two and six hundred, not counting day students, who should not exceed one-third of boarding pupils. This situation permits the boarders to become the nucleus and the tone setters of the school life. The role of the student who resides at home is to bring a new and significant element into the life of the internat. At no time should day and boarding pupils be separated, or preference shown to students in residence. They should study, participate in extracurricular activities, and eat together. The meals should be provided at a special pre-arranged fee.

In 1956 and 1957, so many parents and guardians made application to place their children in internats that there were not enough available. Youngsters without parents, or with only one, or whose parents had experienced special hardships, had priority. Before accepting a pupil, the teachers in the school internats became thoroughly acquainted with the child's environment, his previous school record, if any, his behavior, and his other characteristics. Each potential pupil had a complete medical examination. All of this was very helpful to the regional executive committee who had to arrive at an objective and hopefully correct decision, and also to the pedagogical collective who had to design the first steps of their educational work.

Most of the internats which opened were located in schools, pedagogical institutes, or children's homes. They had to be remodeled to fit the new needs; dining facilities and sleeping quarters had to be added. This transition, in spite of temporary difficulties, was accomplished gradually, and the life conditions created for children were good.

Although it would have been more desirable to build entirely new units, existing schools were being utilized at the time because of the time pressure and the tremendous cost involved.

Since one of the main tasks of school internats is to prepare children for life through active participation in industry and through socially useful work, the pedagogical collective must pay special attention to this problem.

In the near future all internats will acquire farms on which experimental work can be conducted in areas such as animal husbandry and horticulture; these farms will also make the school self-sustaining.

The recruitment of teachers for school internats did not present special difficulties. Many of them were very well qualified, had a great deal of experience in schools or in children's institutions, loved children and their profession, and were enthusiastic about the new system. As a result the school internats were staffed with excellent teachers, many of whom were distinguished in their field.

The teachers in the higher grades were graduates of the higher pedagogical institute, while those in lower grades had a secondary pedagogical education.

The curriculum of the school internats did not differ at all from that of the regular secondary day school. Obviously, not all problems were solved immediately; to this day there is much disagreement about the teamwork of vocational and subject matter teachers.

The problem of finding well-qualified upbringers was a more difficult one. Since they had to have a higher education, their experience was confined mainly to older students and they were not prepared to work with younger ones.

In some cases a schism developed between the teachers of subject matter and the upbringers. The director of the institution had the difficult task of synchronizing the efforts of both and only gradually did they become unified as a collective. Seminars and meetings for discussing educational problems, planning programs, and setting uniform demands for children were all helpful in bringing about the unification.

During the first months of work in an internat setting some upbringers did not pay enough attention to "insignificant" details, such as sloppy dressing habits and poor personal hygiene, forgetting the important role these play in personality development.

Obviously, our upbringer is neither a nanny nor a governess, concerned exclusively with good manners and cultural habits. They must influence the spiritual, ethical, mental, and physical development of the child and must guide and supervise the youngster in accordance with tasks set by Soviet pedagogy. Experience in the school internats proved that many educators are poorly prepared to teach children to work in an industry or agriculture and to fulfill their daily chores, as well as to engage the children in extracurricular activities. All of these shortcomings are the result of the emphasis upon subject matter teaching in pedagogical institutes, which neglects other aspects of bringing up youngsters. The pedagogical institutes use nine-tenths of their curriculum in studying subject content, leaving insufficient time and place for studying educational methods.

Recently, with the adoption of a five-year study course, the pedagogical institutes have improved considerably. This change created the possibility for future teachers to become better trained in areas of work, sports, and the arts, and to receive a greater understanding of problems of upbringing and of methods to solve them.

This does not imply that pedagogical institutes need to establish special departments for upbringers. There is no need to prepare upbringers only, since their work contains elements which the teacher needs also. Instead, we need to intensify the preparation of teachers for the task of upbringing. Perhaps it would be advisable to single out a group of students who plan to work in school internats and give them supplementary training in the area of bringing up children.

The teachers already working there should have an intensive in-service training program, which would emphasize all practical aspects of extracurricular activities in the life of a school internat. In many such institutes already in operation, the educators not only share their experience but also learn arts and crafts and absorb the pedagogical heritage of Krupskaya, Makarenko, and others. Great difficulties were experienced while establishing a workable daily schedule. The students of various backgrounds who entered school internats brought with them habit patterns not easy to change. In many schools younger pupils did not fulfill their chores on time, which disturbed the existing routine. In order to alleviate this, special classes were created in which various routines of daily living were taught. The results were very successful.

Since physical fitness fosters normal growth and development, a great deal of attention must be devoted to it. Unfortunately, not all internats realize its significance. The task of the school internats is to develop physically strong and hardened children. Obviously, one cannot immediately create an advanced method of toughening up children, but a foundation, derived from experience of school and home, must be laid now.

Since physical education is very beneficial, an appropriate place is allotted to it in the curriculum.

The task of the school internats is to give a well-rounded general secondary education which would prepare the youngster for life and productive work. The duration of time is identical with that of a regular day school. The number of students in each class should not exceed thirty.

The work in the internats gets better results when the classes are smaller. This was especially important when learning gaps had to be bridged for many new students in order to bring them up to a higher performance and motivation level. Various methods of individual and group tutoring were employed to try to find the best ways to achieve this. Although improvement was marked, the pupils did not always reach the program standards set by the school. School internats had a lot of difficulties in synchronizing the work of teachers and upbringers. The lower grades have one teacher and two upbringers, and this team constitutes the nucleus of the educational collective, upon whom success or failure mainly depends. To develop a common educational philosophy and approach to various practical problems, they have to develop good communication in the basic team and in the all-school collective of educators.

In order to get acquainted with one another's roles, in some internats the upbringers, who were well prepared for it, taught, for example, arts and crafts, while some of their duties, with additional pay, were delegated to the subject matter teacher. Though the teacher is responsible for the curriculum and the upbringer for all extracurricular activities, experience proves that a strict adherence to this separation of functions is useful neither to subject matter teaching nor to child rearing. On the other hand, some differentiation must be retained, in spite of the fact that both staff members have the same basic goal. Whereas in a day school the teacher leans upon parental help, whose influence upon their children is either good or bad, in a school internat situation he has to rely upon support of the upbringer and on the class collective, and must jointly set goals and choose methods for reaching them.

The development of collectivism, camaraderie, friendship, responsibility, and honesty among pupils in school internats is due not only to the accomplishments of upbringers but also to the achievements of Pioneer and Komsomol organizations. There was a concern among educators that the Pioneer and Komsomol movements would duplicate the work of the student council and vice versa, and some teachers suggested that there be no Pioneer or Komsomol units in school internats. Experience proved that this fear was groundless and that the absence of these organizations weakened the political education of pupils. Obviously some duplication is unavoidable. It is harmless.

Naturally, the work of school internats still has many shortcomings. There is no need to be apologetic, since mistakes are unavoidable in any beginning.

The educational collectives, under the capable leadership of Party organization, are able to raise the standards of life and work in school internats and attain greater success in bringing up a generation which deserves to build Communism.

# 12 School Internats After Five Years

*E. I. Afanasenko and I. A. Kairov*

## § Preface

THIS BOOK is written by educators of the Russian Federal Socialist Republic. This book examines five years of experience of school internats, problems related to the organization of the curriculum as well as to the upbringing process. These include political, vocational, physical, and esthetic education, formulation of scientific attitudes and Communist convictions, as well as the development of socially useful activities and conscious discipline. We tried to emphasize the advantages of school internats as a new institution of learning to point out the fatherly concern the Communist Party and the Soviet State exhibit in the process of rearing the younger generation. Our intention was also to summarize the results achieved in school internats between the Twentieth and Twenty-Second Congresses of the Communist Party—in other words, during the past five years.

This is also a story of raising new individuals to become

E. I. Afanasenko and I. A. Kairov, *School Internats After Five Years*, Izd-vo APN, RSFRS, Moscow, 1961, pp. 5-41.

fighters and workers, active participants in the life of the community—potential builders and citizens of a new Communist society.

## § First Recapitulations of the Work of School Internats

*A New Type of Learning Institution*

We are presently at the eve of the Twenty-Second Communist Party Congress, which will accept a program to conclude the building of Communism in our country.

The contemporary period leading toward Communism is characterized by an unusual upsurge of the industrial power of the Socialist society. Consequently, the Party proceeds firmly to materialize Lenin's policy by creating economic, political, and spiritual prerequisites for the continuous transition to Communism and, on the basis of these prerequisites to form the individual as a Communist of tomorrow. Obviously, the task of educating Soviet people, especially youth, becomes, under these conditions, of utmost importance. "The Party considers the education of the growing generation of special significance in this particular stage. . . . Forming the new individual takes place in the process of active participation in the building of Communism, while he develops Communist principles in his economic and social life, under the influence of the Party, state, and social organizations."*

In recent years the Party made some very important decisions. It determined the new direction of the development of our national educational system, emphasizing the strong need for closer ties between school and life. The new school internats play a very important role in bringing about this improvement.

The main pedagogical reason for developing these new institutions was to create a situation in which all educational influences would be combined. This system assures the valuable well-rounded development of personality as well as character

* Program, Communist Party of U.S.S.R., Gospolitizdat, Moscow, 1961, p. 118.

formation of students, who will represent the Communist ideal of the individual and at the same time will be prepared for practical tasks.

These school internats are very important not only educationally but also politically.

The idea of educating children in school internats is not new. The Marxist principles of creating a new Communist society were established in the beginning of the workers' movement and the proletarian fight for liberation. The basic postulate is to educate the children free in governmental institutions as soon as they are no longer in need of continuous maternal care. From the very beginning of the Soviet government, V. I. Lenin paid special attention to this problem. He called kindergartens, creches, and communal dining rooms the "sprouts of Communism." He felt they should be thoughtfully fostered so as to free the woman from household chores and provide her with an opportunity to participate in industrial work. The idea of a whole day, year-round school became very popular among Marxist educators. Many institutions for children, such as kindergartens, creches, school-communes, experimental pedagogical institutions, childrens' colonies, and finally homes for children without parents, were created.

Children's institutions, headed by Makarenko and S. T. Shatzky, became the base for the Soviet school system and Soviet pedagogy. These creative experiences still retain their value, providing hundreds of thousands of Soviet teachers with meaningful guidance in the area of child rearing.

However, these were only the initial steps on the road to building a universal system of communal education. Obviously, this could become fully implemented only under contemporary conditions, when our country has developed all the necessary material needs as well as the spiritual prerequisites to solve this tremendous task. The U.S.S.R. maintains Socialist economy and organization of work while poverty and unemployment become completely eliminated. The Soviet state has enormous material wealth at its disposal. Therefore, highly qualified teachers and upbringers are able to solve successfully the task of raising children as active builders and citizens of the Communist society.

It would be impossible to overestimate the pedagogical and political consequences of the new school internats. The continuous concern of the state assures their excellent conditions to educate as well as bring up children, to provide an opportunity for a well-rounded development—intellectual, mental, physical, ethical and esthetic—in a collective. Hundreds of thousands of families are reassured about their children and their future.

The system of school internats is growing continuously. Five years have passed since this movement was initiated. Now the educators have to report to the Twenty-Second Congress of the Communist Party about their practical achievements as well as problems they encountered.

The first results of broadening the net of school internats are very characteristic. The seven-year plan, 1959–1965, to develop the national economy, anticipates that by 1965, 2½ million students in U.S.S.R. will be in these schools. During the five years after the Twentieth Congress of the Communist Party, 1990 school internats were established, with a total student population of 500,000. In the last two years the number of school internats increased fourfold, and the number of pupils five times.

The phenomenon of school internats is increasing rapidly in the Russian Socialist Federated Soviet Republic:

| | *School Internats* | *Pupils* |
|---|---|---|
| RSFSR 1956 | 184 | 35,000 |
| 1961 | 1,000 | 350,000 |
| Ukraine 1961 | 379 | 126,000 |
| Azerbaidzhan 1961 | 50 | (4 schools in 1956) |
| Latvia 1961 | 26 | (5 schools in 1956) |

In the last three years the government used, for building dormitories alone, 61 million rubles [$1.10 equals 1 ruble, monetary reform January 1960], which provide space for an additional 231,000 placements; during the current year some 3000 new places will be secured. The percentage of total expenditures for school buildings and equipment is ever growing.. For example: 1959, 14.1 per cent; 1960, 26.3 per cent; 1961, 32.1 per cent.

It is safe to assume that only a Socialist state can afford such high expenditures for education and such a rapid increase. Not only urban communities but also rural ones are fast increasing the numbers of school internats, many of which are built at the expense of the *kolkhozes.*

For the first time in the history of the Soviet educational system, there are institutions of learning which encompass widely diversified age groups under one roof. These school internats provide the youngster with learning experiences from the time he is one year old up to the period of completing secondary schooling and choosing a profession at seventeen years of age.

The plan of the party and of the government is to establish a sufficient number of school internats to enable every parent, who desires, to place his children there.

Though the work done in this area is tremendous, quite a few shortcomings still remain. The tempo of construction lags behind plans. There are many instances when, in an attempt to fulfill the plan, the local department of education issues permits for school internats without the necessary teaching equipment. Some problems inherent in the educational process of school internats are as yet not clearly understood, while the positive experience remains neither sufficiently analyzed nor properly used.

### *School Internats Assure a High Level of General Educational Preparation of Students*

The establishment of any educational institution is a complex and lengthy process, especially when its program calls for total life organization of the attending students—which includes their work, learning, studying, recreation, and rest. These pupils, who come from various families and schools, with a different degree of preparation, and who often do not acquire regular study habits while remaining under the undesirable influence of the street, represent not only a great challenge but also hard educational work for teachers and pedagogues.

It would be unwise to deny that these difficulties do exist. The experience of some of the outstanding schools proves that low achievement can be raised by creating a conducive environment, such as properly supervised study periods.

Children find themselves under continuous guidance and control of teacher and upbringers, who have an opportunity to learn a lot about the youngsters' personality and subsequently use the proper individual approach and render help when needed. School internats create favorable opportunities to tie learning closer to life, while having practical experiences in building Communism.

This continuous control of the quality of learning provides an opportunity to discover learning problems early and to help students individually who lag behind. Another important contributing factor is the team effort of teacher and upbringer to bring about good studying habits in pupils.

Krupskaya wrote: "In order to teach children to use a living, vivid language, they must first be taught to observe." In school internats the upbringers have unlimited opportunities to follow this suggestion to develop their alertness and train their memory.

There are many serious problems related to the curriculum in the middle grades, fifth to eighth, as well as in senior grades, ninth through eleventh. Though it is still difficult to recommend a uniform method (the need for which is rather questionable), it is important to establish basic principles which would underline further improvements in the curriculum.

The schools must definitely overcome their shortcomings, relying upon the positive experience of those who have succeeded in solving them. The main weakness among them is the overstructured curriculum, especially the study period, which should be left entirely to the discretion of the student. Perhaps this was justifiable during the first years when a great number of children needed constant attention and supervision, but now it is inexcusable to convert the time allotted for independent study into additional lessons. Unfortunately, this practice is still in existence in many places.

Obviously, it is much more complicated to organize students to work on home assignments than to do supervised work in the classroom. Space, books, and implements needed must be found for every student, and the teacher or upbringer must make himself available for consultation when requested by the student. It should not be forgotten that developing independence in school children is of great significance for their future life. Many of them, after completing eight grades, will go directly to work in industry; they will receive their future education through corresponding and technical schools, combining studies with industrial work.

Favorable conditions in school internats foster the teaching of foreign languages. The accumulated experience in various schools proves that all school internats can achieve good results. The Council of Ministers of the U.S.S.R. decided in a special resolution to change the teaching of the native language to a foreign one in school internats where there were qualified teachers. Of course, not all, but quite a few subjects were instructed in a different language. This greatly improves the teaching method of foreign languages in schools, especially in school internats. In this way, graduates of most school internats must and will acquire fluency in a foreign language.

### *Vocational Preparation*

One of the main tasks of school internats is to educate children through direct work experiences. It is important not only to teach them to work but also to foster in them good practical habits. The new generation must become psychologically ready to consider labor an organic necessity.

There is a real danger of developing overdependency in the youngsters attending schools on full governmental scholarships. Socially meaningful work proves to be the best method of successfully combatting this danger. By now each school internat has organized all of its daily chores into self-service. Students participate actively in all phases of their life in the school, providing the major labor force. But this is not enough. The school internat must take part in various socially meaningful labor endeavors, such as building parks, squares, villages, cities, and engage in agriculture and industry.

Naturally, students of school internats in small cities or in working settlements do not have many specialties available and, consequently, the principle of voluntary choice is unavoidably affected. Perhaps a plan should be worked out whereby students of the ninth grade have an opportunity to change schools in order to specialize in the field they desire, even if such schools are located outside the district.

There are instances when children become overloaded with work tasks to the detriment of their studies. Teachers and upbringers do not always consider the physical abilities of pupils, especially those in primary grades, when assigning hard and long-lasting physical tasks. Any work must reinforce the health of children, not endanger it. It is important to remember that while the youngster is growing he needs a thoughtful approach, and it is equally wrong to pamper and indulge him as it is to overload him with physical tasks. Obviously, the physician must participate in organizing work programs.

Work remuneration creates a serious pedagogical problem in the school internats. Some schools make grave mistakes by reimbursing the students at an early age when their work is still not very productive and does not bring much gratification. Subsequently, the money involved induces interest in such work, and may even bring about egotism and mercenary motivation.

In view of collective and individual principles of reimbursement, the child's work must be appraised wisely. There is no doubt about the educational value of contributing the earnings to a fund of the collective, as well as its rights to manage and dispose of the money. On the other hand, one should not entirely deny any possibility of individual reimbursement. As they grow older, they want to contribute to the family budget, and they should not be deprived of this opportunity.

Some school directors have established a very fair practice whereby the students receive a certain percentage of their earned wages. Active participation of students in socially meaningful work fosters favorable conditions for their ideological growth, without which work cannot bring positive results. Makarenko wrote, "You may force any man to work as much as you want, but as long as you do not educate him politically and ethically, and as long as he does not participate in the political and social life of the collective his work will remain a neutral process, without valuable accomplishments."*

* A. S. Makarenko, *Collected Works,* Vol. 5, p. 116.

*Ideological Education*

The task of fostering in the young generation conscientious attitudes toward community obligations, concern for the environment, and impatience with shortcomings is especially significant.

Explicit, convincing words, a good movie, impressive radio programs, together with a practical activity for children, are of great help in the process of ethical upbringing.

"Since Socialism," wrote Krupskaya, "is a particular organization, it is of special value to children to become exposed in school to some organizational experience."*

The school should not artificially protect youth from difficulties they will encounter later in life and in work and it should not take away from young people any responsibility for their work, behavior, and actions. The educators must continuously explain to their students that under Communism there is no place for a life of leisure where idleness and inertia rule.

Makarenko points out that the children's collective, independent in character, must be viewed not only as an educational occurrence but also as a phenomenon of communal life, just like any other collective.

Though our country has created the most favorable conditions to develop political maturity in youth, there is still some striving to protect our youth constantly, a fear of allowing them freedom of action, without which self-education, responsibility, and independence cannot be developed.

It is now time to abolish the "lock up" system in school internats. The life of Soviet people establishes new relationships as well as new forms of organization. The society manifests its growing trust in people by continuously increasing self-service without supervision in buses, trolley cars, dining rooms, and stores. These occurrences illustrate explicitly the new Communist organization of society. Since we wish to educate the citizens of the future Communist society in school internats, new forms of social relationships must begin to take roots in this situation also. Everything must always remain open to children: libraries, reading

* N. K. Krupskaya, *Selected Pedagogical Works,* 1955, p. 192.

halls, shops, recreation rooms, and responsibility for the equipment and materials transferred to the students' collective.

Reinforcement of scientifically atheistic attitudes in children should take place in the classroom as well as outside of it. All opportunities to expose the antiscientific essence of religious beliefs should be utilized.

School internats are also called upon to cultivate esthetic education in children. In the better schools esthetics permeate the life of the entire internat collective. The esthetic education of a child is closely related to his upbringing, his ideology, and his aspirations and actions.

### *Daily Schedule*

A sound daily schedule, with blocks of time for work, study, rest, and recreation, is extremely important. Each school follows the recommendations of the Academy of Pedagogical Sciences, which are supported by appropriate medical findings. More attention should be given to the organization of the inner life of the school internat, where the collective of children must become one family. We must still search for more creative methods which would combine wisely certain degrees of organizational regulations with an atmosphere of family comfort.

### *Together with Family and with Society*

The creation of school internats by no means releases parents from their duty toward their children. The state assures all necessary conditions for a free, well-rounded academic as well as practical vocational education, but the family retains its right to raise the children and to be responsible for their destiny.

In a Socialist society, the relationship between school and family is distinguished by limitless opportunities for their close cooperation. In the *Communist Manifesto*, Marx and Engels reply sharply to bourgeois ideologists, accusing the Communists of intending to destroy the family. They wrote: "You state that we want to destroy the most precious human relationships by substituting education in the family by that of the society. But is not your education also determined by society or, in other words, by the social relationships in which you rear the children, as well as by direct and indirect interference of society through your schools? Communists do not invent the influence of society upon raising children, they only change the character of upbringing by snatching it out of the hands of the ruling class."*

The school internats do not isolate parents from their children. The children are placed there only voluntarily, and they meet with parents regularly during their day off and during holidays, as well as during school vacations. Consequently, the educational influence of parents does not stop, it only changes its form. The teachers also turn to parents when the need arises. They get to know each other in the school and during teachers' home visits. The better the upbringers know the family, the more successful is their influence upon the child.

It is very important for the school to propagandize systematically content, principles, and methods of Communist upbringing of children under conditions existing in school internats. It is also advisable to explain to the parents the educational policy of the Communist Party and of the Soviet government to help them, to organize the life of their children correctly while they are at home, and to enlist parents' assistance to the school.

The cooperation of parents with the school begins before the school opens. The upbringers visit the homes of future students in order to acquaint themselves with the conditions of their life.

Many schools wisely conduct series of lectures for parents before the children enroll. They discuss goals, the role of parents in rearing children, work education in school and at home, and daily routines.

### *Teachers and Upbringers*

At the present time the Russian Socialist Federated Soviet Republic employs 35,000 teachers and upbringers. While their number is steadily increasing, the demands placed upon them are growing. The local department of education, as well as the party and professional organizations, must continue their ongoing concern for selection, placement, and increasing qualifications of the entire professional staff in school internats.

Pedagogical science must render serious help to educational

* K. Marx and F. Engels, *Collected Works*, Vol. 4, p. 443.

practitioners. This is channeled through the Academy of Pedagogical Sciences of RSFSR, departments of pedagogy and psychology in universities and in pedagogical institutes and teachers' colleges. They conduct research on a broad scale in various problem areas related to teaching and upbringing in school internats. Last year, by a decree of the Central Committee of the Communist Party of RSFSR and of the Council of Ministers of RSFSR, the Academy of Pedagogical Sciences established laboratory schools.

In the year 1961-1962 the laboratory schools will deal with the most important problem in school internats, namely, with solving the dilemma of selection of the student body. It is well known that these schools often accept pupils who are scholastically poor and undisciplined. Though we are not in favor of selecting only the best students, and desire an average sampling of a variety of students as in any regular day school, it is incorrect to recruit backward pupils primarily. The laboratory school is also searching for an educational curriculum and upbringing methods which are most appropriate in the setting of the new school system, especially highlighting problems such as home assignments, overloading children with curriculum, education for work, and organization of children's self-government.

The laboratory scientific researchers, together with the actively participating teachers and upbringers, make efforts to improve teaching and the quality of learning while trying to diminish the academic load. This research and its practical implementation must be coordinated, while concentrating most on acute problems of further developing school internats as new scientifically educational institutions.

The best pedagogical experience must be popularized even more extensively than it is now. Recently many materials have appeared which deal with work in school internats. Among them are over two hundred books, an abundance of articles in newspapers and magazines, and the Journal *School Internat,* which appears regularly.

The school internats obviously demonstrated their educational advantages in a short time span and proved that without doubt they are the prototype of the school of the future.

Foreign educators and social workers view our new schools

with a great deal of skepticism. The bourgeois press clamored that we Communists tear the children away from the family, that school internats are established to educate the Bolshevik elite, and that by conditioning children early to work we deprive them of their childhood. But five years have passed. Many foreign educators, journalists, and others have visited them and have had an opportunity to observe the new system in action. As a result, they are very enthusiastic. One American journalist remarked during her visit to school internat 12 in Moscow, "Happy faces of children are the highest testimonial for any pedagogical institution."

The school internats, our exemplary learning institutions, continue to grow under the watchful eye and warm concern of the Party and of the nation.

*Part Four*

# *Children's Literature*

The main purpose for including this section is to throw light upon the controversy which existed between the proponents and foes of the right of children to be exposed to fairy tales. Obviously, its impact upon the upbringing of children in the Soviet Union was very great and its significant effect can still be felt. The writings of Kornei Ivanovich Chukovsky and N. K. Krupskaya were chosen because they illuminate the opposing points of view in this controversy.

Kornei Ivanovich Chukovsky, a prominent philologist, poet, and writer of prose, includes among his readers children of all ages as well as adults. Among his writings are fairy tales, poetry, literary criticisms, memoirs, philological essays and books, as well as novels. He is not only a writer but also a translator, who brought Mark Twain, Walt Whitman, and Rudyard Kipling to the Russian reader. It is his gift to see everyday occurrences as something unusual, exciting, and fresh. It is this quality that makes his writings so alive for children and adults alike, no matter what medium he uses to express himself, and no matter what topic he chooses to talk about.

In 1962, Kornei Chukovsky received on his eightieth birthday the most coveted literary award in the Soviet Union, the Lenin Prize. This was for his book *Nekrasov As a Craftsman.* During his visit to England that year he received an Honorary Degree from Oxford University for his contributions to the field of philology, in which he holds a Doctorate.

By now a living legend, he has become an integral part of

the lives of Soviet children through his defense of their right to fairy tales.

In the next section of this book, there is a broader discussion of N. K. Krupskaya and her significance in the development of Soviet philosophies of education and upbringing. Hence, we emphasize here only her role as the outstanding official opponent of the fairy tale.

The poem "The Magic Tree" is a free translation by Helen and Fritz Redl, approved by Chukovsky. "In Defense of Fairy Tales" from the book *From Two to Five,* is a summarized paraphrase of the original chapter, which has also been approved by Chukovsky. This form of presentation of the material was used since it is impossible to render in translation the beauty of his poetry and uniqueness of his prose. These authorizations were the result of consultations between the author and the translator in the Soviet Union in 1963.

# 13 Children's Literature

## *Selections from N. K. Krupskaya and K. I. Chukovsky*

## BASIC DEMANDS FOR CHILDREN'S BOOKS

### *N. K. Krupskaya*

The committee on children's books appointed by the Academy of Pedagogical Sciences worked out the following criteria for children's books, which the collegium affirmed (December 23, 1926).

1. A great quantity of children's books inherited from the old system are unacceptable to us, because of their contradiction with our new educational tasks. We are accepting the most valuable literature of the past and discarding such books that preach passivity, acceptance of evil, etc.

2. The standards for children's books must be equal to those set for adult literature.

3. We consider fantastic fairy tales harmful since they hamper the child's efforts to investigate his environment, develop his superstition and fear, build up unhealthy fantasies, and dull his

N. K. Krupskaya, 1927. Reprinted in N. K. Krupskaya, *Pedagogical Works,* Izd-vo APN, RSFSR, Moscow, 1959, Vol. 6, pp. 75-79, 256-259.

sense of reality. Animal stories are permitted as an artistic method, at the age when the child has already established a clear, realistic concept of the animal kingdom.

4. Children's books should be divided as follows:

a. Books for three to four year olds. Use only the immediate environment (different books for children in rural and urban communities). Picture books are the best desirable form. Illustrations must be realistic, in bright colors, representing people, objects, and animals not personified. The text accompanying the picture, if any, must be brief, simple, and in direct relationship to the picture above.

b. Books for five to seven year olds. In content the book must deal with the child's environment, helping him to broaden his understanding of it. It should cover already existing realistic relationships between objects, since at that age the child begins to show interest in them. It is important to foster children's fascination with life, and to stimulate their engagement in collective games. At this age illustrations play a very important role. The accompanying text is designed for reading aloud to children. The quality of the language read is very significant to the youngster, since it becomes one of the ways to enrich his vocabulary. Any imitation of the child's way of speaking is inexcusable. It must be the regular adult language, simplified on the level of the child's comprehension. When presenting poems (in moderation), they must have good form (rhymes, rhythm, and meter).

c. Books for eight to twelve year olds. At this age the book is very important. Though the youngsters have various interests, in general they are all directed toward the interrelationships between people. People become the center of attention for children in this age group. They have not yet formed their social criteria, and are still defenseless in this respect. Most important are books which are full of life content. The plot must be interesting, and the action fast moving. Ten to twelve year olds are fascinated by novels dealing with social problems and struggles. They must understand what we are fighting for. Fables and ideas at this age level must be presented in a simple and uncomplicated way.

d. Books for Adolescents. In addition to the above-mentioned material, it is pertinent to provide this age group with content which would deal in depth with problems and topics presented to them at the ten to twelve year age level. Of great importance to an adolescent are criticism and evaluation of social occurrences. He often ponders questions such as morals, individual relationships between people and collective. Biographies of famous people stimulate his striving for self-improvement. The lives of people should be presented against the background of social movement to avoid personality cults.

They are fascinated by man's fight with and conquest of nature. They must know the achievements of science in various fields and gain in perspective. "Do It Yourself" books of a technical nature are also important to youngsters in this age group.

# BOOKS APPROPRIATE FOR PRESCHOOLERS

## *N. K. Krupskaya*

In order to produce books appropriate for a given age, writers of children's books must know the vocabulary as well as other characteristics of the particular stage of development of the age for which they are writing.

For very young children, the story or fable plot must at all times remain very simple and include few people and objects. The environment must be one which is familiar to the child. Preschoolers in the four to six year age group need basically the same treatment of objects and people, though the content may be broadened and presented more dynamically, but it must still deal with the child's surroundings. Topics which are far away from him have no meaning as yet, and therefore people and occurrences should be taken directly out of real life situations he already knows.

The selection of fairy tales must be done carefully, avoiding frightening stories which overstimulate youngsters, i.e., witches, devils, etc. It is important to bear in mind that most of them are

N. K. Krupskaya, written in the period 1926-1932. Reprinted in N. K. Krupskaya, *Pedagogical Works,* Izd-vo APN, RSFSR, Moscow, 1962, Vol. 10, pp. 220-222.

saturated with petty bourgeois psychology. It is not frightening to hear stories about talking animals, since the child knows they cannot talk. Fairy tales which enlighten the child's concept of reality are good. Those which confuse him and foster his selfish interests are bad. Anderson's fairy tales are for older children.

Even the older children in a preschool group have trouble with abstract literary concepts. They often do not grasp the meaning of death. They have a need for concrete forms of explanation. While we attempt to widen youngsters' horizons and build their materialistic point of view and Communist morals, we must bear in mind that the children cannot yet conceptualize abstractions.

# THE MAGIC TREE

## *K. I. Chukovsky*

Once upon a time, long long ago, I knew a man who had many children. And for each of them he had to buy shoes. But he had little money and often the children had to run around barefoot or in old, torn, worn out shoes.

I was this man and I got so tired of spending all the money I had for children's shoes, galoshes, rubbers and boots, that out of desperation, to console myself, I finally invented this fairy tale.

At our gate—you see?
Right there, just look,
The Magic Tree.
Magic, magic, gorgeous one,
O gorgeous Magic Tree!

It has no leaves,
It bears no fruit,
But look—a stocking!
Look—a boot!

O, Mother, Mother,
Come and see!
Pluck shoes and boots
From the Magic Tree.

Now father, too,
comes out to reap.
He puts the harvest in a heap.
Look!
Snow boots for Masha
Boots for Zena,
And stockings for Nina!

And for Mourochka?

K. I. Chukovsky, *The Magic Tree and Other Fairy Tales*, Uchpedgiz, Minsk, 1959, pp. 49-50.

Knitted slippers,
Tiny, blue . . .
And with a pom-pom, too!

O, what a treat,
You wonder tree!

Come, all you children,
Come and see!
Your heels are bare?
Your snowshoes rot?
You need new shoes?
This is the spot!

Your boots are ripe,
Your shoes are done.
Stop loafing now,
Come, pluck them, run!

Are you too poor?
Come, pluck a shoe.
Your feet are bare?
Pluck stockings, too!
This is the end
of mended holes,
of biting frost,
of barefoot soles. . . .

# BOOK REVIEW OF CHUKOVSKY'S "THE MAGIC TREE"*

## *N. K. Krupskaya*

What does this fairy tale by Chukovsky mean to an adult?

There are Mashas, Tanyas, and others who receive from the wonder tree—the Soviet government—fancy slippers with bows. There are poor, barefoot children who get only sandals and boots from the government.

Youngsters, on the other hand, will believe that now, just as in the past, children are divided into rich and poor, barefoot and not barefoot.

They will also think that only a miracle can provide them with shoes, but since there are no miracles, there will be no shoes.

Children do not need this nonsense. I find all these very silly fairy tales disturbing and irritating. I think that "The Magic Tree" should not be reprinted.

Moscow, 1926

* The part of this book review by Krupskaya referring to Chukovsky's other fairy tale, "The Slipper," has been omitted here, since this poem was not included in this selection.

N. K. Krupskaya, reprinted in *Pedagogical Works*, Vol. 10, Moscow, 1962, p. 220.

# "IN DEFENSE OF FAIRY TALES," *FROM TWO TO FIVE*

## *K. I. Chukovsky*

The year was 1929. Chukovsky was visiting a group of sick children in a Crimean sanitorium. Sensing their restlessness he began to read aloud to them the *Adventures of Muenchhausen.* The delighted children laughed loudly. Suddenly they were interrupted by the director of the institution, who explained that Soviet children should not be exposed to fantasy and fairy tales. In no uncertain terms the director led him to understand that neither he nor his book about Baron Muenchhausen were welcome there.

Chukovsky never guessed that this incident would start a fight which would continue for more than thirty years. It initiated a struggle between Chukovsky and many pedagogues, the gist of which was, should Soviet children retain their right to have fairy tales as a part of their childhood education? Chukovsky believes that fantasy is the most valuable characteristic of the human mind, and as such needs cultivation from a very early age, because it stimulates imagination and creativeness.

Among the most outspoken foes of the fairy tale was E. Stanchenskaya, noted Moscow educational specialist, who lost no opportunity to express her point of view publicly. She strongly supported the publication of a pamphlet "Fairy Tale as a Factor of Class Education," the main premise of which was the fairy tale is dangerous for Soviet children. As noted by Chukovsky, it is interesting that the son of this educator, having no contact with written fairy tales, began daydreaming, as his mother recorded in her diary.

Chukovsky is convinced that in many games children invent fairy tales and at the same time act them out. Their desire to believe their tale is so great that any attempt of adults to confront them with reality is met with strong protest. Not only games but

K. I. Chukovsky, *From Two Till Five*, Detgiz, Moscow, 1961, pp. 185-220. This material was translated into the third person at the request of the author.

even youngsters' conversations prove their imaginary interpretation of the surroundings, i.e., "When does the alarm clock sleep?" "Does the needle hurt the stocking?"

Fortunately, the efforts of Soviet pedagogues to deprive young children of fairy tales are almost never successful, since the child manages intuitively to sneak them into his life "illegally." In self-defense many children invent imaginary playmates, often animals. This is generally considered a normal occurrence in this age group.

Chukovsky quotes F. M. Dostoyevsky who, shortly before his death, defended the necessity to foster children's imagination and fantasy by exposing them to fairy tales. Addressing himself to a parent: "You claim that fear to develop your daughter's fantasy prompted you to forbid her reading any literary stories. I think this approach is definitely incorrect. Fantasy is a natural human strength which gains special priority over all other talents and abilities during early childhood years. Not satisfying this need of children results either in killing their imagination or in overstimulating its growth out of proportion, which becomes harmful because of its tendency to tax the child prematurely. When children receive information they do not understand and are not ready for, they change it to fit their concepts, as if saying, 'Don't rush me into an adult way of thinking, because I will have to change it into my way, that of fantasy and imagination.' "*

The child deprived of *Adventures of Muenchhausen, Gulliver's Travels,* and *The Little Humpbacked Horse,* says Chukovsky, subconsciously compensates by improvising his own stories full of fantasy, which defeats the goal of pedagogues who deprive him of folk and literary fairy tales. The fairy tale does not vanish from the child's life. It only changes its character from national and literary to primitive, accidentally self-invented.

The authorities setting standards for children's reading material did not seriously consider the possibility of utilizing the fairy tale in its classical form, which is hundreds of years old, as a method to reinforce and enrich the children's creative imagination and fantasy. At the same time, however, they accept the

* Fyodor M. Dostoyevsky, *Letters,* Vol. IV, 1959, p. 196. (Letter to N. L. Ozmidov, August 18, 1888.)

boldest scientific fiction of yesterday as today's reality. We must create a new generation of inspired inventors and dreamers in all fields of human endeavor, says Chukovsky, because without fantasy the pure sciences will become stagnant.

Many Soviet pedagogues have attempted to stigmatize fantasy, claiming it hampers the development of realism in children's minds.

Only people who do not know children would claim that a fairy tale may impair the child's ability to cope with practical life problems, says their famous defender. They view each children's book as a tool which must immediately produce tangible, useful results. They fear fantasy and imagination though they themselves as revolutionaries were dreamers out of touch with the reality that prevailed around them. Their claims that fairy tales are harmful is the most nonsensical fib of all, without any factual support. The only fairy tale we must fight against is the myth created by backward pedagogues. They don't realize that questions such as "How could she breathe if she had no lungs?" or "How could the witch fly on a broomstick without a propeller?" indicate that children are able to orient themselves in their environment, while enriching their imagination.

A grandmother is telling her granddaughter: "He hit the ground and was turned into a falcon." "That is not true," replies the indignant girl. "He just got a bump on his forehead, and that is all."

Chukovsky believes that fairy tales and fables are the best nourishment for children up to the age of seven or eight. They are not "just sweets, but necessary bread," and nobody has the right to deprive them of this food.

The hope that the fairy tale was to regain its important role in the lives of Soviet children grew strong in 1934, especially after Gorky officially came to its defense during the first national meeting of Soviet writers. Many who previously opposed fantasy stories changed sides. Books like *Adventures of Muenchhausen, Hiawatha, Pushkin's Poems, The Little Humpbacked Horse,* and other such stories once again appeared in the bookstores. But it was too early to rejoice. Soon after Chukovsky retold the Greek myth of Perseus, Andromeda, and Medusa in the magazine *YEZH,* the editor received a letter from a school director who stated that his students asked why "this kind of nonsense is printed in a children's magazine. . . . How can one explain to youngsters the incongruity of these ridiculous episodes saturated with superstitution? I think this fable has neither literary merit nor artistic beauty. A. Rappoport."

There are many different ways of introducing this disputed material to the children, but of course this is possible only when the teacher is erudite. When he lacks the necessary information and knowledge, the unfortunate children become exposed to and incited by his prejudice against extremely valuable art creations of which he is ignorant. Furthermore, he also makes a nuisance of himself by writing complaints and protestations to editors of children's magazines.

These ridiculous attacks, under the pretense of demagogical arguments, hide underneath the ignorance of the inventors of this fib.

Chukovsky discusses this letter at length, because he feels this educator uses semirevolutionary slogans to inhibit and distort the literary development of Soviet children.

Chukovsky recalls that while the enemies of fairy tales became less vocal in Leningrad and in Moscow, they still rage in the periphery. Each time the *Children's Literary Press* or the *Young Guard* publishes a children's edition of *Hiawatha* or *Just-So Stories* or *Poems of Pushkin* or *Muenchhausen,* these suppressors of childhood scream, "The revolution is in danger!" and they run to defend the revolution from Pushkin and his poems!

Soon after the new publication of *Adventures of Muenchhausen,* with Chukovsky's interpretation, reached the public, the following open letter was sent to him in care of the newspaper *Communistic Education:*

> Comrade Chukovsky!
> I bought the book *Adventures of Muenchhausen* as a birthday gift for my seven-year-old daughter without reading it previously, since I had no time, and the cover sign indicated "for children." The surprise and also disappointment of my daughter and myself was great when we began to read it together. The excessive lies of this braggart are very confusing to children. For example, his

> head is chopped off and then sewn onto his body again; he flies to the moon, but does not describe its surface, which, though imaginary, might have proven to be of interest to youngsters. He insists that he climbs up on the moon with the help of a bean-stalk and then glides down a straw cord. The presentation of moon inhabitants and their life is sheer nonsense! Muenchhausen's description of Ceylon and his adventures there are just as absurd. At times the book forced the child to laugh while she exclaimed, "What lies!" I think most of his adventures she did not comprehend. I'm interested to find out what was the purpose of translating this book, Comrade Chukovsky!
>
> C. D. Kovalova, Library Supervisor
> (Viazniky, Ivanov Region)

Although he became accustomed to letters like this, he was saddened to discover that she was a librarian. Too bad that in spite of her profession she never heard of Muenchhausen. Of course, he did not argue with Comrade Kovalova, who thinks that, in spite of her ignorance, she qualifies as a judge of good and bad children's books.

This letter presents an excellent example of the demagogy which not so long ago saturated criticisms of children's literature with poison and with which Chukovsky was confronted.

By now it is common knowledge, says Chukovsky, that the fairy tale enriches, improves, and fosters the child's development. While a youngster listens attentively to a story, he identifies himself strongly with its heroes who fight bravely and persistently for a just cause, and this constitutes its basic educational value. No one of these days is fearful of fairy tales and folklore. The children's publications produce a large amount of Ukrainian, Chinese, Indian, and Roumanian tales, as well as French, German, Dutch, and others. Since in general this premise is already fully accepted, attention must be transferred to individual stories and legends which may or may not be harmful to Soviet children. Since the Soviet educators say that their experience in bringing up children has not yet produced scientific principles which would define harmful as well as beneficial influences of various types of fairy tales, this void provides an opportunity for arbitrary public judgment. To illustrate this point, he quotes the following comments in a letter discussing the libretto of the children's opera, "The Chatterbox-Fly."*

> Fairy tales of this kind should not be made into operas, nor should they be written. This story creates in the child empathy for the innocently suffering fly, the "brave" mosquito, and other such parasites. While we have a systematic campaign to exterminate all these parasites, some writers strive through their work to create a feeling of sympathy for them.

When the *Literary Gazette* rejected this letter the writer complained to the higher authority. The result was that the letter found itself in the Children's Literature Section of the Writers' Guild. Chukovsky believes each reader is entitled to criticize a writer's work any way he pleases but, when he arrives at false opinions, the writer has the prerogative to defend the truth.

To Chukovsky's surprise, who thought that the struggle for fairy tales was over, the Committee on children's literature replied in the name of the "National Writers' Guild" as follows:

"The question you raise is a correct one. Unfortunately, some of our writers of fairy tales actually make mistakes, bestowing positive, heroic characteristics upon harmful and dangerous beasts, birds, and insects."

According to this approach, Chukovsky claims that even Pushkin's tale about Tsar Sultan, in which the mosquito is treated sympathetically, or Tolstoy's story about the bear conquering children's hearts, would be banned.

This all happened a few years ago. The present members of the committee for children's books are new and are in no way responsible for the above-described action, though this does not imply that the fight to assure the Soviet children's right to fairy tales is ended.

Chukovsky says the aim of the story teller is to develop in the child, no matter how difficult this may be, humanness—the

* "The Chatterbox-Fly" (a fairy tale in verse), by K. I. Chukovsky. A story about a mosquito who rescues a fly from a spider's grip and then marries her.

marvelous ability to empathize with other people in their fortunes and misfortunes. Fairy tales teach one from early childhood to participate, by the magic of make believe, in the imaginary lives of human beings and animals. This helps him to avoid narrow-mindedness and egocentrism. The child becomes accustomed to taking sides with heroes of worthwhile causes, and learns to identify with the underprivileged, the helpless, and the unfairly treated. Only with these characteristics can a man grow to become a beautiful, sensitive human being, a Chekhov, a Gorky, a Nekrasov. . . .

Before the 1961 edition of *From Two to Five* went into print, the feeling of the editor, as well as Chukovsky, was that the chapter "In Defense of the Fairy Tale" was outdated and therefore should be eliminated. Before they managed to act upon this, however, the *Literary Gazette* received an indignant letter objecting to the new edition of "The Chatterbox Fly." The main objection of the author (an historian) was the distortion of facts of nature—such as a mosquito cannot marry a fly!

There are many other fairy tales in which human beings change into animals, and vice versa. In fact, says Chukovsky, the entire folklore is saturated with such occurrences (i.e., Nursery Rhymes, *Winnie-the-Pooh, Gulliver's Travels, Alice in Wonderland*), but neither children nor adults, while enjoying these fantasy stories, question "the unnatural state of affairs in fairyland" nor do they they find it offensive. However, it should be added that the letters in favor of fairy tales far outnumber those opposed to them.

This letter indicated to Chukovsky and his editor that, unfortunately, the chapter "In Defense of Fairy Tales" still has a great deal of validity, and as such must remain in its pertinent place in the book.

## Part Five

# Pioneers

It is impossible to comprehend fully the contemporary system of Soviet education without tracing its beginnings and knowing about those responsible for the new system. An outstanding Soviet educator who left a heavy imprint upon its philosophical thoughts and practical implementations was the wife of Lenin, Nadezhda Konstantinovna Krupskaya (1869-1939). She and Makarenko remain the most quoted authorities on education in the U.S.S.R. Among her many achievements, Krupskaya was instrumental in organizing Oktyabryata, the Pioneers, and the Komsomol.

The Pioneers, a children's movement designed to select and prepare youngsters for their subsequent membership in Komsomol, was organized by Komsomol in 1922.

In an open letter Krupskaya said: "The Komsomol must strongly influence the children and adolescents to continue their development in a positive direction, help them organize themselves, and bring them up as worthwhile successors. . . . The adolescent is no longer a child, he manifests a strong interest in his environment, is very active and is challenged greatly by new mental as well as physical tasks. One has to learn to utilize and channel his activities constructively, to teach him to work cooperatively, to engage him in socially meaningful tasks, to stimulate his desire to learn, to organize his intellectual as well as physical endeavors. . . . 'Our Soviet children,' she quotes Lenin's wish, 'should grow up as conscientious Communists and knowledgeable, convinced builders of Socialism.'"*

* *Letters to the Pioneers,* Molodaya Gvardya, Moscow, 1938, pp. 5-7.

# 14 Young Pioneers

## N. K. Krupskaya

### § The School and the Pioneer Movement

THE PIONEERS is a youth organization which has its own regulations, goals, and methods of work.

In this organization the children learn to think and act collectively, and to subordinate themselves to the demands and interests of the collective.

The mere existence of this organization is in itself a very important educational means. The child becomes accustomed to keeping in mind continuously the interests of the whole collective and all his activities are closely related to those of his collective. He adjusts himself psychologically to think in terms of the collective, which regulates his behavior, eliminates the feeling of

The excerpts in this section are reprinted in N. K. Krupskaya's book, *The Young Pioneers*, Akademiya Pedagogitcheskich Nauk, Moscow, 1957. Various footnotes indicate the primary source of each selection and its date of publication; the citations and page numbers in brackets refer to the secondary source, *The Young Pioneers,* which is currently available and was used by the translator.

"The School and the Pioneer Movement" is from "Communistic Upbringing of Successors," Moscow, *Molodaya Gvardya,* 1934, pp. 121-126 [*Young Pioneers,* pp. 9-15].

defenselessness and loneliness. The earlier the child is exposed to a life of a collective, the greater are his chances to grow up as a real Communist.

Healthy children growing up in normal conditions have a natural tendency toward organization, which can frequently be observed in children's games.

This is the reason the Pioneer organization captured the imagination and interest of youngsters.

Since the entire environment is permeated by the not so remote past, it is not difficult for children to understand the common objectives of the Komsomol and the Communist Party. It is very advantageous to define goals for children at a young age. An early start brings better results than a later one; hence, as adults their existence is more clearly goal-directed.

Though the festive side of the Pioneer movement is more visible to outsiders, the most important work is accomplished through their everyday work, when their efforts are concentrated on the consistent growth and development of youngsters, upon accumulating knowledge and the deepening of established aims. The close identification of the Pioneer organization with school life and work is its main strength. Without them, this youth movement will become obsolete and lose its appeal.

Correct individual purposes should be tied closely to the common goal. They must be appraised realistically and, as the child grows, increase in complexity. The choice of the goal is a most difficult one. Each Pioneer unit must choose a pertinent, practical task for which the group members are ready and which produces tangible results.

It is incorrect to assume that the movement has priority over the school. This false belief stems from the fact that the problem of systematization and deepening of the content of school curriculum, without which the Pioneers will be unable to reach their objectives, is yet to be dealt with forcefully. To live and work collectively does not suffice in itself. If the Pioneer organization would begin to negate the importance of the school it would change from an avant-guard movement to a reactionary one; covering up spiritual emptiness with colorful rituals. Hence there is a great need for close inner ties and mutual support between school and Pioneer movement.

The school, as well as the Pioneer organization, strives for the same goal—to bring up worthy successors, to continue the historical tasks set before them. The school supplies them with theoretical and practical knowledge, while the other teaches them how to implement successfully all they have learned. The Pioneer organization provides the school with students strongly motivated. Their human dignity, quest for knowledge, and curiosity becomes intensified. They become self-disciplined and serious toward learning. These pupils become much easier to work with.

To stimulate the students' learning process, it is sufficient for the teacher and the Pioneer or Komsomol leaders to point out to them the differences existing between the old bourgeois and the new Soviet school (the ideology, aims and purposes, as well as the curriculum). When the students and teachers comprehend clearly the significance of this close relationship, the school will become life itself, just as the Pioneer movement. In the process, the school will become more precious and indispensable to its pupils.

The teacher who wants to make the school a new one in content has to bear in mind that this can be accomplished only together with the students. Since the Pioneer movement is making the achievement of this goal easier for him, the teacher has to cooperate and give his support to the Pioneer organization and help draw into its orbit all students. The Pioneer leader, on the other hand, has to clarify in children's minds the main objective of the new Soviet school—to make the youth better able to help their country through building the new school.

The question of curriculum content is already decided upon, but many others are not yet solved. For example, the self-government of students remains unresolved. Another very significant problem not yet dealt with is how to combine most successfully the school curriculum with the practical work experience of youngsters. Since 1917, the problem has been under deliberation, but still remains not fully resolved. Here too the experience of the Pioneer movement may be of great help.

Pioneers set for themselves concrete, socially necessary goals. In this area the accumulated experience is rather weak, and existing evidence is still insufficient. There is no doubt that the Pioneer leaders will create new methods to develop children's initiative. When they succeeed in setting socially necessary labor tasks for youngsters, the work of the school will improve. With this goal in view the efforts to tie the Pioneer groups closer with school curriculums should be intensified. Both have the same goal and their paths to achieve it are closely interwoven. Neither can accomplish the task singlehanded; hence the necessity for their union. Only with the help of both can the youth of U.S.S.R. prepare itself to succeed in the great tasks set before them.

## § In Life to Have Knowledge Is Just as Necessary as to Have a Gun During a Battle

Dear Children,

The school year began a month ago, and the excitement of the beginning weeks seems to have subsided considerably. You settled down to study and work, and that is precisely what I would like to talk about.

The student in a Soviet school knows how important it is to acquire knowledge. He realizes how powerful knowledge is. He must know a lot to understand his environment well, read interesting books, find out how people live, how the outstanding ones fight for a better, more enlightened tomorrow for all, just as Lenin did. . . . In order to live a bright, enlightened, happy life, one has to learn how to work with his head and with his hands.

This is the reason why one should attend school regularly. Skipped school days are lost, since it is difficult to make up for squandered time.

The undivided attention of the student to the teacher's explanations during class periods helps to facilitate learning. Any distraction during the lesson disturbs other students. Homework

"Pioneer Pravda," September 22, 1938, No. 129 (2123) [*Young Pioneers*, pp. 42-45].

must be done neatly, carefully, and be well organized. A sloppy half hour spent on home assignments may mean three hours of conscientious work. It is not right to do the assignments carelessly. Neither is it correct to dawdle on them. The Stakhanovites work not only thoroughly but also fast. Students should help classmates, especially those who remain behind, not only because they are apt to slow down the learning progress of the whole group but also because the class in a Soviet school is a cooperating collective. Previously, students were self-centered, but now every classmate is the responsibility of every other classmate. It is strange to think that some may consider extending help by prompting and permitting weaker students to copy assignments. This is not help, it is cheating, and great harm is done to students who completely give up studying, relying on "help."

The task of the Soviet teacher to bring up youngsters as real "Leninists" is not an easy one. The teachers study, frequently consult with other faculty members, share experiences, and try to convey to the children all that is most important and most essential. The students must respect their teacher, help in his work in the classroom, and guard, not waste, his time. This regard for the teacher must have an outward manifestation which reflects itself in a cordial relationship, and his instructions obeyed.

The Soviet school is one of many strong Soviet institutions, and as such it must maintain order and obey rules and regulations. First of all, outward order has to be established. Students must never be late, and immediately after the bell they should proceed to their rooms. Only with a teacher's permission may the pupils leave the room during the class period. All home assignments should be submitted to the teacher upon his first request. Participation in class discussion should proceed in an orderly manner, under the teacher's leadership. Order must be maintained at all times in laboratories and shops as well as in the cafeteria, on field trips, and during recess. But one should not stop there. There is a need to establish an ongoing concern of all students in the life of the school and their active participation in its continuous improvement. There must be a realization by each pupil that he is engaged in the process of growth and maturation, which leads him to become a cultured, purposeful human being.

Students must abandon petty quarrels and arguments, forget the foul language and hooliganism and instead become socially conscious, the way Lenin wanted it. He told this to the Komsomol, requesting their help in libraries, kindergartens, wherever the need may be. There should be a collective decision to choose appropriate tasks which are realistic and do not disrupt studies. Often youngsters want to have amusements most of the time. This of course is not right. The children must attend movies or theater only when the play is worthwhile. By frequent attendance one may lose time needed for studying. Extending help when needed and socially meaningful work provide great satisfaction, since they make every classmate an accepted member of the class collective. The Soviet school must become an example of the solidifying work of the collective.

Greetings, dear children! May you succeed in growing up to become true Leninists!

## § Pioneer Movement— An Educational Problem

We often say that the goal of the school and the pioneer movement is the same. While the school puts heavy emphasis upon learning, the pioneer movement stress is upon upbringing. These closely related processes, though complementary to each other, represent, nevertheless, two distinctively different problems.

While adults are being re-educated in the spirit of socialism, a very special effort has to be made to bring up the young generation in the same vein.

What does socialistic education mean? Lenin summarized it very simply: "One for all and all for one."

These few words contain the essence of our educational problem. We must bring up our children as collectivists. The question of how we can achieve it is a very serious one.

"Communistic Upbringing of a New Generation," Moscow, "Young Guard," 1934, pp. 129-133 [*Young Pioneers*, pp. 76-80].

The aim of Soviet upbringing is to foster in each child his ability, to raise the level of his performance, of his consciousness, to emphasize well-roundedness in his personality, and to stress individuality. Therefore we employ entirely different educational methods from those utilized in bourgeois schools. The bourgeois society stresses primarily the "I" of individuals, who set themselves apart from the masses. The Communist upbringing uses other methods. We believe that the child's personality can reach its fullest development only in the collective. The collective strongly influences only the quality and the content of the child's upbringing and at no time does it make any attempt to absorb his personality.

The Pioneer movement is able to contribute greatly in this regard. Every Pioneer leader must make sure that all members of his group have common group experiences. This does not mean that the young Pioneer group should be constantly "amused." The essence is not in observing festive colorful rituals, but rather in concentrating on a meaningful content; otherwise the group will soon fall apart.

Instead of using Pioneer meetings to discuss problems of discipline, smoking, and teaching rules and regulations of the Pioneer movement, it is advisable rather to devote their meetings to the teaching of songs, games, reading aloud, etc. These activities, when meaningful, are significant in bringing the children closer together, just as a common happy or unhappy experience does. The group leaders must bear in mind that less formality and more content produces better results. The games introduced should be the ones which develop the instinct of collectivism, not individualism. Books used should emphasize important values.

Common experiences, such as field trips, group studying and reading, putting out newspapers and yearbooks, also play an important role in bringing the group members closer together. In such instances it is pertinent to make sure of active participation. Responsibility and the subordination of the individual interests to the common goal of the collective are problems the leader is confronted with.

Other aims of the Pioneer movement: Resolving the problem between individual work and that of the collective; coordinating and following up progress reports of work; exerting mutual control; fostering collaboration of all economic aspects of life; and developing conscious discipline.

The engagement of Pioneers in socially significant work, where they can implement their accumulative knowledge and exhibit correct work habits in a collective, is another task of the Pioneer movement.

The success of bringing up children in the collective is very dependent upon help of adult workers as well as that of the school.

All of the questions discussed above conceal in themselves very grave problems which must be worked out by Pioneer leaders and by teachers.

## § Collective Work of Children

Children, when engaged in play, are sometimes reproached by grownups for being lazy or idle. The adult does not realize, however, that what to him is just a game is interpreted by the child as work.

When the children begin a joint project adults should not interfere, because the children, unable to compete with adults, realize their limitations, become frustrated, and lose interest. However, when children turn to adults for advice, it is important that they treat the problem seriously.

The practical Americans realize the value of children's collective work. The children get together for creative work, their common bond a special interest or talent such as American Indian lore or painting. Sometimes they work together on a project as long as a month. Such purposeful projects are frequent in American schools.

I am not sure how reliable my information is (I read about it many years ago), but if it is true, this is an example we should follow.

When children initiate by themselves joint purposeful projects, these efforts should be supported and aided. Getting used to

"Our Children," 1928, Nos. 2-3, p. 2 [*Young Pioneers*, pp. 80-83].

working together is extremely significant, even when the projects are only temporary and the goal is a childish one.

The organization of our lives on the collective basis is the best assurance of avoiding poverty and other hardships connected with a divided, unorganized life, where man is against man. To achieve our goal we have to begin collective work simultaneously in all aspects of our life.

We must begin early to bring up our children in the spirit of collective work, in order to reinforce our social structure and the building of socialism.

We are still unable to meet the needs of preschoolers and build many kindergartens, children's clubs and workshops. But we can start by setting up across the country small groups of children who will work collectively on projects. These children's units become a very effective way of combating hooliganism. Later the school and the pioneer movement will be able to channel these collective working units into a larger organization. When the habit of collective work takes root in youngsters, the task of the school becomes an easier one, and the work of the children improves greatly. We must learn to respect and help children in their work.

## § Necessary Routines

1. *Keep order.*

Order must reign in school, at home, and in all other places. "Each thing in its place." This very important habit children must acquire as early as possible.

2. *Clean Up.*

After every work or play activity a cleaning up period must be established. Save every scrap of material. Nothing must be wasted.

Suggestions submitted to *Narkompros*, 1928 [*Young Pioneers*, pp. 85-90].

3. *Hygiene and Sanitary Rules.*

Observe personal hygiene and keep up sanitary conditions of the environment.

### WORK PROGRAM

1. School (Work tasks in: classroom, school, library and other areas)
   mutual help of students.
2. Preschool:
   taking care of pets, garden, flowers, science corner
   preparation for play
   mutual help of students.
3. Household chores:
   cleaning up, cooking, baking, care of siblings, etc.
4. Socially meaningful activities:
   realistic appraisal of plan and strength, selecting ways of fulfilling the task, division of labor, use of accumulative knowledge.
5. Initiative and creative work:
   formulation of child's inquiries and interests.
6. Skills to be acquired:
   a. 3 R's
   b. physical fitness
   c. knowledge of the environment
   d. understanding of people
   e. good working habits in collective work, wisely selecting aims and over-all goals, exercising self-discipline.

### AIM OF WORK

Each task should be socially centered and have a worthwhile goal. Aims must be designed collectively by children themselves, because their motivation and conscious discipline, as well as their personal development, depend upon them. The desire of children to help each other comes as the result of conscious behavior rather than of superimposed moral obligation.

The better thought-out the goals and steps of action, the stronger the chances of succeeding.

## § Progressive Tasks of the Pioneer Movement

The task of the Soviet school is manifold. It concentrates not only on subject matter, but also provides them with an understanding of their surroundings, and to a certain degree, with a Marxist point of view. Since children do not yet comprehend the Marxist terminology, we can give them only its essence and understanding, explaining it on their level. It is possible to interpret the environment from a Marxist point of view without using words too difficult for the children to grasp. Lenin thought that the main task of National Commissariat of Education is to create a new school curriculum which would faithfully reflect life. In reality this method represented a true interpretation of the basics of Marxism. To translate the complex concepts of Marxism into simple terms and to use easily understood examples is a difficult undertaking. A new curriculum evolved as a result of these efforts. When it went into effect, the teachers approached it seriously, though they complained about the difficulties connected with the transition period.

The Pioneer movement is all for improving and strengthening the school, which then could be used to the maximum by the Pioneers. The Pioneer leader must know the school curriculum well and create a close relationship with teachers, and the program of his group must be tied closely to that of the school.

Pioneer leaders, through common experience, can bring the children's collective much closer together than the teacher can in a school situation. The new school needs the Pioneer movement, which helps the students to develop positive characteristics such as independence, ability to work in a collective, organization, and inner discipline.

In my many talks with teachers, I encountered a great deal of jealousy. They thought that the students were moving away

Speech, Second Congress of Pioneers, 1925 [*Young Pioneers*, pp. 112-131].

from them. I tried to point out that in order to teach the children to subordinate not only to the teacher but also to the interests of the collective, the Pioneer movement must remain independent of the school. Though the majority of teachers understand the uniqueness of the organization and its importance, many still resent it. Only after a great deal of experience will they finally become convinced.

The Communists have three major tasks—*to learn, to propagandize, and to organize.* The first task is to learn. This is correct, but I do not approve when youngsters write: "Lenin said—we must learn, learn, learn," which is what the teachers tell them. He meant it as a task for adults. The Pioneer leader must reinforce certain areas of school teaching that need additional clarification.

The second task of Marxism is to propagandize. The teaching of this approach must begin when the children are very young. Often the Komsomol and Pioneer erect barriers, because they consider themselves better than the broad masses of children and youth. They forget that the main task of the Communist Party, of Komsomol and of Pioneer, is to create a classless society. Socialism means organization without any class divisions. The younger the age, the more important becomes the inclusion of members belonging to various strata of society. A forty-year-old man has a more difficult time in changing than does a twenty-year-old, while a twelve-year-old has no past yet to hamper change. The Pioneer movement should make the effort to attract these children. The Pioneers must learn and share their acquired knowledge with others.

The third task is to organize. There are many kinds of self-government of students. Some collectives create a self-government which functions as a policing force. Others activate only a small part of the members, the elective officers; the rest remain completely passive.

The self-government of the Soviet school must strive to become a genuine one. The whole school collective must actively participate; each student must have special duties and responsibilities delegated to him. This is the only way the school environment can stimulate youngsters to search for an important goal and find the best way leading to its accomplishment.

To build and develop a self-government in the spirit of Communism is very difficult. The teacher can only advise; the real work remains with the Pioneer movement.

To create a definite plan of action and to proceed accordingly is very important, since we Russians have yet to develop the habit of planned work. The school may give the children these good habits, but it is a must for the Pioneer organization to engage in developing this approach in the entire school life.

Not every Communist is able to work with children. I know many who have no conception of child psychology, education, or upbringing of children. The Komsomols are much better equipped, because the youngsters feel closer to them. It should be taken into consideration that members of the Komsomol, as natural authority figures, exert a strong positive influence upon youngsters. Therefore, the Party should define only the general direction of the children's movement, and its main content, leaving the rest to the Komsomol and Pioneer; otherwise it would deprive the movement of its independence and hamper its growth.

It cannot be denied that our Soviet school at the present time does not yet meet its goals, and the teachers are often confused when using new methods. Though our task has just begun, the majority of teachers already understand and agree with the main premise. The teachers study eagerly, which gives us assurance of rapid progress. In many instances program overloading occurs, when the teacher, not comfortable with the new curriculum per se, adds it on top of the old one with which he is so much more familiar. This must disappear, and it will as the work with teachers continues.

The self-government of the school must form in the students a habit of collective work and goals. Without them we will be able to achieve very little, because we have not yet learned the real meaning of the collective. Many tasks could never be reached without collective goals.

The school in our old system did not concern itself with self-education of its pupils or with the students' ability to work collectively. Lenin characterized the transition to socialism as a transition to mass cooperation. To achieve it, re-education and unification of efforts into a collective goal must take place, and here the role of the school can become very important. The collective has even greater significance in children's institutions, when the life of youngsters is organized on a collective basis with a purposefully designed schedule. These institutions should not be isolated islands. They must be closely tied to the surrounding community, to all organizations existing therein, and to the children who are outside the institutions.

The question should be raised whether to allow the development of children's organizations other than the Pioneers, which could also include children who remain outside the youth movement. For example, the young naturalists aim to explore nature, a goal entirely unpolitical in character. Pioneers whose interests are in natural science should join this group and try to permeate it with the Pioneer spirit.

The organization of population in accordance with diversified work goals is very significant. Any effort to suppress this development is a definite goal distortion of our present transitional period to socialism. The Pioneer organization, though it is a children's movement, is also a political organization. Therefore, no other groups which are political in character are needed for youngsters.

A strong emphasis should be placed upon developing apolitical groups; without it we would not be able to work in depth. Forbidding is easy, but it does not solve the problem. For example, someone from a village located in the Leningrad region wrote: "Could measures be taken to prohibit the Baptists preaching among the Finns, since they seem to be very successful in their work?" The writers of this letter want to embark on the way of least resistance. At the same time the analysis of the situation existing in the village proved that the Finns do not have a representative in the village council. Furthermore, not a single member of this council speaks Finnish, and as a result this Finnish group remains apart, cut off from the whole community and from the building process of the new system. Since the whole re-education work is done exclusively in Russian, no effort was made to establish a newspaper in Finnish or to recruit Pioneers. In spite of this thoughtless approach the people are still surprised that the Baptist influence is gaining strength. I selected this example to prove that prohibiting is not the best way to deal with a problem. To outlaw this Baptist movement would not accomplish anything, except to foster its growth. Instead we should intensify our work there and try to correct our mistakes.

Though the task of outlawing any children's organizations seems to be a simple one, it is important to keep in mind that this may drive them underground, which may prove to be very unhealthy. There is no need for outlawing them. Instead, send Pioneers who have the same interests.

There is one more problem I would like to mention here, which I did not cover in my speech; namely, that of national minorities and the relationship to children belonging to these groups. The result of a recent study in this field proved that not enough attention is devoted to this problem. I am afraid this is also true in respect to the participation of children belonging to national minority groups in the youth movement. I strongly feel that the Pioneer movement must draw all children together and not divide them into national groups. The school and pioneer organization must work harder in these situations than in any others, because the children's movement is of special significance.

## § Learning to Work Mentally and Physically

Dear Children:

The values of the old social system downgraded any manual labor while holding in high esteem any mental work. Now we do not have any division of labor into more and less important, into more and less revered. All labor is equally respected, though sometimes workers of physical labor are brought forward. The character of manual labor is now changed completely, as a result of great technical and scientific advancement. To be "handy"

"Letters to the Pioneers," Moscow, *Molodaya Gvardya,* 1938, pp. 35-40 [*Young Pioneers,* pp. 213-217].

in our time is not enough; one must also have theoretical knowledge.

Marx, Engels, and Lenin discussed at length the education for labor in view of contemporary technique, as well as the disparity existing between mental and physical work. Now our most important task is to enlighten the masses. Though compulsory education became the law of the land and great attention is devoted to schoolwork, it does not mean that our children should grow up without practical experience in physical labor. We need children who use both their head and their hands.

Though in a socialistic system everybody must work, the existing conditions of labor stimulate a deep interest and personal involvement, because the gain is for all, not the individual.

You Pioneers must gain experience in both physical and mental labor, utilizing all available resources. You must be brought up as workers of socialistic, well-organized labor. Without technical knowledge, you will be lost as builders as well as defenders of our socialistic country.

## § Qualifications for Pioneer Leadership

Every Pioneer leader must frequently review and analyze his leading ability, discover his strengths and weaknesses. Of course, mistakes are unavoidable, but he must learn not to repeat them. To meet the requirements he must have a basic general education, and be well-versed in politics. It is the responsibility of Komsomol to send Pioneer leaders for special training to help them to grow continuously.

Not every Komsomol member has the making of a Pioneer leader. To be a real activist, who has proven himself in work and deed, to set an example for Pioneers, and to show great interest and understanding in building socialism is not enough. He must understand children, be able to use the correct approach

Speech, Meeting of Pioneer Leaders of Moscow, November 17, 1933 [*Young Pioneers*, pp. 285-295].

to influence them, and his authority must be respected by youngsters. In short, he must know and utilize child psychology.

Lenin said "Communistic morals mean that every accomplishment of socialism, such as building the system, fighting for workers' causes, etc., becomes of great importance and that readiness to defend socialism is ever present." To bring up children in the spirit of Communism, the desire must become deeply imbedded in the youngsters.

Many times children create disturbances. Instead of finding out why they do so, often they are excluded from the organization. To effect re-education, and make him an earnest, eager member of the group, knowledge of child psychology is of help. It does not of course mean that the leader has to be well-versed in the entire psychological theory. He must concentrate mainly on the part which is applicable. For example, in many instances the leader judges the physical strength of Pioneers in comparison with his own, thinking they can walk and run just as long as he does, forgetting completely that they are much younger. To avoid these mistakes he must learn what are the realistic expectations at various ages.

The leader must select purposeful tasks which give the children an opportunity to develop.

I think that competition among Pioneer leaders is good. It stimulates their awareness and self-improvement, and as a result the quality of work in Pioneer groups becomes elevated.

I wish you success in your goal—to bring up the growing Soviet generation in the spirit of Communism.

## § Toward Deepening the Content of the Pioneer Work

Summarizing, the following may be said: There is no question that the Pioneer movement must continue to pursue the same goals which we formulated in the very beginning.

From lecture to the Central Committee of the Communist Party, January 23-24, 1928 [*Young Pioneers*, pp. 143-148].

It is also correct to assume there is no need to duplicate the school tasks. There are many important and necessary work habits which must be learned, but which the school does not teach, and therefore it is wiser to concentrate on them. The Pioneer leader must teach the children the best way to reach goals chosen by them.

Discipline is another important problem for the pioneer leader. When we talk about discipline we have in mind two kinds. The first kind, forced upon from without, is a remnant of the old capitalist system, which does not produce results, in lieu of reward and punishment. The new system needs discipline also, but a different kind. It must reflect voluntary self-discipline. There are many instances in our lives which demonstrate the second kind of discipline. For example, when the organized masses subordinate their individual interests to that of the collective. Pioneers must be brought up in the spirit of this voluntary discipline, and Pioneer morale should be built solely upon it without resorting to rewards or punishments. Our basic task is to substitute the discipline of the old system with a new one, which has a much higher motivation.

It is time that we stopped considering the teachers and the Ministry of Education responsible for the school, while the Komsomol is responsible for the Pioneer movement. In order to make our educational institutions a real Soviet school, and Pioneer not a club but a strong organization where the youngsters learn to work collectively from an early age, we need the support of all our population. Only this help will bring desirable results in areas as important as the correct upbringing of our new generation.

All of the problems under discussion here are by no means deliberated in full. Our work in this area is far from finished. Though there are many other related problems left to tackle and clarify, I think the results of this conference were very fruitful.

## § How to Bring About the Well-rounded Development of Children

How often we go from one extreme to another! Previously, we believed that children were ready almost in infancy to become politically conscious. We discussed serious topics with them which they really could not comprehend, tried to make Communists out of them during the preschool period. This approach was wrong. Now we have switched to the other extreme. We minimize their understanding, assuming they are almost slow witted. We must explain a great deal to children, brighten their horizons, and help them to become socially conscious. We feed them too much with fairy tales, while the reality around them is much more interesting. Furthermore, there are great differences among fairy tales. Some are good and others are very harmful. Some help to understand people and the surroundings; others confuse the children greatly. Life demands children's participation, and we cannot deny them this.

In order successfully to avoid misrepresentation and misunderstanding, books must be selected wisely for school libraries, taking into consideration children's interests, and their level of comprehension, and we must let them choose freely. I do not believe that each age has certain "must" and "must not" books. One should not protect children too much. They have to retain initiative in choosing reading matter of interest to them.

It is important to keep in mind the child's stage of development. When presenting a tale, for example, remember the age of the children and build upon what they already know without overburdening them with too many new and unfamiliar concepts. On the other hand, avoid talking down to them.

There also are other ways to learn about life. Field trips, games, and nature studies should be utilized as a part of extracurricular activities, rather than remain a continuation of the

"Pioneer Leader," 1937, No. 6, pp. 10-13 [*Young Pioneers*, pp. 295-301].

formal lesson in which the leader teaches while the group members listen attentively but passively.

Unfortunately, we pay too little attention to the various stages of child development and their specific characteristics. There are a lot of complaints that child psychologists approach child development solely from a theoretical point of view without a concern for its practical implications. We must remember that without theoretical knowledge, we cannot help the youngsters to grow correctly.

It is important to bear in mind that singling out and favoring specially talented youngsters very often proves detrimental to their development. We must not convey to them that they are special and because of it deserve privileges. We must give them the best well-rounded education to help them in their chosen field. One cannot determine very early which girl should become a ballerina and which boy should become a scientist. We must show equal concern for all children, giving every one the most we can.

Initiative and creativity should be supported, and their interest should be guided. Parents should not spoil children with too much entertainment, most of which they do not understand. Less amusement, but on their level of development and comprehension, is more advisable and produces better results. Overstimulation creates irritability.

We must strengthen all children's technical workshops, and have many trips to explore the immediate environment. Pioneer Palaces must maintain rooms where children may become engaged in their chosen activity.

We must bring up the children to continue our tasks. Lenin hoped that our children will become even better fighters and workers than their fathers.

One should pay more attention to bringing up children in the spirit of socialism. Raise them as collectivists, and mature, socially conscious workers with strong characters and a firm desire to be useful. Our children are wonderful. We must only learn to understand them to help them grow as fighters for our cause.

15

# *To Inspire Children*
## *(A Pioneer Leader's Notebook)*

*S. A. Shmakov*

### § Together but a Little Bit Ahead

IT IS IMPOSSIBLE to assess immediately the results of the creative and complex task of the teacher. Sometimes it takes many years to receive gratification. This may happen at an accidental meeting with a former pupil or member of a Pioneer group, now an adult, who expresses praise and appreciation of the teacher's or Pioneer leader's role in his life. How pleased was the Pioneer leader of the hero Yuri Gagarin, when he paid tribute to her.

Pioneer leader—these words imply not only a profession and work but also a calling and a service. Can we consider this leadership a profession? Yes. A senior in a secondary school, a University student, a factory worker, actor, writer, engineer who is a real friend of children and, as such, becomes their conscience for a long time, is educating children politically.

Gorky and Dzerzhinsky were among our famous Pioneer leaders. A broad field of action lies ahead of any wise, brave,

S. A. Shmakov, *To Inspire Children,* XI Series. Pedagogika .Izd-vo "Znanye," Moscow, 1963, pp. 3-46.

and cheerful individual who commits himself to this very responsible task.

To lead children does not imply guiding them by the hand. It means helping them to grow and to develop as well as awakening their thinking, and formulating their soul, heart, and intellect. In the Pioneer organization the length of service is not counted by decades, but by years and even months.

This book does not contain a unified plot or one major hero. Instead my numerous "comrades in arms" are the ones I will talk about here. In spite of the great differences existing among them in age and character, their love for young Pioneers is the common bond. They are the people who walk together with the children, but a little bit ahead of them.

## § Let the Children Grow as Communists

To bring up children as Communists is to develop in them a feeling of vital concern for problems such as vandalism, waste, the fight for freedom in the Congo.

In political education, discussions and gatherings are much less important than actual performance of meaningful tasks.

The strength of children's imagination is so great that it can overcome any difficulty. The child becomes stronger in his own eyes when he can fulfill his duty, no matter what. In a Pioneer summer camp, the girl on flag duty did not leave her position, even when her mother arrived unexpectedly. She asked to relate to her mother, "I am on guard duty, the change will come in two hours, please don't feel hurt and wait, or come tomorrow."

Makarenko was right when he said, "Respect for the banner symbolizes not only love toward our country, but also efficiency in performing a task in the collective."

## § Do We Need Work Dodgers?

Children who manifest listlessness, passivity, and inertia, and a pronounced indifference to their surroundings, have been called dodgers or slackers by Makarenko.

Slackers are a special category. On the surface they may appear to be all right. Their performance is "average." They do not fight, neither are they rude. Since their overt behavior is different from that of "hooligans," "wild ones" and "incorrigibles," they may pass by for a long time without being noticed. They do not know the true meaning of friendship and honor. They lack spiritual fortitude and stability, which must be fortified in children from a very early age, since it is important not to miss the stage of development when the youngster is most receptive.

Since in twenty or thirty years these children will govern our country, we cannot afford to bring them up as slackers and dodgers of responsibility.

## § Look for the Good in the Child

Very often the main goal of all our educational measures is to run everything smoothly without commotion and trouble. We appease our conscience by "influencing" the mind of the child "educationally," namely by reprimanding him, dressing him down, and warning him. As a rule this is all done by adults. Why not delegate some of these unpleasant tasks to children, or even transfer some of the responsibilities of adults to young Pioneers.

Independence is the basic premise of the Pioneer movement. Unfortunately this is not implemented sufficiently in practice. Our children do not have opportunities to experience the joy of independence. Everything in the summer Pioneer camps is done before they arrive. The Pioneer camp is "a temporary field quarter, a bivouac," where self-service is the only way of doing things. The Pioneer motto, "always be ready," deepens its meaning in this camp setting.

Our school curriculum is sharply differentiated. Though the physical and intellectual loads are attuned to the developmental stages of pupils, the system of guiding the Pioneers has not been thoroughly thought out. For example, the tasks do not take into consideration the differences between children in the third grade and adolescents in eighth and ninth grades.

Recently, the trend in upbringing has been directed toward the child's personality and the old worn out method of wholesale education is on its way out. This has brought about a new problem—how to get through to a child, especially the "difficult" one. Since there is a way for each child to be reached, if we look long enough, we will find it.

The question may be posed: Has the Pioneer leader the right to risk safety of children? Where should the line be drawn between educational courage and recklessness?

The leader must always proceed slowly, carefully, think through every step, plan all preparation in advance, considering also the children's readiness for hardship, the fostering of which should start with small tasks in everyday life. Otherwise it will not work.

It is no secret that our children lack the ability to endure difficulties. We often shortchange them, deprive them of hardships which develop courage.

## § They Do Not Want Anything

Perhaps it is time to re-examine the program when we complain that the children in our groups do not want anything. Subsequently, we will probably discover, to our dismay, that we do not always try to find out *what* they want. In order to find out what interests them we must view the youngsters not only as Pioneers and pupils but also as individuals, who have their own world of childhood joys, sorrows, plans, interests, projects, and thoughts.

Since life changes continually, the experiences which seemed full of excitement ten years ago do not interest the children today. The educator has a difficult task to keep up with the new developments, but this is the only way to maintain the children's interests.

The interests of children have grown tremendously during the last few years, and the questions they pose in various technical, political, and esthetic areas indicate that no incident escapes their attention. For example, "Why has President Nasser imprisoned the Communists in his country while at the same time he is defending the interests of his nation?"

After sharing our experiences, we often wonder whether we reply correctly to children's inquiries.

The pedagogical dialects are complex, we cannot pause even one moment for fear of lagging behind. A Pioneer leader must continue to learn. Some just wait for seminars and recommendations, while others observe, explore, and search on their own. When we strive to know all about something and something about all, then we will not complain that "they do not want anything."

## § The Boys Go to Sleep

Boys are very restless. The camp is getting ready for the night. Most children are already in their rooms. One, barefooted, remains in the hall.

—Where are you going?
—To wash my feet.
—Why are you without slippers?
—But I walk only on tiptoes.

From the corner room one can hear voices still discussing the happenings of the day and things they read or heard about. Slowly they are settling down. There is no need to rush them. They will fall asleep by themselves and dream. The last light is turned off.

The natural exchange of opinion is often much more valuable than any "special" discussion or a lesson; hence we should not "destroy" it by shouting or preaching.

## § We Are for the Game

Children like to play. In their games, they mix creativity and fantasy. Undoubtedly, the pedagogically skillful implementation of games not only satisfies the unused need of Pioneers to play games but also revitalizes the Pioneer program.

The favorite games are those where reality and imagination merge. Makarenko said that a true collective of children cannot exist without games. It is valuable educationally when children are not self-conscious about their play. We need games not only in Pioneer camps but in schools also.

There is no doubt that games are an essential element of upbringing. The program built around play is unusually broad and variable. It is rather primitive to consider only games such as volleyball, "gorlet," and "salka." But educators are still debating whether games are lowering the serious process of upbringing.

One should remember that games do not only amuse. They also teach useful things, develop feelings, and unify the collective. We must regard Pioneer games as absolutely necessary in the life of the child, for whom they are a free and creative activity, full of important and realistic experiences.

Games in Pioneer work must maintain their role of great significance, wrote Krupskaya. "The Pioneer life must be beautified. . . . Art and games must occupy a much more important place in the Pioneer organization than they have now."

## § The Boys Like to Take Oaths

Boys like to demand an oath as proof of trustworthiness. Kataev, in *The Lonely White Sail,* describes how Gavrik forces Petya to eat dirt and to pronounce a frightful curse, "May the devils tear me to bits." Boys enjoy using flowery words and inspiring mottos which they retain for a long time, sometimes forever.

Slogans must be clear and enticing. Perhaps each developmental stage needs its own maxims and watchwords. We talk to children a lot about the need for mottos to guide their lives, but it is more important to show them than to tell them.

## § They Received a Genuine Welcome

Two Pioneer camps are located side by side. They are divided only by a road running between them. Though their life and the rules and regulations are the same, sometimes they are at war with one another.

It happens sometimes that the "cold" war changes into a "hot" one, and cones and layers of turf fly.

We somehow ignore it and function in our collective within the boundaries of our own territory, blinded to all that goes on beyond our fence. The results we achieve are nothing to brag about. When visitors come from across the road the behavior of children and Pioneer leaders leaves so much to be desired that it is embarrassing.

The feeling that Pioneers everywhere constitute the same big family must become deeply imbedded within them as a basic characteristic of members of the Soviet society.

We must treat our visitors as very important guests and not spare efforts to receive them with a real genuine welcome as becomes Pioneers and their leaders.

## § Gifts Under the Pillow

The children's collective is a family, and as such it needs various traditions. It is important to know the birthdays of all the children, especially since parents sometimes have difficulty in coming to the camp on these special days. When there are many children in the camp, one special day is chosen to celebrate all birthdays falling within their stay in the camp. Pioneer leaders plan this special day carefully. Under the pillow of each birthday child there will be a small package of sweets. This simple gift will warm the hearts of children.

We talk a lot about our love for children. Our hollow talk often covers up our disregard for their inner world. Sometimes we have to admit we search for the love of a child and attain it, but even then we still maintain a certain distance. In the family it is different; one gives love without regard to any pedagogical theory, and it manifests itself by sacrifice, unselfishness, and action.

## § If All the Boys in Our Country

The upbringing of our children is the responsibility of us all. Not every youngster is growing up under the same conditions. Some of our boys are developing without supervision of a father figure and, while they require care, love and attention, what they need most is firmness, reasonable demands, and manliness. The Pioneers of today are tomorrow's adolescents who have a harder task to face while actively participating in new endeavors. To prepare them for this responsibility they have to become active swimmers, skiers, hunters, pathfinders, explorers. All these activities foster physical toughness and endurance, and clear, independent thinking. Unfortunately, we often neglect this part of our children's education.

To educate an individual, to develop his character and formulate his convictions is much more important than building cities, developing new machinery, and sending rockets into the cosmos. Since the school alone cannot accomplish this tremendously complex task of the utmost importance to us, we all must help. Good intentions and ceremonial meetings only will not accomplish it. Children, mainly adolescents, need older, genuine friends, not "kings for an hour" or talking-down Pioneer leaders who think they do a favor when they meet with youngsters once a week. Pioneer leaders must wholeheartedly volunteer their free time.

The most serious obstacle which frightens away many adults is the difficulty involved in the job. It is not easy to ignite the hearts of children. To do so one needs to have the ability to find the right approach, the key to which is knowing what makes the children tick. Dignity, friendship, and mischief—important factors in growing up—must be handled with delicacy and sensitivity.

There are people who devote their lives to Pioneer leadership. These men occupy a special place, since one good Pioneer leader today means hundreds of wonderful people tomorrow.

RENEWALS 458-4574